THE KORPORATE KANNIBAL KOOKBOOK

Also by Brad Blanton

Radical Honesty: How to Transform Your Life by Telling the Truth

Practicing Radical Honesty: How to Complete the Past, Live in the Present, and Build a Future with a Little Help from Your Friends

The Truthtellers: Stories of Success by Radically Honest People (editor)

Radical Parenting: Seven Steps to a Functional Family in a Dysfunctional World

Beyond Good and Evil: The Eternal Split-second Sound-light Being

Honest to God (with Neale Donald Walsch)

Some New Kind of Trailer Trash: And Some New Trail of Kinder Trash

The Korporate Kannibal Kookbook:

Recipes for Ending Civilization and Avoiding Collective Suicide

Brad Blanton, Ph.D.
Author of *Radical Honesty*

Sparrowhawk Press
Stanley, Virginia

Grateful acknowledgment is made to all the great authors whose material is reprinted in this volume.

Dedication

To all those who have ever killed anyone
to protect children from being harmed.

The game on top of the world that controls the minds of men and is destroying human life on earth and damaging all of life is called Corporate Capitalism. I call it Korporate Kannibalism because that more aptly describes what it is. It is a simulated form of life that has "a life of it's own" in the minds and hearts of humans. It is an infection. We must amputate. Quickly. The patient will die if we do not amputate. If we kill a mere one thousand of these billionaires and take their shit and redistribute it and restore balance, we could save 3 billlion children from dying from the predictable and inevitable result of failing to act, violently, precipitously and immediately. One thousand guilty murdering fat fucks or three billion children? ... See you in the emergency room. —Brad Blanton

Acknowledgments

I thank you, my friends and colleagues and coaches and tutors and mentors and helpers and clients and workshop participants, from the bottom of my heart, for sustaining me and teaching me that love is queen, though, as a subject, I have faltered many times.

To Stephanie Gunning, my editor and friend, thank you for your kind and persistent willingness to assist in helping me clarify meaning and content and sources and manner of presentation.

Thank you, Vicki Valentine, for this great cover and for the other covers of books of mine you have done.

Thanks to Derrick Jensen for you endorsement and support along the way, and for your great books that have inspired and depressed and sustained me along the way for five years now. Thanks to all who I have named in the text and quoted and listed in the end notes.

Thanks to Keith Moon for always being on hand to help and for reading earlier drafts and making suggestions and helping me with the Internet.

Thank you Mike Lewinski for getting the vision and for coming on as CEO of Radical Honesty Enterprises to give me time to write this book, and for helping me be willing to understand marketing.

Thank you, Gene Marshall, for your thoughtful reflections and reliable independent opposition to both what I had to say and how I said it, and for being a good friend and mentor and a model for the life of faith.

Thanks to all the participants in the Blanton for Congress discussion group online, for reading my rants and missives and for giving me such good links to pursue and for keeping in contact with me these years since the campaign.

Thanks to all the members of the Luray Caverns Country Club, even the goddamned Republicans among you, for playing golf with me and giving me shit and giving me all that money when I beat you (and screw you for all you took!)

Thank you Maria for all those times I stayed there in Sweden with you and Bruno and all the jetlagged hours in the middle of the night. I had a place to write day and night, and to get nourished by loving Bruno and welcoming him into the world with you. And thank you for loving Bruno and doing your best to have me be with him as much as I can and as often as I can come there because the love of that little boy has given me heart. I love him so much the rest of the world is included.

Thank you, Elijah, for going to Sweden with me in the summers and talking with me and playing the guitar and being my loving son and kind critic and a million other things.

Carsie, thank you for all your wonderful songs and poetry and performances and ongoing cheerful affirmative attentive loving way of being with humans and dogs and Jon and all your friends and me too.

Thanks Shanti and Seth and Liam and Zolly for putting me up and putting up with me, and letting me be with you all in California, and for your sharing of how your life is and for your loving way of being a family.

Thank you Amos for having me come do that therapy session with you and your therapist, and for calling me to account for how I raised you, for calling me a narcissist, and for loving Amy and Carsie and Elijah so much and with such kindness.

Thanks to all those who have been in workshops with me over the last couple of years while this book was aborning.

Thanks to all the members of Sustainable Shenandoah for our gardening and learning projects over the last couple of years, and the parties at my Yurt.

Thanks Jack Stork for being a great friend and mentor and a loving husband to my sister Anno to the very end, and for your honesty and grieving and sharing with all of us in her family so kindly and informatively during the process of her dying and since then. Thanks for the feedback on my rants and sections of this book over the last couple of years, too, and for what you contributed.

Thanks to Lee McWhorter and Jerry Griffin and Susan Guest and particularly Rick Woodward for stopping by the Yurt and having a drink, and talking about the ongoing flow of life and commerce and the slow decline of the state of affairs of our community and friends and country.

Thanks to Joe Bageant for being a fellow Redneck Scottish-heritage reprobate and a great, great writer, barfly, guitar player, and friend.

Thanks to all my friends at The No Mind Festival at Angsbacka in Molcolm, Sweden, for having me there to present seminars on Radical Honesty and The World Café and whatever else I was interested in at the time, and for allowing me and Elijah to participate in your wonderful programs for the last seven years, and for sharing your hearts and your wisdom with me and mine.

You all, every one of you, have helped me a lot and I am grateful. This book could not have been brought into being without all of your help. So if anyone bitches about it, I will tell them who to blame.

Love, Brad.

"A great industrial nation is controlled by its system of credit. Our system of credit is concentrated. The growth of the nation, therefore, and all our activities are in the hands of a few men who, even if their action be honest and intended for the public interest, are necessarily concentrated upon the great undertakings in which their own money is involved and who, necessarily, by very reason of their own limitations, chill and check and destroy genuine economic freedom.

We are at a parting of the ways. We have, not one or two or three, but many, established and formidable monopolies in the United States. We have, not one or two, but many, fields of endeavor into which it is difficult, if not impossible, for the independent man to enter. We have restricted credit, we have restricted opportunity, we have controlled development, and we have come to be one of the worst ruled, one of the most completely controlled and dominated, governments in the civilized world—no longer a government but a cabal ruled by the opinion and duress of small groups of dominant men."

—*Woodrow Wilson*

"The end of the human race will be that it will eventually die of civilization."

—*Ralph Waldo Emerson*

"Abstracted too many levels from its source, language maroons us in a factitious fantasy world, an unconscious story that turns us into its victims."

—*Charles Eisenstein*

"When a well-packaged web of lies has been sold gradually to the masses over generations, the truth will seem utterly preposterous and its speaker a raving lunatic."

—*Dresden James*

"All great truths begin as blasphemies."

—*George Bernard Shaw*

Preface

"The money powers prey upon the nation in times of peace and conspire against it in times of adversity. It is more despotic than monarchy, more insolent than autocracy, more selfish than bureaucracy. I see in the near future a crisis approaching that unnerves me, and causes me to tremble for the safety of my country. Corporations have been enthroned, an era of corruption will follow, and the money power of the country will endeavor to prolong its reign by working on the prejudices of the people, until the wealth is aggregated in a few hands, and the republic is destroyed."

—William Jennings Bryan

The preceding quotation often has been attributed to Abraham Lincoln, when, in fact, it was written by William Jennings Bryan, who served as Secretary of State from 1913–1915 under president Woodrow Wilson and was a great orator.[1] Known as the Great Commoner, Bryan gave a speech on what a growing number of us know now: that the rich shall always be with us, just like the poor.[1] In fact, if the rich are with us it is a certainty that a lot of poor folks will be also. If it were not for the rest of us to take from, where would the accumulation of money for the rich come from? They exist from ripping off others. The tool that the rich use to rip poor people off is called "interest." Calling it that is a masterpiece of double speak. It's called interest because it is one of the most boring goddamned things in the world.

Eternal vigilance means to keep bringing down the rich and pulling up the poor over and over again. Kind of like tilling the soil, if we are responsible, loving human beings we are plowing under the rich and elevating the poor constantly. And if we do it just exactly the right way, we won't deplete the soil. Sadly, this kind of action is usually just one of the kinds of agriculture that extends the lifetime of the soil for a longer period of time so folks don't notice the gradual decline, from Eden to dust bowl. Both industrial farming and eternal vigilance are ultimately unsustainable and destructive without the renewal that only their death can provide.

We need a more radical form of "crap rotation" right now because the soil that is our society soon will no longer be nurturing. When I say "we," I mean all of us, and most specifically, I mean the disappearing middle class. We are the last ones left to get that the same wealthy upper class scum who are the perpetual traitors of our poorer brethren are ripping us off too. Profiting from rip-offs is the essence of corporate capitalism. And corporations don't die. The Supreme Court says they are people. So they are people who never die. It's no wonder then that as each new generation of young people come up they are so easily fucked over by these persons, many of whom are way over a hundred years old, and practiced in the art of taking and not giving back.

As long as we keep using the system invented ten thousand years ago of locking up the food, private ownership, and waging war to protect the store, the eternal conflict between the rich and the other rich will keep on keeping on and those of us in the middle will keep on paying for it. To hell with the poor and the middle class, unless they are needed for cannon fodder or to build something for the rich. This is soil depletion of the worst kind. But it is slow enough that, like the frog in the infamous heating water in the pot story (which is a lie, by the way) that is too weak to jump out of the pot before realizing he is being boiled alive.

The terrible message of current times, demonstrated by the weakness and impotency of President Barack Obama to pull off any of his campaign promises during his first years in office, is that we have no choice but to re-empower the "money powers that prey upon the nation" if we want to keep the poor and middle class from losing their shelter and their means of getting around and declining to the point of dying out. Propping up the banks and the car companies is like trying to restore slavery so the slaves can survive. In fact, it *was* restoring slavery so the slaves could survive. That is what Barack Obama has been doing since being elected, including making health insurance companies and pharmaceutical companies more entrenched and protected than ever in the name of health care "reform." The first black president is the ultimate achievement of the rich. They have attained dominance. The rich have won. The class war is over. They have all the money and all the troops. And what they have structurally in place cannot be beaten from within. *This system cannot be reformed from within.*

Here is how the system works. Here are three steps you can use to fuck more and more people out of their money and have it accumulated by fewer and fewer people.

1. Form a corporation that lives forever. Start fucking people out of their money. If they litigate, keep the court case going until they run out of money or time and die waiting. Remember, you live forever and have access to almost unlimited resources, but they are limited to a mere lifetime and what they can scrape together.

2. Make sure political campaigns in your system are financed by contributions. As long as you can keep this up, corporations will control the political system and the economy, simply because, with extremely rare exceptions, no one can win an election without corporate money.

3. Keep fucking the people out of their money; only talk them into paying you for keeping it from them as well. Let a few new people in now and then who want to have some of the money you are fucking other people out of. These are called bankers and accountants. That's why they call it, when you get fucked out of all of your money—*bank*ruptcy. Keep up recruitment of hucksters to maintain control. Reward them with big bonuses for being good at ripping off from others an amount much greater than what they get.

These three steps are a habit network that is ensconced in corporate capitalism and sustained by the law of the land.

The only thing being elaborated on now is that the corporations that keep track of the money that people are being fucked out of can fuck them out of a little bit more with loans. The so-called banking industry gets paid for (1) keeping track of just how much the original corporations have fucked people out of, and then (2) loaning un-payable amounts of play money to the fuckees when they can't make ends meet, and then (3) using the bad loans to create more phantom wealth based entirely on lies. These packages of worthless lies are then sold to investors with the claim that they have value. These are called derivatives. It means rich crooks derive more money by stealing it from whoever of the other crooks has a little bit left.

An ever-increasing number of people worldwide are having the slowly-dawning realization of just how true all of this is, and with it there is a growing anger at the perpetrators. And soon, no amount of lying in commercials and other forms of propaganda will serve to prop things up anymore. This system is destined to self-destruct. It is unsustainable. We are going down.

Can't We Come up with Something Better than This?

As one last impotent, sheepish, and whiny protest, as the great majority of us are flushing down the toilet bowl of economic history, I ask: Can't we come up with something better than this system? Particularly since the rich corporate cannibals are now, without any doubt, destroying the world, as we speak. Is just letting that happen really the best we can do?

We just say, "Yes, Massah... Whatever you say, Massah... Here have another bite of my child, Massah... Hope you enjoy your meal, Massah... Thank you for letting me serve you my children, Massah..."

Cannibalism Exits Right Now

The truth is that a rapacious form of cannibalism currently exists and is growing more powerful every day. This system is run by fools and psychopaths who are laughing all the way to the bank and, once there, they are laughing like hell with the bankers.

We are all in need of a worthy substitute for this system (and I do mean all of us, even the rich) or we shall all be eaten soon, and suddenly, billions of us at once. We must bring about the end of rich people rule in some quick, ecologically-sound fashion or we are almost all going to die from it. This system is called corporate capitalism or, as I have become fond of calling it, korporate kannibalism.

Corporations are the front for personal greed and the malice aforethought of rich, greedy people. And even worse, evidence provided in this book seems to indicate that, given the right circumstances almost all of us would be fundamentally the same as rich, greedy people. Apparently, according to valid research, almost all of us would fuck people out of their money until they died, given the chance, and knowing we could get by with it. This is, as they say, "only human nature." We apparently cannot "heal" or "cure" or "change" this form of cannibalism in any reliable way. Our best hope is to simply use it.

The *Korporate Kannibal Kookbook* is about the problem being its own solution, or, in other words, cannibalism being the answer to corporate cannibalism. It is also about the greater virtue of this new cannibalism, which is the essence of compassion because it is, by far, the most humane approach to the upcoming big die-off for humanity, which is structurally in place and without drastic interference, bound to happen. Without radical change to the current course of history, without radical intervention, we are doomed, soon, to almost all (or all) die at once and lose our chance at further, more cooperative, and more conscious participation in evolution.

The cannibalism I advocate merely involves feeding a very small number (relatively speaking) of rich people to a whole lot of poor people, and also taking all of those rich people's property and re-distributing it to the rest of us. This is simple, elegant, appropriate, just, fitting, and virtuous, and I expect you will be as convinced as I am, perhaps in another paragraph or two.

The Empire Is Consuming Us, So Let's Name Names and Get Cookin'

Believe me. The numbers are mind blowing. Just the top twelve hundred richest people, or just the leaders of the top one hundred or so corporations is all we have to do in! By my estimates, killing and eating less than .001 percent of humanity, and taking all their shit would solve damned near all of our problems! Redistributing their wealth and possessions could save half of humanity! That is, by killing and eating less than .001 percent we save 50 percent of humankind! The scheme involves sacrificing twelve hundred and ninety-two people, almost all of whom are rich, fat, thieving scum, to ensure the lives and well being of three billion other people, mostly children.

This is the simplest, most effective, and tastiest solution (if we cook 'em right) to damned near everything that is killing us by the tens of thousands on a daily basis and soon to be threatening the entire future of humanity.

Then, when our delicious solution is carried out properly, using the fairest system of justice the world has ever known, (this book goes into detail about six other big ideas other than eating corporate cannibals.) The system of justice I referred to above is based on actually knowing the truth about what is going on—coming right up in chapter 8, "The Truth Machine" —so we can re-establish balance.

Those of us who remain can establish a maximum amount of property that any human being (or collective of human beings, such as a corporation) is permitted to own. We will have the option of eating anyone who violates the standard. And we can revoke the corporate charters of any institution that surpasses the limit of what may be earned and kept. They can be discorporated, much like their leaders will have been, unless they pay the bribe to avoid being consumed.

This book is a guidebook on how really to be a consumer—with some taste and refinement—and to keep consumerism from consuming us by consuming a bit more selectively.

What the Hell Happened to Me?

I hardly know myself anymore. I used to be known by some great labels—Civil Rights Leader, Non-violent Anti-war Protestor, Psychotherapist, Author of Books and Articles about Love, Forgiveness, and Permissive Child Rearing. I was the picture of compassion.

I Googled myself to rediscover my identity, and even that didn't work. I am fed up with being owned and operated by assholes, even if they are like I would be if I was them, and I have come up with a solution to our mutual problem. It is a good solution, but it has damaged my image a bit. Damned if I know what happened. Something happened to me.

I think what happened to me is something like what might have happened to you. A rude awakening to reality occurred. My idealism fantasy died. I got pissed off at people for hurting people I loved and after I worked at it and forgave a lot of enemies, one day I didn't fucking get over it anymore. This is a big shift, maybe backwards, from my former self, the author of popular books in the Radical Honesty series written over the last twenty years.

One thing that happened was I grew older. Like Sigmund Freud and dozens of other clinical practitioners throughout history, as I grew older, I found my initial interest in healing and helping people turning from individual and family and marital problems to community and global and universal problems. And now the source of both sets of problems appears to be the same. It's called civilization. When Freud wrote *Civilization and Its Discontents* he was pretty much disillusioned with human beings too.

The fundamental prescription offered in my previous books was based on my experience as a clinical psychologist in Washington, D.C. where I helped a lot of people live happier lives. I have books of stories of lives changed for the better. I know that what I did with people worked most of the time. People who were suffering found relief. Radical Honesty was about listening, connecting, and being fully present—like good parents, teachers, therapists, uncles, or aunts listen to the people they care about and the children they love. The best book of mine where the outcome of good listening shows up is *The Truthtellers: Stories of Success by Radically Honest People* (Sparrowhawk Publications, 2004). In that book people tell stories of the results of reconnecting with people from whom they have been alienated and through undoing lies and being honest, forgiving them. This honest listening and honest response is done in order to solve both individual personal problems and conflict of a social nature in families.

All this healing being brought about, I realized, *was occuring, nestled in the context of the merciless and murderous corruption of the government of the United States in the last half of the twentieth century and the first part of the twenty-first.*

The theme of all my earlier books was always the same. It was about redemption and forgiveness through honesty. I wrote that people, by being radically honest, can escape the jail of their constantly judging minds, listen and connect, actually hear what others are saying and get what they are feeling, and become friends with the people around them, have empathy for them, and bond with them anew. They start out wanting to break through the barriers of habit and the phoniness of their established, superficial relationships based on lies and pretence. They end up feeling that the other person has actually broken through to them, and stuck with them, and both parties are grateful for it.

Now I think this same kind of therapy offers a healing greatly needed on a larger social scale for the sake of our survival as a species. And, as did Freud and Jung and Erikson and Maslow and many others, when I attempt to apply what worked to make people in families and relationships less miserable, anxious, depressed, and conflicted—and to make some even happier—it appears that what works on a smaller scale looks like it could work fine on a larger scale. *That could be simple, except for one thing: the negative influence of rich people and their wars and deprivation-based economy. We can't simply forgive rich people for past sins and then let them continue on in the same way. The escalation of their ways and means of murder for profit is now killing the world.*

That is why, after having spent a lifetime helping people bring renewal, love, and forgiveness into being, I now write a book about killing and eating rich people—because the wealthy ones I am suggesting we eat are themselves eating people at a merciless and continuously escalating rate! Their apparently endless appetite will only expand unless we do something drastic about their mercenary, murderous, and wasteful ways. They kill children for breakfast. They fuck children for entertainment (literally and figuratively, as they include the Catholic Church and sex trafficers, and other gigantic gangland corporate entities) before lunch, and fuck over children for supper. And they kill some of them for amusement in the evenings and starve thousands upon thousands at night through neglect and unconsciousness.

I cannot begin to make this sound as bad as it actually is. I can only hope to offend your sensibilities to the core in hopes that you will awaken and join us and help get the goddamned barbeque pit ready for these perverse monsters.

For the sake of all children and innocents, and all the other current victims of predatory capitalism, I say let's kill and eat the cannibals who are killing and eating our children as we speak. The most efficient and compassionate thing to do for the sake of humanity is to immediately capture coporate capitalists and kill them and redistribute their wealth and their protein. We need to shoot them right now to stop them from killing more of our children. I can think of nothing more humane and effective or merciful than the immediate slaughter of the slaughterers in the midst of their slaughter. There is not enough time to try to inform them and transform them. They are incurable anyway. Corporate capitalism is a generic disease implicit in civilization. The United States of America has just formalized it more effectively than ever before in history. We *are* the evil empire.

What is this? Have I gone insane? No. I am in the process of going sane! It may be hard for you to recognize this from the standpoint of your own craziness, but if you can suspend judgment and consider the possibility that I might have a point, and take in a little more data... Just get this one thing: Killing of humans by humans is happening and will continue for sometime into the future regardless of what you or I do. We can only influence who gets killed and save as many innocents as we can. This is the way things are.

This level of compassion is not the dreamworld of non-violence in which I myself have been a delusional participant for forty years. That has not worked. To the degree that it did work it was because a violent threat loomed on the horizon and the retreat of the perpetrators of classist violence was able to avoid a bloodier defeat. I am tired of corporate capitalists killing my children, my brothers and sisters, my beloved friends, my fellow human beings, and my fellow living creatures. Rich Americans are my enemy and yours and the enemy of humankind. The killing fields the world over are created out of, and for the sake of, greed for greater wealth for the already wealthy.

I will give you the complete evidence in this book, which is based on thorough research by people I love and trust, so that you can see why I want to kill corporate capitalist cannibals and feed them to the hungry and what is left of the middle class, and eat my share of the motherfuckers myself, in a ritual designed to deepen my compassion and committment to loving others. I know this sounds crazy and I put it that way because I want you to see the contrast writ large. Stick with me a little longer and see if this makes sense once you have more information. It at least makes much more sense than conventional wisdom and morality.

The Dilemma of Empathy Bringing about Murder

We are all fundamentally empathic beings. All of us. Even the ones who are too sick to know it. Even many corporate capitalists. Almost all of us have some compassion, except for the true sociopaths, who unfortunately are primarily the ones now in charge because they have organized to control the rest of us mere neurotics. By writing their own self-protection into law, they have built a system to sustain their uncaring and ill-informed form of cannibalism. Dick Cheney is a prefect example.

We all need intimate affiliation with others in order to be healthy and happy. But, as I have pointed out in a half dozen other books, we live in a culture in which intimacy is blocked at every turn, because phoniness, secrecy, and lying are contrary to intimacy and they are the social norm. If intimacy is to happen within the system, someone has to charge for it and make a profit. Intimacy for sale, since intimacy requires honesty, is a very hard thing to pull off, because a huckster has a hard time being honest when getting the sale is the most important thing. What results from that attempt is a pathetic sentimental substitute for intimacy and a kind of prostitution that is not even that much fun. Corporate capitalism is what has provided the opening for the sociopaths to take charge and set up the worldwide economic order to assure that things will stay that way—commercial, cheap, phony entertainment instead of love, truthiness instead of truth, husk instead of seed, bullshit instead of honesty.

At both the individual and collective levels, we are living in a world where we are entertained by each other's performances in front of each other in the daily dance of routine superficiality, but we don't get nourished by contact at a simpler and deeper level. This discrepancy between the "act" and the actual experience of being in contact is now institutionalized, codified, and taught in every second in school, at home, on television, and even on the Internet. Civilization now depends on TV and the Internet. As long as we remain civilized, we will remain defeated and doomed.

How do we fix that? Most people know the sensation of disconnection vaguely and intuitively and feel like they are starving, but they consider it to be normal because everyone else is disconnected and starving, too. And like any good AA member will tell you, the first step is to "admit that we have a problem."

First, we have to somehow withdraw from the ongoing booming, buzzing confusion of the world game we are all playing, where we live in abstractland instead of our bodies, and we are not related to gravity and each other as present-tense, noticing beings. In my work, I have called the mutual breakthrough to contact with sensation, gravity, and others "radical honesty." Honesty is the basis of all intimacy. And intimacy is the basis of happiness, and we are only happy if we are authentically connected because we are essentially social animals.

Without authentic intimate contact with others, we shrink up and die. The institutionalization of the shrunken and the dead is called corporate capitalism. It tries to substitute entertainment-for-a-fee, for the nourishment of commonplace experience in contactful relationships with others.

The wisdom my clients and I have gained from thirty years of clinical practice and doing tons of workshops, does apply to healing the social alienation and our murder-for-profit culture. *But not without full confrontation and taking back from the bloody hands of our oppressors—by any means possible—that which has been taken from us. Our empathy with the great majority of the oppressed must bring us to stop the opressors and put into place something that keeps them down.*

I want to be fair, including being fair to rich people. What I am proposing can be done so much more fairly than the careless slaughter currently in place and sanctioned by the fat fucks in commerce and Congress who are engaged in conventional corruption. Some of these goddamned killers and child molesters need killing—and quickly—and I know how we can do it. We could save billions of lives by redistributing the wealth and protein of perhaps as few as a thousand people. Can you believe it? It's true! I'll show you!

This is tough love, tough compassion. The toughest. But practical. It's a new system for killing and eating old fat fucks, rich from a lifetime of murder, instead of letting them kill children. It is a terrible, but necessary form of practical compassion, and a hell of a lot less terrible than the slaughters, poisonings, torturous killing, and deprivation of innocents going on as we speak.

But you might as well nip your peacenik tendencies in the bud. If you think you can save the children without killing the fat fucks, and fighting, killing, and eating some of their goddamned goons as well, you are delusional. I am not just a guy in a diner. I am a good man, an intelligent person, someone who loves people, a clinical psychologist, a best-selling author, father, friend, and successful member of the human community of my time. I was born in the lower class in America and have advanced to the middle class—if you can call that an advance. I have degrees and enough money to live well and travel the world. This is my considered professional opinion after a lifetime of service to others: Eat the rich! Now! Take all their shit and pass it around! Give it back to the people it has been stolen from!

There are good reasons why I have reached this conclusion. Here, is one, just one, example of more information to come: a simple beginning fact for you to chew on. This is the way wealth is distributed right now, today, in the United States of America. As Joe Bageant says in his book *Rainbow Pie* (Portobello Books, 2010), "Given the terrible polarization of wealth and power in this country (the top 1 percent hold more wealth than the bottom 45 percent combined, and their take is still rising), we can no longer even claim equal opportunity for a majority. Opportunity for the majority to do what? Pluck chickens and telemarket to the ever-dwindling middle class?" [2]

The polarization of wealth needs to be faced and handled on a global scale immediately, because it is absolutely deadly to our own citizens and to people throughout the rest of the world.

Soon there will be a mass realization of a simple fact: There are a hell of a lot more of us than there are of them. We could change who is being served and who is serving this meal. I am going sane. Come on and join me. If you can't beat 'em, eat 'em! Let's get cookin'.

Brad Blanton
Sparrowhawk Farm
November 1, 2010

INTRODUCTION

The Question for Our Time (and a Much Too Reasonable Answer)

The world is going to hell in a hand basket and we are set up to have a big die-off of human beings in just a few years. Unless we come up with a better plan, poor people all over the planet soon will start dying like flies. Two to three billion people are in danger of dying at once, within months of each other, sometime within the next ten years.

The poorer half of humanity is in grave danger of going to their graves—or dying and just rotting where they are—at some point within the next ten years. There is a pandemic of non-human species dying off that also shows no signs of diminishing. These billions of people and these thousands upon thousands of entire species are going away forever soon, and very quickly, possibly, or probably, whether or not we try to do something about it.

Tragedies like global warming, pandemics, the accumulation of nuclear waste and other sources of poisoning, the very likely occurrence of nuclear holocaust in several danger zones, the total and complete economic collapse of the existing banking/military/industrial/governmental/media complex (based on theft, murder, and unending growth), methane burps (already starting) putting gigantic amounts of previously unpredicted global warming gas into the atmosphere, peak oil resulting in greater demand and decreased supply on an ever growing basis, ocean destroying oil spills and related tragedies, and a few other independently catastrophic events, are on the horizon. And the likelihood of not more than one big tragedy happening at a time is very, very low. Just to be clear, the probability of more than one of these things happening at the same time and interacting with each other to create greater tragedy is very very high.

A cumulative combination of sets of upcoming tragedies occurring at the same time is actually statistically unavoidable, and any two at a time will wreak havoc in the world like nothing we have ever seen. Win, lose, or draw, threats to the life of humanity and the planet are on the way, most are inevitable, and the liklihood of simutaneous and interacting tragedies is also practically inevitable. The shots have been fired. All we can do now is try to dodge the bullets or take the hits with the least amount of damage.

There is no certainty but let us assume that this is simply the truth. What must we stop doing and what must we do?

Our dire circumstances have been brought about by our so-called civilization, which essentially involves too many people living in city-states stealing resources from surrounding land bases, and killing off the inhabitants who live there in order for the city-states' way of life to survive.

The current worldwide corporate capitalist economy, based almost entirely on this type of violence and theft, is without a doubt coming to an end whether or not we end it consciously. Our standard of living in the West, which is based on the on-going, ever-increasing murder and enslavement of other humans and species, and on the devouring of the earth's resources, is patently unsustainable.

The only thing to be determined by us is the time it takes for these bad things to happen, how it gets done, and what is left after it is over. The question for our time is: *How do we get to a post-civilized world and have a social and physical environment that sustains and preserves humans and other species, and protects all from further human destruction?*

This is the main orienting question for this entire book. My suggested plan involves dodging some bullets we have already fired and taking some hits with relative equanimity, and I go into some detail about what is likely to happen and what can be done.

There exists no solution that avoids these upcoming tragedies. I do have a very reasonable plan for reducing their magnitude significantly, controlling to some extent how traumatic they will be, and preventing billions of human deaths and the extinction of tens of thousands of species.

As I already told you in the Preface and title, the key to handling these inevitable upcoming threats to the very life of humanity itself is simple: feeding rich people to poor people. Cannibalism is the answer. We do this until a complete redistribution of wealth and food occurs, and a locally sustainable way of living is created for the remainder of humanity, by consent and with the protection of a worldwide majority.

Obviously, for the plan to work, this must not take quite as long to accomplish as the timeline for human extinction currently in place. Again, listen. This is important. The redistribution of wealth and power must not take as long to accomplish as the process of human extinction that is currently occurring. So, in this book I will tell you about the timeline that is currently in place. It is not good news. And it is the reason for the pressing need for this book. I will also tell you about how long we have to redistribute the wealth and protein of rich, powerful people and take back what belongs to us from corporate murderers for profit.

The plan I advocate is as *just* as it is *simple*. It is more viable than any other current ways of thinking I know of, and much fairer than the current plan—or lack thereof. Consider this. In a world without the quick reversal of our current form of cannibalism, a third or more of humanity (two to three *billion* people) dies suddenly in the midst of a total economic collapse, while experiencing the chaos of famine, starvation, disease, and massive "natural" disasters resulting from global warming. Most of these victims will be poor people. The next biggest group of victims will be middle class people. The smallest group of victims will be rich people. There are fewer of them and they are better protected. Even under the current no-plan plan, more of the rich and powerful will still die in the mess we are headed for than would die up front if we fix the situation with korporate kannibalism! So this benefits everyone—even the rich! We can significantly affect these overall statistics and the extent of the tragedy so that almost everyone wins! But we must act quickly.

We must create very quickly conditions and requirements enforced by law and military power, where the rich can only bribe their way out of being eaten by giving up almost *all* of their money and becoming relatively poor. (They will give up billions, but be allowed to keep a little stipend if they come along nicely.) They can avoid being eaten and have almost *all* of their possessions taken anyway and still have a good life. *Then, at the very most, less than a few hundred rich people die and get eaten, because most will volunteer to pay the bribe, and the restoration of balance and a new beginning for the world and humanity will be brought about much more efficiently, humanely, and justly.*

I am advocating cannibalism as a practical matter as well as to get your attention, so that we not waste this murder of murderers, but use their bodies as well as their stolen wealth to feed hungry people and grow good food and restore the earth, *and to care for those billions of the rest of us* fortunate *enough to be poor or of modest means.* But that is only the beginning of this book. This book is also about several very important and very hopeful additional social and scientific innovations that could save us from our current technological and psychological path to ecocide.

History in a Cul de Sac called Corporate Capitalism

So far, a new emerging view of history shows that humanity has always had and still has a great will to destroy and a death wish. Unfortunately sociopaths most stricken with these obsessions are currently entirely in charge of the economic order and the political systems. Let's not only face this truth, but also apply it as leverage to change the guard. In his book The Power of Conscious Feelings (Hohm Press, 2010), Clinton Callahan says that coming out of our numbness is an important first step that must be taken before we can make change. Even though the psychological change is not social change itself, coming out of our denial and delusion about the tough situation we are facing in the world today is going to motivate us to act swiftly and decisively for social change.1 Waking up is hard to do. Acting upon awakening is even harder, but not impossible.

The Korporate Kannibal Kookbook is full of information about both why and how to cook the cannibals who are currently devouring the living earth and the rest of us. The recipes for what kind of meal to make out of these folks are not ironic by accident. There are suggestions for how to butcher butchers, to eat eaters, poison poisoners and to select and consume merciless consumers, so that their deaths might be considered in relation to how they lived and treated other people, and taken as instruction, as well as nurturance.

There are instructions on how to prepare your feast in ways that are particularly appropriate to the kind of life the particular cannibals you are consuming have lived. Tasty recipes are offered that use owners, executives, stockholders, and employees of insurance companies, pharmaceutical companies, credit card companies, banks, oil companies, and media conglomerates as ingredients. Most of these people from the banking industry will be butchered by being squeezed to death. Special preparations are made for lobbyists, weapons manufacturers, oil company folks, right-wing media stars, and more lobbyists. The book includes a great list of potential dishes. (The recipe "*Lobbyist from Soup to Nuts!*" comes to mind.)

We even include a few suggested things to mention when saying grace over your meal, as a matter of honoring our fellow cannibals, much like Native Americans spoke to the bodies of the creatures they hunted and killed, to honor their spirits before butchering the animals and eating their meat.

Top on the list of candidates for cooking are all of the capitalist cannibals who have previously decided who lives and who dies purely on the basis of profit. Next come all those who profited immensely from helping the capitalists, their Eichmann-like obedient servants. (Adolf Eichmann was the German Nazi who was such a talented organizer that he was able to design and conduct the Holocaust on behalf of his boss, Hitler). Every one of the capitalist bureaucrats who profits from participation in the system, unless they give up all their money immediately, will qualify to be eaten, and still have their wealth taken and redistributed anyway. (Some of the stupider ones who don't take the deal may need to be parboiled longer than others for tenderness.)

There is a pretty good supply of these goddamned rich, civilized, sociopathic murderers, but there are a hell of a lot less of them than there are of us who are poorer and slightly less malicious. So, as a practical matter, this is not only a very good life-saving idea, it will clearly improve the quality of the kind of people the rest of us have to put up with as well.

It is striking, almost unbelievable, how few people we have to kill (or threaten and let bribe their way out of becoming the main course for the evening) for my plan to work. Starting off with merely the top twelve hundred of the richest of these rich folks would make a gigantic difference in the worldwide quest for sustainable living! Their property and assets would cancel the entire world debt of all nations and all individuals and families with plenty left over to provide for our future for enough years until new structures are in place to continue the reform. There is a list of a thousand of them in a special edition of Forbes magazine (March 10, 2010) in an article entitled "The World's Billionaires." There is one version of our goddamned list right there!

They either give up all but enough to live on, to avoid being eaten, or else we eat them and take all their money. Either way, the world wins. If they cheat, we eat. If they are stubborn or foolish enough to refuse to make their contribution to healing the world voluntarily, we get a good meal and a nice group of homes and gardens for poor folks to live in from every one of them.

We can have a new "consumer index," a truly meaningful measure of economic health, for the first time in history. And we'll be able to love our enemies, just like Jesus said we should—with a little extra flavoring, butter, olive oil and excellent sauces.

As we, the great majority, get hungrier, angrier, and wiser, we need to follow a step-by-step plan to use these murdering thieves to feed, shelter and clothe those we care about and ourselves. In this way, we will begin to restore balance, rather than just having to endure chaos, mob rule, death and destruction for decades while poor people slaughter each other and protect the rich for pay. If the great die-off occurs, and if we don't make this eat-the-rich plan a reality, that's what we are in for, you can rest assured it will be poor people in front.

This is a very reasonable solution (too many people, not enough food, people as food). So the question is: Which people get to eat and who gets eaten? Using rich people as food and fertilizer, as well as seizing their assets to pay off the entire worldwide debt, gives the rest of us more land and life to grow on, and what we might call a meat and potatoes kind of solution. Food to feed more and kill less shows up for dozens of reasons once we get really fed up, so to speak, and the korporate kapitalist fictional figureheads are consumed.

With a new system of justice based on sustainability (proposed in chapter 4) we can do this fairly. Avoiding ecocide and saving billions of people is actually attainable by killing fewer than a thousand people. The overshoot on the Earth's capacity to survive the overpopulation of people will be improved instead of damaged further by the ignorant captains of industry who are currently in charge of the big lie—that the "free" market rape and murder of the world will self correct. Capitalist rapists will not reform capitalism.

Human population decline, which is necessary for our survival and renewal can occur on a much more reasonable basis than the current prevailing plan of consuming our surroundings and each other until everything is gone and we all die after a period of disorganized cannibalism. When I say "our" I mean it with a capital "O," which means *all us living beings on the planet*, not just human beings.

Making Choices

There are honest cannibals and there are korporate kannibals. Pick your group. One bunch is going to devour the other one way or another. This is a "how-to" book that will put some of the korporate kannibals into a real pickle (see "How to Pickle Kannibals").

Here are the chapter titles with brief synopses. These chapters lay out the potential solution to all our problems and provide the scientific evidence for the viability of this way of handling a tough job as tastefully as possible.

Table of Contents

Preface

PART ONE—FOOD

Chapter 1 Feeding Rich People to Poor People: The Just Solution to Poverty, Global Warming, War, Species Extermination, and a Few Dozen Other Problems—Why It Is Necessary and How It Could Work

This is a detailed overview of the necessity and benefits of this particular diet for a small planet.

Chapter 2 Ethics and Aesthetics: Broad Guidelines for a New System of Justice to Decide Whom to Eat, How to Choose Which Current Butchers to Butcher, How to Prepare Them, and How to Cook Them

Hahaha! "How to Prepare Them, and How to Cook Them"! Get it?

Chapter 3 How to De-Face the Hard Case Who Has Defaced the Land Base (and How to Save Face)

Hey! Don't give me any lip!

Chapter 4 Special Places, Special Recipes: The Fat Cat Crematorium, The Hot Dog Plant, Broiled Banker, Corporate Capitalist Consume, Attorney on a Gurney, Fillet of CEO, Grilled Lobbyist Caesar Salad, Deep Fried Freeze Dried

Rawhide from Countrywide.

Chapter 5 Lobbyists from Soup to Nuts! Weyerhaeuser Waffles, Trawler Tripe, Pork Skins and Men Skins from Napalm Producers, Spaghetti and Meatballs from Factory Farm Owners/Managers—and Other Hole Foods

Chapter 6 How to Conduct a Bender with a Blender Party: A Celebration Where Who Comes to Eat and Who Comes to Be Eaten Remains Vague Until the Very Last Minute, and Fun Is Had by All!

In one version of this, guests get to decide democratically who gets to eat and who goes hungry, so to speak. (Hahaha! GOES hungry! Get it? Hahaha!)

Chapter 7 Sweet Revenge and Just Desserts

Particularly good to eat in every way are desserts and munchies made from those who currently hire, brainwash, bribe, or force our children to soldier for them to protect them from the rest of us, to guard their stolen properties and resources, and to kill native populations who are trying to get their stolen resources back. This chapter is topped off with recipes for "Blue Blood Pudding" and "Cereal from General Mills Executives."

PART TWO—FERTILIZER

Chapter 8 The Raw Foods Revolution: Making "Rich Soil" (Good Shit Out of Bad Shits) for Spectacular Gardens

Each memorial marker or carved stone memorializing those who gave their lives so others might live will explain how each of these people soiled themselves—so to speak.

Chapter 9 Crap Rotation: How to Poison, Purify, Process, and Prepare Monsanto Executives—The New Agricultural Revolution

We'll have a special plot in more ways than one for how to make sure these dudes are genetically modified in such a way that no more of them can be grown again without our seal of approval.

Post Script

This is script to be written on a post for future interplanetary travelers to read if they happen to drop by, in order to explain how we disappeared, just in case we don't have the guts to eat the eaters, take the takers, and consume the consumers. It will be humanity's tombstone, so to speak, if we fail to cannibalize the cannibals.

Appendix

Later in the book, there will be a list of the top twelve hundred or so people who are first in line to be served (along with an excellent recipe for Korporate Kapitalist Kchitlins) and a list of the year's top ten worst corporations. We have more than our limit for the first big cook-off right here! Check it out.

In addition to canceling world debt for all nation states, the redistribution of the wealth of the thousand or so people at the top of the line would pay off all the mortgages the whole world over, and still be enough to provide food, education, health care, shelter, and child care for everyone in the world, on an ongoing basis, long enough to establish a world order that sustains all those things ongoingly.

Published by the KKK (The Kannibal Kookbook Korporation)

"In a world gone insane, anyone going sane is seen as insane—and of course, some of them are."

—Korporate Motto

Note: Of course, that is not the real table of contents. I just couldn't stop making up little dumb-assed brainchild chapter titles for menus from the fundamental concept. As you will see, once you get started it is hard to stop finding candidates for supper every-goddamned-where you look.

So I lied. That's not the table of contents. The whole book, and the real table of contents, deals with everything I have mentioned so far, but more than what I have cooked up here. Keep going. It gets better. Trust me.

Mwahahahahahahahahahahahahahahaaa!

Korporate Kannibal Kookbook

Actual Table of Contents

Preface 11

Introduction: The Question for Our Time in History (and a Much Too Reasonable Answer) 21

PART ONE : DESIGNING THE WAY OF THE COLLAPSE

Chapter 1 Getting Hangry: Clues for Whom to Eat for a Special Treat 35

Chapter 2 Feeding Rich People to Poor People: The Just Solution to Poverty, Global Warming, War, Species Extermination, and Other Problems—Why It Is Necessary and How It Could Work 41

Chapter 3 Discontent and Its Civilization: Dissed Appointments 55

Chapter 4 Okay, Okay, We Can't Eat 'Em Goddammit: How about Just Killing Them? 87

PART TWO: INTEGRATING A NEW VISION

Chapter 5 A New Story for a New Beginning on the Other Side of Civilization: Human Photosynthesis 99

Chapter 6 The Work of Stanley Milgram: Obedient Servitude or Moral Integrity Based on Knowing Your Own Heart 107

Chapter 7 The Conservative Way: The Pathway to Oblivion 117

Chapter 8 As Long as You Have Obedient Servants You Can Forget about Justice: Then How Bad Is the System of Survival We Have in Place? 133

Chapter 9 The Truth Machine: How We Can Know What Is True 145

Chapter 10 Called by Each Other to Our Higher We: Permanent Structures for Citizen Dialogue and Deliberation 159

Chapter 11 The Machine Stops: A Story by E.M. Forster 177

PART THREE WHAT'S THE BIG IDEA?

Chapter 12 A Simple Question: Can We Heal or Replace the Collective Mental Illness Called Corporate Capitalist Civilization? 207

Chapter 13 Radical Honesty as a Prelude to Deep Democracy: The Antidote for Compliant Cowardice 219

Chapter 14 Examples of Hardheartedness and Irresponsibility: The Opposite of Empathy 225

PART FOUR: SOME GOOD NEWS AND POSITIVE RESULTS FROM BIG EXPERIMENTS

Chapter 15 Conscious Participation in Evolution: How Can We Help? 241

Chapter 16 The Pathway to Salvation, If There Is One: Rooting Out a Route 255

Chapter 17 Summary of What I Have Said, What Others Have Said, What I Have Said about What Others Have Said, and What We Should Do About It: A Final Framework for Feasible Failure 269

Notes 278

Recommended Resources 287

About the Author 288

Part One

Designing the Way of the Collapse

You know how there are these truisms that simply are not true, yet they persist, like "We only use 10 percent of our brain capacity"? This is not true, but everyone believes it. Collectively we have dozens of them—things that we "know" and operate according to, which simply are not true.

Often these "memes" unify and control us, and help us to focus and do things collectively that are not really good for any of us. Well, one or two may benefit a few folks for a little while, so those few folks sell the idea to the ones that pay the cost. The rest of us participate in getting ripped off, and then brag about it—like poor, ignorant, brainwashed, pitiful Rednecks voting Republican because they believe "it's the Christian thing to do."

This problem of folks working against their own self-interest simply because of tradition is no longer a small thing. We have to take charge of our lives together and undo a bunch of these dumb-assed memes right away in order to have only a small bunch of us die, instead of almost all of us. We need to come up with some better memes to substitute for the massively self- and planet-destructive ones.

This Book is a Gigantic Recipe for a Special Feast Called "Love in the Aftermath"

Okay, here is what this book is really about. There are seven subjects, related to each other. Korporate kannibalism is one of the seven. It is a necessary, but not sufficient condition. Here is the list of ideas that interlock to make up the big idea of this book.

I give you this list in advance, dear reader, and without explanation. Further explanation, item by item, will come in the section coming up called "What's the Big Idea." Then the entire remainder of the book explains the explanation. This is much closer to the real table of contents than that first one I lied about to get your attention.

If you don't want to read the rest of the book to understand what I am talking about, then don't.

If you do, thank you. I would like to hear from you so I don't feel so lonesome.

Here is the list.

(1) Campaign finance reform and permanent lobbyist control by citizens
(2) Corporate cannibal cannibalism
(3) A new system of justice based on sustainability
(4) How to build and begin to use a Truth Machine
(5) A new, deeply democratic form of government that has never existed before
(6) The establishment of a world commonwealth that is not international
(7) The establishment of a worldwide meritocracy

The last section is the vision of how these ideas interlock and reinforce each other to create heaven on earth, just on the other side of the hell we must go through to get there, and includes hell in it as part of the design.

CHAPTER 1

Getting Hangry: Clues for Whom to Eat for a Special Treat

Thinkers throughout history have been aware of the human tendency to consume ourselves. A few examples of this are mentioned in the following excerpt from Raj Patel's book *The Value of Nothing* (Picador USA, 2010).

> "Jean-Jacques Rousseau turned this [Hobbe's idea of nature as a state of war] on its head. Although he shared with Hobbes the view that people were generally unsociable, he disagreed that humans were inherently machines of infinite want. It was possible, he argued, for people to feel that they've got 'enough.' Being sated is something that people can learn—and it is after they have managed to control their instincts and impulses in the best interests of themselves and society that they are truly free—precisely the opposite of Greenspan's vision. Rousseau also went on to argue that 'artificial people' were, in fact, precisely possessed of the characteristics that Hobbes saw in the state of nature. Entities like corporations and governments were nasty and brutish. Worse, because they didn't have to eat or sleep, and could never die, artificial people were more worrisome because they could never have enough.
>
> "Rousseau wasn't the first to worry about insatiable nonhuman creatures living among us. Almost every cultural tradition has cautionary tales of similar beings with appetites run riot. In what is now called western Canada and the United States, indigenous cultures told of Weendigoes. A giant, hungry spirit, a Weendigo had lips that were bloody from its constantly gnashing jaws, and

> its hunger became deeper with every drop of human blood it drank. Weendigoes were cannibals, people whose desires had so entirely become the core of their being that they were prepared to eat others in order to survive. Weendigo tales were told as a reminder that unbridled consumption in harvest months meant less food for everyone in leaner seasons, which meant that eating more than your fair share today was effectively a kind of cannibalism inflicted on the rest of the tribe in the future. Basil Johnston, an Ojibwe scholar, argues that Weendigoes are alive and well. Few people in North America have seen giant spirits, but many more people have seen their modern incarnation, giant creatures with few interests beyond the satisfaction of their immediate appetites, even if this prevents tomorrow's hunger from being met. The modern Weendigo, Johnston suggests, is the multinational corporation.
>
> "Other cultures also have icons of insatiable and constantly suffering beasts. Thai and Japanese Buddhists tell of hungry ghosts, once covetous people who when they die become ghosts with mouths as small as the finest needle's eye and who are cursed with perpetual hunger. These mythic people weren't blind to the world—they merely saw it through the optic of their own desires, desires that outweighed any care they might have had to the damage they caused. Like Asia and the Americas, Europe also has an example of a creature like this, and when Marx wrote about capitalism's progeny, he drew on it directly. For him, capitalism bred vampires."[1]

More contemporary among thinkers than Hobbes and Marx is Paul Krugman. If you don't know him please allow me the pleasure of introducing you. He has a way of looking into things with a kind of shocked and appalled critical mind like all great essayists and thinkers. He often casually, and even-handedly, reports incredible ignorance in a simple, merely descriptively way, such that it induces fury and disbelief on the part of the reader. And he rightfully calls ignorance treason, when it is.

Betraying the Planet
By Paul Krugman *(New York Times,* June 29, 2009)[2]

So the House passed the Waxman-Markey climate-change bill. In political terms, it was a remarkable achievement.

But 212 representatives voted no. A handful of these no votes came from representatives who considered the bill too weak, but most rejected the bill because they rejected the whole notion that we have to do something about greenhouse gases.

And as I watched the deniers make their arguments, I couldn't help thinking that I was watching a form of treason—treason against the planet.

To fully appreciate the irresponsibility and immorality of climate-change denial, you need to know about the grim turn taken by the latest climate research.

The fact is that the planet is changing faster than even pessimists expected: ice caps are shrinking, arid zones spreading, at a terrifying rate. And according to a number of recent studies, catastrophe—a rise in temperature so large as to be almost unthinkable—can no longer be considered a mere possibility. It is, instead, the most likely outcome if we continue along our present course.

Thus researchers at M.I.T., who were previously predicting a temperature rise of a little more than 4 degrees by the end of this century, are now predicting a rise of more than 9 degrees. Why? Global greenhouse gas emissions are rising faster than expected; some mitigating factors, like absorption of carbon dioxide by the oceans, are turning out to be weaker than hoped; and there's growing evidence that climate change is self-reinforcing—that, for example, rising temperatures will cause some arctic tundra to defrost, releasing even more carbon dioxide into the atmosphere. Temperature increases on the scale predicted by the M.I.T. researchers and others would create huge disruptions in our lives and our economy. As a recent authoritative U.S. government report points out, by the end of this century New Hampshire may well have the climate of North Carolina today, Illinois may have the climate of East Texas, and across the country extreme, deadly heat waves—the kind that traditionally occur only once in a generation—may become annual or biannual events.

In other words, we're facing a clear and present danger to our way of life, perhaps even to civilization itself. How can anyone justify failing to act?

Well, sometimes even the most authoritative analyses get things wrong. And if dissenting opinion-makers and politicians based their dissent on hard work and hard thinking—if they had carefully studied the issue, consulted with experts and concluded that the overwhelming scientific consensus was misguided—they could at least claim to be acting responsibly.

But if you watched the debate on Friday, you didn't see people who've thought hard about a crucial issue, and are trying to do the right thing. What you saw, instead, were people who show no sign of being interested in the truth. They don't like the political and policy implications of climate change, so they've decided not to believe in it—and they'll grab any argument, no matter how disreputable, that feeds their denial.

Indeed, if there was a defining moment in Friday's debate, it was the declaration by Representative Paul Broun of Georgia that climate change is nothing but a "hoax" that has been "perpetrated out of the scientific community." I'd call this a crazy conspiracy theory, but doing so would actually be unfair to crazy conspiracy theorists. After all, to believe that global warming is a hoax you have to believe in a vast cabal consisting of thousands of scientists—a cabal so powerful that it has managed to create false records on everything from global temperatures to Arctic sea ice.

Yet Mr. Broun's declaration was met with applause.

Given this contempt for hard science, I'm almost reluctant to mention the deniers' dishonesty on matters economic. But in addition to rejecting climate science, the opponents of the climate bill made a point of misrepresenting the results of studies of the bill's economic impact, which all suggest that the cost will be relatively low.

Still, is it fair to call climate denial a form of treason? Isn't it politics as usual?

Yes, it is—and that's why it's unforgivable.

Do you remember the days when Bush administration officials claimed that terrorism posed an "existential threat" to America, a threat in whose face normal rules no longer applied? That was hyperbole—but the existential threat from climate change is all too real.

Yet the deniers are choosing, willfully, to ignore that threat, placing future generations of Americans in grave danger, simply because it's in their political interest to pretend that there's nothing to worry about. If that's not betrayal, I don't know what is.

This Makes Me Hangry

Doesn't that just piss you off? How did these ignorant, shit-for-brains people get elected to public office?

If you work on it, when you read shit like this, you can start feeling hungry for some good ol' barbeque spare ribs like they make real good in Georgia, where they call it "Piggin' out on Pig!" A few drinks beforehand... maybe some fine wine to go along with the main course... and lots of napkins. We could videotape the meal and the conversation, and send it out to the world to let these smug, ignorant fuckers know their ignorance is no longer as completely protected as it used to be.

Menu for the evening: Dumb Fuck Congressman from Georgia.

Just kidding again, of course. Try not to think about it. Heh heh heh.

My friend Susan Campbell, author of *Getting Real* (H.J. Kramer/New World Library, 2001), and many other books, and a Radical Honesty trainer, was originally repulsed by the whole idea of corporate cannibal cannibalism. But she eventually asked, "How big is the eco-footprint of the average aristocrat?" (*That is a very good question!)*

She continues, "There are other more radical ideas for diehard carnivores. *Time to Eat the Dog?* (Thames and Hudson, 2009) is the title of a new book by Brenda and Robert Vale, two New Zealand environmentalists. (Several recipes from Korea are available, should you choose to follow this path.) The eco-pawprint of a large dog is the same as that of a 4.6-liter SUV driving 10,000 kilometers, according to the authors, who are both scientists at Victoria University of Wellington. They state that an average dog eats 164 kilograms of meat and 95 kilograms of cereals every year, which means that it takes 0.84 hectares (a football pitch) of arable land and tens of thousands of liters of water to give the dog his Pedigree Chum."[3]

Hey! I guess we can eat the fat folks' pets along with them! Now we're getting somewhere! As Susan and I continued our discussion by email, she wrote, "I was at a lecture this past Sunday at the science and non-duality conference here by a man named Le Baaba (an African teacher with intimate experience with Indonesian and African tribes), who, when making 'first contact' with a tribe in Indonesia, participated in a hunting/killing the neighboring tribe and eating their flesh ritual. His tale was fascinating. So the theme of cannibalism is emerging in the culture—sort of like vampirism is also a current theme. What do you make of this?

"I imagine we're sensing that overpopulation is coming to get us and we're running out of food. Archetypal themes often presage changing cultural beliefs. And cultural beliefs often have a very self-serving function. Maybe eating the rich isn't such a bad idea after all."

Then, she concluded. "I'm so hungry I could eat a Brahmin."[4]

So, I say we need a "piece of reconciliation commission" of citizens drawn at random to determine who gets eaten and who eats. These temporary panels could be called once a year and we could feast on the cream that has risen to the top over the last year. More importantly, we could also save some pets.This is a killer idea!

CHAPTER 2

Feeding Rich People to Poor People:
The Just Solution to Poverty, Global Warming, War, Species Extermination, and Other Problems—Why It Is Necessary and How It Could Work

What are the benefits of my suggested high-protein, high-fat diet for a small planet?

To start out, here is the essence of the dilemma we face, discussed in a dialogue by two very bright, very wise Brits, George Monbiot, a syndicated columnist and bestselling author known for his environmental and political activism, and Paul Kingsnorth, an author, environmentalist, and poet.

Is There Any Point in Fighting to Stave off Industrial Apocalypse?
By George Monbiot and Paul Kingsnorth[1]

The collapse of civilization will bring us a saner world, says Paul Kingsnorth. No, counters George Monbiot, we can't let billions perish... Their dialogue was published in *The Guardian/UK* (August 19, 2009).

Dear George,

On the desk in front of me is a set of graphs. The horizontal axis of each represents the years 1750 to 2000. The graphs show, variously, population levels, CO_2 concentration in the atmosphere, exploitation of fisheries, destruction of tropical forests, paper consumption, number of motor vehicles, water use, the rate of species extinction, and the totality of the human economy's gross domestic product.

What grips me about these graphs (and graphs don't usually grip me) is that though they all show very different things, they have an almost identical shape. A line begins on the left of the page, rising gradually as it moves to the right. Then, in the last inch or so—around 1950—it veers steeply upwards, like a pilot banking after a cliff has suddenly appeared from what he thought was an empty bank of cloud.

The root cause of all these trends is the same: a rapacious human economy bringing the world swiftly to the brink of chaos. We know this; some of us even attempt to stop it happening. Yet all of these trends continue to get rapidly worse, and there is no sign of that changing soon. What these graphs make clear better than anything else is the cold reality: there is a serious crash on the way.

Yet very few of us are prepared to look honestly at the message this reality is screaming at us: that the civilization we are a part of is hitting the buffers at full speed, and it is too late to stop it. Instead, most of us—and I include in this generalization much of the mainstream environmental movement—are still wedded to a vision of the future as an upgraded version of the present. We still believe in "progress," as lazily defined by western liberalism. We still believe that we will be able to continue living more or less the same comfortable lives (albeit with more wind farms and better light bulbs) if we can only embrace "sustainable development" rapidly enough; and that we can then extend it to the extra three billion people who will shortly join us on this already gasping planet.

I think this is simply denial. The writing is on the wall for industrial society, and no amount of ethical shopping or determined protesting is going to change that now. Take a civilization built on the myth of human exceptionalism and a deeply embedded cultural attitude to "nature"; add a blind belief in technological and material progress; then fuel the whole thing with a power source that is discovered to be disastrously destructive only after we have used it to inflate our numbers and appetites beyond the point of no return. What do you get? We are starting to find out.

We need to get real. Climate change is teetering on the point of no return while our leaders bang the drum for more growth. The economic system we rely upon cannot be tamed without collapsing, for it relies upon that growth to function. And who wants it tamed anyway? Most people in the rich world won't be giving up their cars or holidays without a fight.

Some people—perhaps you—believe that these things should not be said, even if true, because saying them will deprive people of "hope," and without hope there will be no chance of "saving the planet." But false hope is worse than no hope at all. As for saving the planet—what we are really trying to save, as we scrabble around planting turbines on mountains and shouting at ministers, is not the planet but our attachment to the western material culture, which we cannot imagine living without.

The challenge is not how to shore up a crumbling empire with wave machines and global summits, but to start thinking about how we are going to live through its fall, and what we can learn from its collapse.

All the best, Paul

Dear Paul,

Like you, I have become ever gloomier about our chances of avoiding the crash you predict. For the past few years I have been almost professionally optimistic, exhorting people to keep fighting, knowing that to say there is no hope is to make it so. I still have some faith in our ability to make rational decisions based on evidence. But it is waning.

If it has taken governments this long even to start discussing reform of the common fisheries policy—if they refuse even to make contingency plans for peak oil—what hope is there of working towards a steady-state economy, let alone the voluntary economic contraction ultimately required to avoid either the climate crash or the depletion of crucial resources?

The interesting question, and the one that probably divides us, is this: to what extent should we welcome the likely collapse of industrial civilization? Or more precisely: to what extent do we believe that some good may come of it?

I detect in your writings, and in the conversations we have had, an attraction towards—almost a yearning for—this apocalypse, a sense that you see it as a cleansing fire that will rid the world of a diseased society. If this is your view, I do not share it. I'm sure we can agree that the immediate consequences of collapse would be hideous: the breakdown of the systems that keep most of us alive; mass starvation; war. These alone surely give us sufficient reason to fight on, however faint our chances appear. But even if we were somehow able to put this out of our minds, I believe that what is likely to come out on the other side will be worse than our current settlement.

Here are three observations: 1) Our species (unlike most of its members) is tough and resilient; 2) When civilizations collapse, psychopaths take over; 3) We seldom learn from others' mistakes.

From the first observation, this follows: even if you are hardened to the fate of humans, you can surely see that our species will not become extinct without causing the extinction of almost all others. However hard we fall, we will recover sufficiently to land another hammer blow on the biosphere. We will continue to do so until there is so little left that even Homo sapiens can no longer survive. This is the ecological destiny of a species possessed of outstanding intelligence, opposable thumbs, and an ability to interpret and exploit almost every possible resource—in the absence of political restraint.

From the second and third observations, this follows: instead of gathering as free collectives of happy householders, survivors of this collapse will be subject to the will of people seeking to monopolize remaining resources. This will is likely to be imposed through violence. Political accountability will be a distant memory. The chances of conserving any resource in these circumstances are approximately zero. The human and ecological consequences of the first global collapse are likely to persist for many generations, perhaps for our species' remaining time on earth. To imagine that good could come of the involuntary failure of industrial civilization is also to succumb to denial. The answer to your question—what will we learn from this collapse? —is nothing.

This is why, despite everything, I fight on. I am not fighting to sustain economic growth. I am fighting to prevent both initial collapse and the repeated catastrophe that follows. However faint the hopes of engineering a soft landing—an ordered and structured downsizing of the global economy—might be, we must keep this possibility alive. Perhaps we are both in denial: I, because I think the fight is still worth having; you, because you think it isn't.

With my best wishes, George

Dear George,

You say that you detect in my writing a yearning for apocalypse. I detect in yours a paralyzing fear.

You have convinced yourself that there are only two possible futures available to humanity. One we might call Liberal Capitalist Democracy 2.0. Clearly your preferred option, this is much like the world we live in now, only with fossil fuels replaced by solar panels; governments and corporations held to account by active citizens; and growth somehow cast aside in favor of a "steady state economy."

The other we might call McCarthy world, from Cormac McCarthy's novel *The Road*, which is set in an impossibly hideous post-apocalyptic world, where everything is dead but humans, who are reduced to eating children. Not long ago you suggested in a column that such a future could await us if we didn't continue "the fight."

Your letter continues mining this Hobbesian vein. We have to "fight on" because without modern industrial civilization the psychopaths will take over, and there will be "mass starvation and war." Leaving aside the fact that psychopaths seem to be running the show already, and millions are suffering today from starvation and war, I think this is a false choice. We both come from a western, Christian culture with a deep apocalyptic tradition. You seem to find it hard to see beyond it. But I am not "yearning" for some archetypal End of Days, because that's not what we face.

We face what John Michael Greer in his book of the same name, calls a "long descent": a series of ongoing crises brought about by the factors I talked of in my first letter that will bring an end to the all-consuming culture we have imposed upon the Earth. I'm sure "some good will come" from this, for that culture is a weapon of planetary mass destruction.

Our civilization will not survive in anything like its present form, but we can at least aim for a managed retreat to a saner world. Your alternative—to hold on to nurse for fear of finding something worse—is in any case a century too late. When empires begin to fall, they build their own momentum. But what comes next doesn't have to be McCarthyworld. Fear is a poor guide to the future.

All the best, Paul

Dear Paul,

If I have understood you correctly, you are proposing to do nothing to prevent the likely collapse of industrial civilization. You believe that instead of trying to replace fossil fuels with other energy sources, we should let the system slide. You go on to say that we should not fear this outcome.

How many people do you believe the world could support without either fossil fuels or an equivalent investment in alternative energy? How many would survive without modern industrial civilization? Two billion? One billion? Under your vision several billion perish. And you tell me we have nothing to fear.

I find it hard to understand how you could be unaffected by this prospect. I accused you of denial before; this looks more like disavowal. I hear a perverse echo in your writing of the philosophies that most offend you: your macho assertion that we have nothing to fear from collapse mirrors the macho assertion that we have nothing to fear from endless growth. Both positions betray a refusal to engage with physical reality.

Your disavowal is informed by a misunderstanding. You maintain that modern industrial civilization "is a weapon of planetary mass destruction." Anyone apprised of the Paleolithic massacre of the African and Eurasian megafauna, or the extermination of the great beasts of the Americas, or the massive carbon pulse produced by deforestation in the Neolithic must be able to see that the weapon of planetary mass destruction is not the current culture, but humankind.

You would purge the planet of industrial civilization, at the cost of billions of lives, only to discover that you have not invoked "a saner world" but just another phase of destruction.

Strange as it seems, a de-fanged, steady-state version of the current settlement might offer the best prospect humankind has ever had of avoiding collapse. For the first time in our history we are well-informed about the extent and causes of our ecological crises, know what should be done to avert them, and have the global means—if only the political will were present—of preventing them. Faced with your alternative—sit back and watch billions die—Liberal Democracy 2.0 looks like a pretty good option.

With my best wishes, George

Dear George,

Macho, moi? You've been using the word "fight" at a Dick Cheney-like rate. Now my lack of fighting spirit sees me accused of complicity in mass death. This seems a fairly macho accusation.

Perhaps the heart of our disagreement can be found in a single sentence in your last letter: "You are proposing to do nothing to prevent the likely collapse of industrial civilization." This invites a question: what do you think I could do? What do you think you can do?

You've suggested several times that the hideous death of billions is the only alternative to a retooled status quo. Even if I accepted this loaded claim, which seems designed to make me look like a heartless fascist, it would get us nowhere because a retooled status quo is a fantasy and even you are close to admitting it. Rather than "do nothing" in response, I'd suggest we get some perspective on the root cause of this crisis—not human beings but the cultures within which they operate.

Civilizations live and die by their founding myths. Our myths tell us that humanity is separate from something called "nature," which is a "resource" for our use. They tell us there are no limits to human abilities, and that technology, science, and our ineffable wisdom can fix everything. Above all, they tell us that we are in control. This craving for control underpins your approach. If we can just persuade the politicians to do A, B, and C swiftly enough, then we will be saved. But what climate change shows us is that we are not in control, either of the biosphere or of the machine that is destroying it. Accepting that fact is our biggest challenge.

I think our task is to negotiate the coming descent as best we can, while creating new myths that put humanity in its proper place. Recently I co-founded a new initiative, the Dark Mountain Project, which aims to help do that. It won't save the world, but it might help us think about how to live through a hard century. You'd be welcome to join us.

Very best, Paul

Dear Paul,

Yes, the words I use are fierce, but yours are strangely neutral. I note that you have failed to answer my question about how many people the world could support without modern forms of energy and the systems they sustain, but 2 billion is surely the optimistic extreme. You describe this mass cull as "a long descent" or a "retreat to a saner world." Have you ever considered a job in the Ministry of Defense press office?

I draw the trifling issue of a few billion fatalities to your attention not to make you look like a heartless fascist but because it's a reality with which you refuse to engage. You don't see it because to do so would be to accept the need for action. But of course you aren't doing nothing. You propose to stiffen the sinews, summon up the blood, and, er … "get some perspective on the root cause of this crisis." Fine: we could all do with some perspective. But without action—informed, focused, and immediate—the crisis will happen. I agree that the chances of success are small. But they are non-existent if we give up before we have started. You mock this impulse as a "craving for control." I see it as an attempt at survival.

What could you do? You know the answer as well as I do. Join up, protest, propose, create. It's messy, endless and uncertain of success. Perhaps you see yourself as above this futility, but it's all we've got and all we've ever had. And sometimes it works.

The curious outcome of this debate is that while I began as the optimist and you the pessimist, our roles have reversed. You appear to believe that though it is impossible to tame the global economy, it is possible to change our founding myths, some of which predate industrial civilization by several thousand years. You also believe that good can come of a collapse that deprives most of the population of its means of survival. This strikes me as something more than optimism: a millenarian fantasy, perhaps, of Redemption after the Fall. Perhaps it is the perfect foil to my apocalyptic vision.

With my best wishes, George

Who Are These Men?

I just love this whole dialogue for its clarity and mutual nastiness presented in such a civilized way while speaking of imminent tragedy. Here is the description of who they are from the footnote to the article: "Paul Kingsnorth is a writer, environmentalist, and poet. He has written widely for publications worldwide. His book, *Real England*, was published by Portobello in 2009. George Monbiot is the author of the bestselling books *The Age of Consent: Manifesto for a New World Order* (HarperPerennial, 2004) and *Captive State: The Corporate Takeover of Britain* (Pan Books, 2001), as well as the investigative travel books *Poisoned Arrows (1999), Amazon Watershed (1991), and No Man's Land (2003).*"

The entire dialogue between George and Paul is a serious conversation about the heart of the matter concerning our current human pell-mell trip straight to hell. It seems overwhelming to propose that we actually change our founding myths. Makes you want to say, "What the hell? Maybe it would be easier to just go ahead and die."

I especially like Monbiot's comment: "I still have some faith in our ability to make rational decisions based on evidence. But it is waning." Have faith George! What you point out about humanity, primitive or civilized, being the big eater of everything and the destructive source of all our own problems has in it the very key to our most rational survival plan! Let's destroy our destructiveness. A just form of cannibalism!

Monbiot says, "However faint the hopes of engineering a soft landing—an ordered and structured downsizing of the global economy—might be, we must keep this possibility alive." I agree. But the harshest wrenching change is required by that mild-mannered assertion, and it will require a new and very quick creation of an alternative system of justice to replace the sham that keeps the current destructive economic order in place. (That new economic order and system of justice are two out of nine big ideas I will lay out a bit further along in this book.)

Both of authors just quoted agree on something I want to make more explicit. When civilization collapses psychopaths will take over. So what's new about that? Nothing! Civilization itself is a stairway to heaven for psychopaths already. Psychopaths (or sociopaths, if you prefer) are people without conscience. They lack the capacity for empathy. They don't care what it takes to win in terms of cost to other people. As my friend Clinton Callahan says, "It's not that power corrupts. Corrupt people seek power." Leadership in hierarchically arranged civilizations, where those who lock up the food are able to control the others, is always done by psychopaths. That context invites and empowers psychopaths to make their way to the top.

Now, let's pursue further the evidence for the futility of the recent, most stylishly civilized attempt to dodge the bullet we have already fired. Adam Sacks cheers us on by telling the whole truth about both the problem of climate change activism and the problem with attempted solutions so far—a very grim truth indeed.

The Fallacy of Climate Activism
By Adam D. Sacks *(Grist Magazine,* August 23, 2009*)*[2]

In the twenty years since we climate activists began our work in earnest, the state of the climate has become dramatically worse, and the change is accelerating—this despite all of our best efforts. Clearly something is deeply wrong with this picture. What is it that we do not yet know? What do we have to think and do differently to arrive at urgently different outcomes?[3]

The answers lie not with science, but with culture.

Climate activists are obsessed with greenhouse-gas emissions and concentrations. Since global climate disruption is an effect of greenhouse gases, and a disastrous one, this is understandable. But it is also a mistake.

Such is the fallacy of climate activism[4]: We insist that global warming is merely a consequence of greenhouse-gas emissions. Since it is not, we fail to tell the truth to the public.

I think that there are two serious errors in our perspectives on greenhouse gases:

Global Warming as Symptom

The first error is our failure to understand that greenhouse gases are not a cause but a symptom, and addressing the symptom will do little but leave us with a devil's sack full of many other symptoms, possibly somewhat less rapidly lethal but lethal nonetheless.

The root cause, the source of the symptoms, is three hundred years of our relentlessly exploitative, extractive, and exponentially growing technoculture, against the background of ten millennia of hierarchical and colonial civilizations.[5] This should be no news flash, but the seductive promise of endless growth has grasped all of us civilized folk by the collective throat, led us to expand our population in numbers beyond all reason and to commit genocide of indigenous cultures and destruction of other life on Earth.

To be sure, global climate disruption is the No. 1 symptom. But if planetary warming were to vanish tomorrow, we would still be left with ample catastrophic potential to extinguish many life forms in fairly short order: deforestation; desertification; poisoning of soil, water, air; habitat destruction; overfishing and general decimation of oceans; nuclear waste, depleted uranium, and nuclear weaponry—to name just a few. (While these symptoms exist independently, many are intensified by global warming.)

We will not change course by addressing each of these as separate issues; we have to address root cultural cause. [Italics mine. —BB]

Beyond Greenhouse-gas Emissions

The second error is our stubborn unwillingness to understand that the battle against greenhouse-gas emissions, as we have currently framed it, is over.

It is absolutely over and we have lost.

We have to say so.

There are three primary components of escalating greenhouse-gas concentrations that are out of our control:

Thirty-year Lag: The first is that generally speaking the effects we are seeing today, as dire as they are, are the result of atmospheric concentrations of carbon dioxide in the range of only 330 parts per million (ppm), not the result of today's concentrations of almost 390 ppm. This is primarily a consequence of the vast inertial mass of the oceans, which absorb temperature and carbon dioxide and create a roughly thirty-year lag between greenhouse-gas emissions and their effects. We are currently seeing the effects of greenhouse gases emitted before 1980.

Just as the scientific community hadn't realized how rapidly and extensively geophysical and biological systems would respond to increases in atmospheric greenhouse-gas concentrations, we currently have only a rough idea of what that 60 ppm already emitted will mean, even if we stopped our emissions today. But we do know, with virtual certainty, that it will be full of unpleasant surprises.

Positive Feedback Loops: The second out-of-control component is positive (amplifying) feedback loops. The odd thing about positive feedbacks is that they are often ignored in assessing the effects of greenhouse-gas emissions. Our understanding of them is limited and our ability to insert them into an equation is rudimentary. Our inability to grasp them, however, in no way mitigates their effects, which are as real as worldwide violent weather.

It is now clear that several phenomena are self-sustaining, amplifying cycles; for example, melting ice and glaciers, melting tundra and other methane sources, and increasing ocean saturation with carbon dioxide, which leads to increases in atmospheric carbon dioxide. These feedbacks will continue even if we reduce our human emissions to zero—and all of our squiggly light bulbs, Priuses, wind turbines,

Waxman-Markeys, and Copenhagens won't make one bit of difference. Not that we shouldn't stop all greenhouse-gas emissions immediately—of course we should—but that's only a necessity, not nearly a sufficient response.

We need to find the courage to say so.

Non-Linearity: The third component is non-linearity, which means that the effects of rising temperature and atmospheric carbon concentrations may change suddenly and unpredictably. While we may assume linearity for natural phenomena because linearity is much easier to assess and to predict, many changes in nature are non-linear, often abruptly so. A common example is the behavior of water. The changes of state of water—solid, liquid, gas—happen abruptly. It freezes suddenly at 0°C, not at 1°, and it turns to steam at 100°, not at 99°. If we were to limit our experience of water to the range of 1° to 99°, we would never know of the existence of ice or steam.

This is where we stand in relationship to many aspects of the global climate. We don't know where the tipping points—effectively the changes of state—are for such events as the irreversible melting of glaciers, release of trapped methane from tundras and seabeds, carbon saturation of the oceans. Difficult to pin down, tipping points may be long past, or just around the corner. As leading climatologist Jim Hansen has written, "Present knowledge does not permit accurate specification of the dangerous level of human-made GHGs. [Greenhouse-gases. —BB] However, it is much lower than has commonly been assumed. If we have not already passed the dangerous level, the energy infrastructure in place ensures that we will pass it within several decades."[6]

Evidence of non-linearity is strong, not only from the stunning acceleration of climate change in just the past couple of years, but from the wild behavior of the climate over millions of years, which sometimes changed dramatically within periods as short as a decade.

The most expert scientific investigators have been blindsided by the velocity and extent of recent developments, and the climate models have likewise proved far more conservative than nature itself. Given that scientists have underestimated impacts of even small changes in global temperature, it is understandably difficult to elicit an appropriate public and governmental response.

Beyond the Box

We climate activists have to tread on uncertain ground and rapidly move beyond our current unpleasant but comfortable parts-per-million box. Here are some things we need to say, over and over again, everywhere, in a thousand different ways:

Bitter climate truths are fundamentally bitter cultural truths. Endless growth is an impossibility in the physical world, always—but always—ending in overshot and collapse. Collapse: with a bang or a whimper, most likely both. We are already witnessing it, whether we choose to acknowledge it or not.

Because of this civilization's obsession with growth, its demise is 100 percent predictable. We simply cannot go on living this way. Our version of life on earth has come to an end.

Moreover, there are no "free market" or "economic" solutions. And since corporations must have physically impossible endless growth in order to survive, corporate social responsibility is a myth. *The only socially responsible act that corporations can take is to dissolve.* [Italics mine again. —BB]

We can't bargain with the forces of nature, trading slightly less harmful trinkets for a fantasized reprieve. Geophysical processes care not one whit for our politics, our economics, our evening meals, our theologies, our love for our children, our plaintive cries of innocence and error.

We can either try to plan the transition, even at this late hour, or the physical forces of the world will do it for us—indeed, they already are. As Alfred Crosby stated in his remarkable book, *Ecological Imperialism*, Mother Nature's ministrations are never gentle.[7]

Telling the Truth

If we climate activists don't tell the truth as well as we know it—which we have been loathe to do because we ourselves are frightened to speak the words—the public will not respond, notwithstanding all our protestations of urgency.

And contrary to current mainstream climate-activist opinion, contrary to all the pointless "focus groups," contrary to the endless speculation on "correct framing," the only way to tell the truth is to tell it. All of it, no matter how terrifying it may be.[8]

It is offensive and condescending for activists to assume that people can't handle the truth without environmentalists finding a way to make it more palatable. The public is concerned, we vaguely know that something is desperately wrong, and we want to know more so we can try to figure out what to do. The response to *An Inconvenient Truth*, as tame as that film was in retrospect, should have made it clear that we want to know the truth.

And finally, denial requires a great deal of energy, is emotionally exhausting, fraught with conflict and confusion. Pretending we can save our current way of life derails us and sends us in directions that lead us astray. The sooner we embrace the truth, the sooner we can begin the real work.

Let's just tell it.

Stating the Problem

After we tell the truth, then what can we do? Is it hopeless? Perhaps. But before we can have the slightest chance of meaningful action, having told the truth, we have to face the climate reality, fully and unflinchingly. If we base our planning on false premises—such as the oft-stated stutter that reducing our greenhouse-gas emissions will forestall "the worst effects of global warming" —we can only come up with false solutions. "Solutions" that will make us feel better as we tumble toward the end, but will make no ultimate difference whatsoever.

Furthermore, we can and must pose the problem without necessarily providing the "solutions." [9] I can't tell you how many climate activists have scolded me, "You can't state a problem like that without providing some solutions." If we accept that premise, all of scientific inquiry as well as many other kinds of problem solving would come to a screeching halt. The whole point of stating a problem is to clarify questions, confusions, and unknowns, so that the problem statement can be mulled, chewed, and clarified to lead to some meaningful answers, even though the answers may seem to be out of reach.

Some of our most important thinking happens while developing the problem statement, and the better the problem statement the richer our responses. That's why framing the global warming problem as greenhouse-gas concentrations has proved to be such a dead end.

Here is the problem statement as it is beginning to unfold for me. We are all a part of struggling to develop this thinking together:

We must leave behind ten thousand years of civilization; this may be the hardest collective task we've ever faced. It has given us the intoxicating power to create planetary changes in two hundred years that under natural cycles require hundreds of thousands or millions of years—but none of the wisdom necessary to keep this Pandora's box tightly shut. We have to discover and re-discover other ways of living on earth.

[Note: Those italics above are mine, Brad Blanton, the author of this book. They are there to stress their importance, because I think that statement is the heart of what we have to do. We have to take drastic action immediately because we don't have much time. We need a new system of justice based on sustainability and we need a police force and judges to carry it off, enforce it, butcher and eat all of the old guard that oppose it, and destroy every last remnant of the previously existing system. More on that later. —BB]

We love our cars, our electricity, our iPods, our theme parks, our bananas, our Nikes, and our nukes, but we behave as if we understand nothing of the land and water and air that gives us life. It is past time to think and act differently.

If we live at all, we will have to figure out how to live locally and sustainably. Living locally means we are able get everything we need within walking (or animal riding) distance. We may eventually figure out sustainable ways of moving beyond those small circles to bring things home, but our track record isn't good and we'd better think it through very carefully.

Likewise, any technology has to be locally based, using local resources and accessible tools, renewable and non-toxic. We have much re-thinking to do, and re-learning from our hunter-gatherer forebears who managed to survive for a couple of hundred thousand years in ways that we with our civilized blinders we can barely imagine or understand.[10]

Living sustainably means, in Derrick Jensen's elegantly simple definition, that whatever we do, we can do it indefinitely.[11] We cannot use up anything more or faster than nature provides, we don't poison the air, water, or soil, and we respect the web of life of which we are an intricate part. We are not separate from nature, or above it, or in any way qualified to supervise it.[12] The evidence is ample and overwhelming; all we have to do is be brave enough to look.

How do we survive in a world that will probably turn—is already turning, for many humans and non-humans alike—into a living hell? How do we even grow or gather food or find clean water or stay warm or cool while assaulted by biblical floods, storms, rising seas, droughts, hurricanes, tornadoes, snow, and hail?

It is crystal clear that we cannot leave it to the technophiliacs. It is human technology coupled with our inability to comprehend, predict, and prevent unintended consequences that have brought us global catastrophe, culminating in climate disruption, in the first place. Desperate hopes notwithstanding, there are no high-tech solutions here, only wishful thinking—the tools that got us into this mess are incapable of getting us out.[13]

All that being said, we needn't discard all that we've learned, far from it.[14] But we must use our knowledge with great discretion, and lock much of it away as so much nuclear weaponry and waste.

Time is running very short, but the forgiveness of this little blue orb in a vast lonely universe will continue to astonish and nourish us—if we only give it the chance.

Our obligation as activists, the first step, the essence, is to part the cultural veil at long last, and to tell the truth. [Italics mine. —BB.]

The Absolute First Step

As the Grandpa of Radical Honesty, I agree with Adam Sacks that telling the truth about our predicament is the absolute first step for any chance we have to soften our crash landing. The crash of civilization doesn't necessarily have to destroy all of humanity and most of the living beings on earth. How many survive the crash is quite unpredictable but it doesn't look good.

This is the doctor coming from the operating room with bad news. We have to face this truth of certain upcoming trouble and probable death, with radiation and chemotherapy the lousy least worst options. If there is light at the end of this tunnel it pretty much depends on what we do now, at the beginning of the tunnel.

CHAPTER 3

Discontent and Its Civilization: Dissed Appointments

"The enemy is us," says Adam Sacks. I agree. The problem is civilization, culture—human attachment to absolutely destructive ways of living. I agree. We must be honest about all this and face the music. I agree. Couldn't have said it better myself. And I haven't. Not in six previous books.

Sacks also says, "Desperate hopes notwithstanding, there are no high-tech solutions here, only wishful thinking—the tools that got us into this mess are incapable of getting us out. All that being said, we needn't discard all that we've learned; far from it. But we must use our knowledge with great discretion, and lock much of it away as so much nuclear weaponry and waste."[1]

We can use some knowledge, but lock most of it away. And perhaps new combinations of technology can actually do restorative work. There is some technology—a combination of physical and social technology—like the one example in Brazil (reclaiming the rain forest) that Monbiot mentioned and that I go into in detail later in this book—that could possibly deliver us from ourselves. But before we get into that, we should read just one more article by one more very bright and articulate person, to round out this picture...

Looking deeper into our entanglement in the big meta-cultural lie called civilization, let's read this next essay by Charles Eisenstein, author of *The Ascent of Humanity* (Panenthea Productions, 2007). I reprint it here because, again, I would like to quote damned near every paragraph of it. It is a better articulation of my life's work than my own writing.

This essay offers both brilliant thinking and brilliant writing. I want to use it as a starting point to talk about what I think the function of Radical Honesty could be in the world that is now collapsing around us, and how a new honesty might be the key to dampen and modify the growing inferno that seems so unstoppable that it threatens to turn the earth into hell and burn it up altogether.

The Ubiquitous Matrix of Lies
By Charles Eisenstein (*Reality Sandwich*, June 24, 2009)[2]

Let's begin with beer. Near my home I drive past a billboard advertisement for Coors Light. The slogan is, "Coors rocks Harrisburg."

Now, does anybody actually believe that Coors does in fact "rock Harrisburg"? No. Does the Coors corporation itself believe it? No. Does anyone believe that Coors believes it? No. It is a lie, everyone knows it is a lie, and no one cares. Everyone automatically writes it off as an ad slogan, an image campaign.

The next sign advertises Miller Beer with the phrase, "Fresh beer tastes better." Does anyone actually think Miller is fresher than Budweiser, Coors, or Pabst? No. Does anyone at Miller Brewing think that? No. It is another obvious and unremarkable lie, beneath the threshold of most people's awareness. But it contributes to a feeling of living in a phony world where words don't matter and nothing is real.

Here is another beer slogan, for Carlsberg: "Probably the best beer in the world." Obviously, the word "probably" has been chosen to suggest that someone devoted great consideration to this question, sampled all the world's great beers, and finally issued an impartial judgment. Of course, nothing of the sort happened. No one thinks it did. Everyone knows that actually what happened is a bunch of advertising pros thought up a slogan in an effort to create an "image." Isn't it remarkable that lies are still effective even when no one believes them? Unfortunately, when it hardly matters whether words are truth or lies, then words lose their power to convey the truth.

Continuing on my way, I drive past the Colonial Park Mall, a generic, boxy edifice amidst a vast expanse of concrete. There is no park here, nor is there actually any connection with anything "colonial," a word chosen to evoke an image of simple times, kind folk, and quality craftsmanship. The mall is home to a food court called "Café in the Park," a name chosen to evoke (who knows?) a Parisian café with outdoor tables under the shade of the trees. Basically, the entire name is a lie. No café, no park, nothing colonial. And this lie is, again, completely unremarkable.

Increasingly, words don't mean anything. In politics, campaigning candidates make statements that flatly contradict their actions and policies, and no one seems to object or even care. It is not the routine dissembling of political figures that is striking, but rather our near-complete indifference to it. We are as well almost completely inured to the vacuity of advertising copy, the words of which increasingly mean nothing at all to the reader. Does anyone really believe that GE "brings good things to life?" Or that a housing development I passed today— "Walnut Crossing" —actually has any walnut trees or crossings? From brand names to PR slogans to political code-words, the language of the media that inundates modern life consists almost wholly of subtle lies, misdirection, and manipulation.

We live in a ubiquitous matrix of lies, a sea of mendacity so pervasive that it is nearly invisible. Because we are lied to all the time, in ways so subtle they are beneath conscious notice, even the most direct lies are losing their power to shock us.

The most shocking thing about the lies of the Bush administration was that those lies were not actually shocking to most people. Why do we as a society seemingly accept our leaders' gross dishonesty as a matter of course? Why does the repeated exposure of their lies seem to arouse barely a ripple of indignation among the general public? Where is the protest, the outrage, the sense of betrayal?

It is certainly not to be found in the person of Barack Obama. Just as there is little difference between Coors and Miller, so also is there little difference in the policies of Bush and Obama. I realize that this statement will provoke outrage from many of my readers. Sure, there are some differences between them—enough to establish Obama as a new brand—but the basic course of empire, of finance, the military, medicine, law, education, of all the defining institutions of our society remains unchanged.

Significantly, during the campaign most of the media commentary on his speeches was about the image they created, their emotional effect, and not their content. Today, the content barely matters except for what image it creates. Words become merely emotive signs, not semantic ones.

Therefore, even though I don't think Obama tells deliberate lies, as did his predecessors, the change in the way we use and receive language makes it impossible for him to tell the truth either. Everything is heard through a filter of meta-interpretations; we hear not words but code-words, not semantic meaning but signals and "messages." Words don't mean what they mean. Speaking into such a listening, it becomes impossible to really tell the truth. Even if a politician speaks plainly, we hear an attempt to create an image of plainspokenness.

Thus it is that people detect a certain indefinable insincerity underneath Obama's words—insincerity is now built in to the language of politics. (It is also inherent in the contradictions of our civilization's deep ideology, but that is a different matter.) Playing by the rules of the political game, as Obama most definitely does, he can do naught but lie. His "hope" and "change" will be exposed as the brands they are. People will see that there is little cause to hope, and that not much has changed. The despair, cynicism, and sense of betrayal that will result will foment a dangerous crisis and, in the end, a profound renewal of public discourse that demands truth and has no patience with inauthenticity.

Above I asked, "Where is the indignation, the outrage, at the lies in which we are immersed?" Clearly, the answer lies deeper than the machinations of one or another faction of the power elite. It lies deeper than the subversion and control of the media. Part of our society's apathy arises from a subtle and profound disempowerment: the de-potentiation of language itself, along with all other forms of symbolic culture. Words are losing their power to create and to transform. The result is a tyranny that can never be overthrown, but will only proceed toward totality until it collapses under the weight of the multiple crises it inevitably generates.

As we acclimate ourselves to a ubiquitous matrix of lies, words mean less and less to us, and we don't believe anything any more. As well we shouldn't! We are facing a crisis of language that underlies and mirrors all the other converging crises of the modern age. Just as a growing profusion of material and social technology has failed to bring about the promised Utopia of leisure, health, and justice, so has the profusion of words and media failed to bring about better communication. Instead, the opposite has happened.

We are faced with a paradox. On the one hand, in a technological society, words are themselves actions. The entire modern world is built on language, on symbol. Any endeavor requiring the coordination of human activity beyond a very small scale requires language. You cannot build a microchip, run an airport or a government, wage a war, organize a peace movement, or build a wind turbine without a vast apparatus of codified instruction books, technical manuals, educational curricula, time schedules, planning documents, memos, instructions, measurements, and data. If the President decides to bomb Iran, do you know how he will do it? With words. He literally has the power to speak a war into being. Like the Old Testament Jehovah, we create the world with our words. Neither the President nor Congress really ever does anything but talk (and write). Unless you work with your hands as a carpenter or garbage collector, you are probably the same.

What are we to do, then, when words, our primary creative tool in the modern world, have become impotent? Surely political activists must ask this of themselves, as they shout the truth from the rooftops, loud and clear, to so little effect (yes there are some small victories, but the inferno rages on). We feel the urge to stop talking and get out there and do something. But to do is to speak. An exception might be the activists who, impatient with all the talk, go out there and sabotage tractors and spike trees. Ironically, the main impact of such operations usually comes from their symbolic power, which has quickly diminished (in the public consciousness) to the status of gimmicks and stunts.

Something similar might be said of mass protests, which began to lose their power after the civil rights and antiwar movements of the 1960s. Originally, marches and demonstrations were intended not only to attract media attention, but carried the threat of actual physical action. Their essence was, "We're sick of sitting around talking, we're going to do something about this!" But as protests turned into media events, whose success was defined by the amount and kind of coverage, they became just another form of talking: they "raise awareness" and "send a message." Not since Seattle in 1998 has the physicality of street action had much of an effect. (In other parts of the world it is a different story. In China, for instance, protestors in rural villages are wont to [literally] tar and feather corrupt local officials. In Europe, mass demonstrations paralyze commerce and government.) It is not that the symbolic aspect of such actions is unimportant, but when they become wholly symbolic, the symbol loses its connection to—and impact on—reality.

It is not only that the powers that be so completely dominate the narratives of our time that any dissent seems irrational or illegitimate. The words of the dominant powers are losing their potency as well! The primary method by which governments increase their control is by creating fear. In this atmosphere, it is easy to declare new wars, impose new restrictions on freedom, make people accept new sacrifices, etc. With this in mind, I was gratified to see the utter failure of the "terrorism threat level" color-coding system to instill panic. You may have heard the message in airports: "the Department of Homeland Security has raised the terror alert threat level to orange..." Does anyone say, "Oh my God, it is orange! That's just one step short of a red alert!"? No. The words impact us as the buzzing of a fly. Another example is the recent failure of government scaremongering about the swine flu, a fine opportunity to implement mandatory vaccination programs, build mass quarantine facilities, etc.

Perhaps the most significant failure of the language of the rulers is the futility of their rosy economic pronouncements to reverse the progressive unwinding of the global financial system. (For money, too, is a story, a system of meanings and symbols that assigns roles, focuses collective intentions, and coordinates human activity.) When governments fail, such as in the breakup of the Soviet Union, a terminal symptom is the failure of the credibility of their leaders' words. When reality conflicts more and more obviously with the pronouncements of leaders, then when they say, "This shall be," no one believes that either. Laws, authority, currencies, and so on are all systems of symbols. When they break down, what remains is as Chairman Mao described: "Power comes from the barrel of a gun." That is why I think the finale of the de-potentiation of public speech will be an interlude of rule by naked force.

I note as an aside that it is not only public language that is losing its power and suffering a crisis of meaning. The same is happening to all symbolic communication. To quote from *The Ascent of Humanity,* "Another symptom of the breakdown of semantic meaning is the routine use of words like 'awesome,' 'amazing,' and 'incredible' to describe what is actually trivial, boring, and mundane. We are running out of words, or words are running out of meaning, forcing us into increasingly exaggerated elocutions to communicate at all."

We might say that the crisis of our civilization comes down to a crisis of language, in which words have seemingly lost their ability to create. We have all the technology and all the knowledge we need to live in beautiful harmony with each other and the planet. What we need is different collective choices. Choices arise from perceptions, perceptions arise from interpretations or stories, and stories are built of words, of symbols. Today, words have lost their power and our society's stories have seemingly taken on a life of their own, propelling us toward an end that no sane person would choose and that we seem helpless to resist. And helpless we are, when all we have are impotent words.

It is as if, as in "The Emperor's New Clothes," the boy has cried, "The emperor is completely naked" and everyone hears him but no one cares. The parade marches on, an increasingly contrived and ruinous spectacle that no one, not even its leaders, truly believes in.

What, then, are we as writers, as speakers, as humans, to do? Shall we stop writing? No. But let us not labor under any illusions. The truth has been exposed again and again, but to what effect? What have forty years of correct analysis of the environmental and political state of the world brought us? The reason that the entire staff of *Counterpunch, The Nation*, and *Truthout* is not in a concentration camp is that it is not necessary. Words themselves have been robbed of their power. Thoreau said, "It takes two to speak the truth: one to speak and another to hear." Who hears now but the already-converted?

A picture is worth a thousand words—perhaps the image can rescue us from the crisis of language. Unfortunately, it cannot. The same air of unreality has come to infect the realm of images as has debilitated the power of words. In an age of virtual reality, immersive video games, on-line interactive worlds like *Second Life*, computer 3D animation, and routine graphic depictions of violence on screen, images of real atrocities are losing their power to shock. For the viewer, there is little observable difference between images of real violence and its on-screen simulation—both are just a set of pixels and neither impacts the viewer's off-screen reality in any tangible way. It's all happening in TV-land. Perhaps this explains the absence of any national sense of shame or soul-searching in the wake of Abu Ghraib. For many, it was just another bunch of images, just as 600,000 Iraqis dead is another string of digits.

Like words, images have become divorced from the objects they are supposed to represent, until the very word "image" itself has taken on connotations of inauthenticity: a corporate image, a politician's image. In a world of lies and images, nothing is real. Immersed in such a world, is the political apathy of the American public so difficult to understand?

The danger when we operate wholly in a world of representations and images is that we begin to mistake that world for reality, and to believe that by manipulating symbols we can automatically change the reality they represent. [Italics again! My italics. —BB] We lose touch with the reality behind the symbols. Grisly death becomes collateral damage. Torture becomes enhanced interrogation. A bill to gut pollution controls becomes the Clear Skies Act. Defeat in Iraq becomes victory. War becomes peace. Hate becomes love. Slavery becomes freedom.

The Orwellian ambition to render language incapable of even expressing the concept "freedom" has nearly been fulfilled. Not by eliminating the word, but by converting it into a mere image, an empty shell, a brand. How can the voices of protest be effective when everyone discounts all speech as image, spin, and hype? Whatever you say, it is in the end just words.

Take heart: the evisceration of the language that makes our tyranny impregnable also ensures its eventual demise. The words, numbers, and images over which it exercises complete control are less and less congruent to reality. Such is the folly of the infamous "Brand America" campaign, designed to burnish America's "image" abroad. The image has become more important than the reality. Bombs blow up innocent civilians to send a "message" to the "terrorists." No matter that this message exists only in the fantasies of our leaders. They are, like those they rule, immersed in an increasingly impotent world of symbol and cannot understand why the world does not conform to their manipulation of its representation, the pieces on their global chessboard.

However we play with the statistics to cover up the converging crises of our time, the crises continue to intensify. We can euphemize the autism crisis away, the obesity epidemic, the soil crisis, the water crisis, the energy crisis. We can dumb down standardized exams to cover up the accelerating implosion of the educational system. We can redefine people in and out of poverty and manipulate economic statistics. We can declare—simply declare—that the forests are not in precipitous decline. For a while we can hide the gathering collapse of environment and polity, economy and ecology, but eventually reality will break through.

As we rebuild from the wreckage that follows, let us remember the lesson we have learned. The power of the word, like all magical powers, will turn against us or wither and die if not renewed by frequent reconnection to its source.

Abstracted too many levels from its source, language maroons us in a factitious fantasy world, an unconscious story that turns us into its victims. Those of us dedicated to creating a more beautiful world must not lose ourselves in abstraction. Let us not imagine that we are more intelligent than the Neo-cons in their think tanks or the liberal professors in their universities. They are just as clever as anyone else at manipulating logic. All they say follows logically from their premises. It is the premises that are at fault, and these cannot be reasoned out. Remember that the Neo-cons too believe they are creating a better world. Only arrogance would say that we, being smarter than they are, can do better. Indeed, it is arrogance that defines them, and the opposite of arrogance is humility, and to be humble is to constantly open to new truth from the outside, from the real world and not one's interpretation of it.

That is the only thing that can keep us honest. Horror results when we get lost in a world of axioms and ideals. Many before us on left and right have reasoned atrocity out to a nicety. We stay honest by grounding ourselves again and again in the reality outside representation. When environmentalists focus on cost-benefit analyses and study data rather than real, physical places, trees, ponds, and animals, they end up making all the sickening compromises of the Beltway. Liberal economists with the best of intentions cheer when a poor country raises its GDP; invisible to their statistics is the unraveling of culture and community that fuels the money economy. Visit a real "mountaintop removal" operation and you know that there is no compromise that is not betrayal. Visit a real third-world community and the vacuity of free-trade logic is obvious. See the devastation of a bullet wound or a bomb strike, lives strewn across the street, and the logic of national interest seems monstrous.

Increasingly isolated in a virtual world, the people fear authenticity even as they crave it. [Jesus! Ain't it the truth! —BB] Except in the young, the fear usually prevails over the craving until something happens to make life fall apart. Following the pattern experienced by Cindy Sheehan, the fundamental corruption of first one, then all of our civilization's major institutions becomes transparent. I have seen this many times in various areas of activism. Someone discovers that the pharmaceutical industry, or the music industry, or the oil industry, or organized religion, or Big Science, or the food industry is shockingly corrupt, but still believes in the basic soundness of the system as a whole. Eventually, in a natural process of radicalization, they discover that the rot is endemic to all of these and more. Each institution supports, affirms, and draws its own legitimacy from the others. So we discover eventually that the wrongness permeates every institution, and we desire to find and uproot its source.

As activists for the truth, we are midwives to this process. It is not quite true that no one heeds the boy's cry that the emperor is naked. Those who are ready to hear will hear, and they are made ready when their world crumbles. The exposing of all that is wrong serves an important purpose in guiding people from the old world to the threshold of a new—but only to the threshold, not across it. To enter into the new world requires that we recover the tools of world-creation: first and foremost, the power of word.

A nicer term for a "ubiquitous matrix of lies" would be a "ubiquitous matrix of stories." I am not suggesting that we abdicate the creative power of language. Language is an essential means to coordinate human activity, for beauty as well as for destruction. The stories we tell with words unite masses of people toward a common goal, and assign the meanings and roles necessary to attain it. To be sure, images, music, and art, both representational and non-representational, contribute to the weaving of a story, especially evoking the emotional energy that powers it, but information is indispensable as well. In a new world we will not cease to tell the story of what is and what shall be, but we will become conscious of our storytelling. The sequel to this essay will explore what I call "storyteller consciousness" on a cultural and personal level, so that we may prepare to tell the story of a more beautiful world, and to speak that world into existence as presidents and kings have spoken wars into existence for thousands of years. As these old stories fall apart, the time ripens for new ones. And the old stories are indeed falling apart, of which our increasing immunity to political and commercial speech is a symptom. No more or less significant a symptom is the crumbling of our great social institutions—education, politics, medicine, money—that are themselves built of a matrix of stories. When stories fall apart, the world falls apart.

As the crises of our age converge and infiltrate the fortresses we have erected to preserve the virtual world of euphemism and pretense, the world is falling apart for more and more people at once. The stories that have defined us and bound us are dying. We sense, as counterpart to the existential anxiety that comes as the old world and our identity within it disintegrates, an invigorating newness close at hand. So let us cease to be afraid as we stand at the threshold. It is time to learn the technologies, linguistic and otherwise, of world-creation.

Reality Is Not a Dream

Damn! Isn't this clear? Isn't Charles Eisenstein inspiring? The stories are dying! The words are dying! The house of cards all of us have become used to believing is reality is about to fall, though many Band-Aids are being applied to keep it together. Those of us who have been out of the house of cards now and then and are grounded in the beautiful real world of gravity and compassion will be standing there when the house finally and inevitably falls down. People are about to be made ready to hear the truth. We had better be ready to tell it.

All of the brilliant writers whose work I have reprinted in this and the preceding chapter, every one of them has mentioned honesty as the core of recovery. The problem has been stated and the solution, I think, inferred. As far as words are concerned, the honesty they are suggesting has something to do with honesty of a descriptive kind, referring to real things in the material world. They also suggest being honest about the premises of interpretation in the world of framing or contextualizing, and then honest about the fact that the interpretation itself is an expression of opinion.

The solution they point to has something to do with paying attention to what is experientially real by virtue of being witnessed, heard, and sensed. It has to do with not avoiding seeing, hearing, or being present to information because we are not blinded by our biases, but admitting all along that they are temporary arrangements to further our cooperation in creative enterprise.

In a radically honest world such as this, we would also be conscious of the ever-likely occurrence of being sucked back into the old stories and away from witnessing reality. Even sharing new ideas in order to play together in reality our tendency is to again start believing our wishes because we prefer them to reality. I had a gay man in therapy with me one time, who said, "I didn't really mean to become homosexual. I just kinda got sucked into it." That is funny as hell and also the reason "getting sucked in" is such a good metaphor. The ubiquitous matrix of lies has such power to suck us back in because we want to have the distanced lightweight daydream "reality", which we have the illusion we are in control of, win out over what is really real. We are afraid and want to feel safe even if the safety is an illusion that is killing us.

Our current houses of cards have to do with bad stories, bad fitting stories, bullshit rationalization stories, crafted lying stories, and stories about responsibility created by the irresponsible. The list goes on forever. Secrets and lies. CIA. Closed room meetings. Closed mind requirements for entry into meetings. Secret keepers and liars. Lying to children to make them fit the stories. Punishing non-believers. Killing dissidents. Phony town halls. Speeches. Politics. Business as usual. Mind-numbing slop-filled television. Commercials. The list is damned near endless! Were I not a member of On and On Anon, I would keep going on and on.

What should we do with all these assholes that keep these stories alive? I think it is a good idea to kill the motherfuckers and eat them. End of story. End of storyteller, end of story. Of course, that alone won't work; in large part because it would mean suicide for most of us.

But if we build a new story to end an old story, that may work. We are going to have to start using what Eisenstein calls "storyteller consciousness" in order to make a new story. (Or else volunteer to be eaten ourselves after every essay we write is digested, so to speak.)

So we have to start out affirming what is true. One way to affirm this noticeably and shockingly enough to get the attention of the walking dead, would be to kill and eat a few storytellers and story maintainers, and then make a new story. So the first story I propose to get this program started is one called "How about cannibalism?" I think there are many, many people who don't deserve to die and they need protecting. And there are many people who have already earned the right to be eaten, as well as many more working away at the ongoing murder of innocents right now who need to be killed and eaten, or made into fertilizer to grow more food, immediately.

Flies and ants and all kinds of insects and animals eat their own when they die or are killed. It is something we can watch happen. It seems to come quite naturally to them and they don't appear to get too sentimental about it. All we need to make this work for humans is a principle or two of selection that would serve to pick out the ones to take out. What we humans have, if we adapt ant survivability to ourselves, is *the capacity to be selective about whom we eat according to a system of justice most of us agree upon—one that is grounded in reality more than words!*

I am outlining the solution to these problems and the pathway to it by telling some stories about what is possible in the rest of this book. I propose a new system of justice, new terms of condemnation, and new kinds of punishments. I am going to come up with an imaginative way to fairly and systematically take the money and possessions of the stupid story fucktards who kill for profit. There is no way around killing a lot of stupid story fucktards, even though killing them will not in and of itself end the stupid story. It creates an opening to replace a dead end story (literally) with one that is less deadly and more functional. This one will end too, but much less tragically.

My New House of Cards Is Six Stories High

So we have six interlocking stories. (Campaign finance reform, humanitarian cannibalism, a new system of justice, a new technology for knowing the truth so the system of justice and system of government can be more just than any that have existed before, a new form of government based on a kind of revolving jury duty where citizens dialogue and deliberate in designed contexts, campaign finance reform in all separate nation states along with a meritocracy to replace former bureaucracy, and a new world commonwealth with more power than any nation state based on representation of the people of the world rather than nation states.) As houses of cards go, this is a good one because all of the stories support each other and they are all out loud and not hidden and have built into them structures to avoid secrecy, which is like termites in most houses of cards, including the one falling down around us.

We already know a lot of the perpetrators of death-for-profit, and with the Truth Machine system I am about to explain in an upcoming chapter, we can find the rest. We can find out easily who is lying for profit and getting away with it in secret, and hold them accountable. (I suppose we will still have to grill some of them to find out. Heh heh.) And as each liar who lies to profit from murder of people and planet is found out, because of the reliability of our new technology for knowing when people are lying, we will be able to cash them in and redistribute their wealth. We need to do this quickly and save the lives of billions of people and thousands upon thousands of innocent species that were doomed to die form the continuation of the perpetrators of the old stories. Because of developing a Truth Machine (a way to discriminate using a combination of social and scientific technology based on observation-bound concepts), with a high degree of certainty about who is lying and who is telling the truth, we will no longer need a long time for appeals. We'll know when they're guilty just as certainly as we know when they are innocent. We'll know both guilt and innocence with a greater degree of certainty than ever before and more quickly than ever. We can kill and eat some of them within the week of judgment.

This speeds up justice while at the same time making it more just. The time for appeals shouldn't take more than another week or two, and then we can then get on with the dismantling of the bad business created by the bad businessperson and begin to create good ones. We can eat the biggest hogs first. Then we can use what they have stolen to take care of those from whom they have taken it. We can reuse their flesh and bones and property to maintain and restore the earth and the health of those people have been damaged by the slaughterhouse of corporate capitalism.

Wait a minute! This cannibalism thing was supposed to be a joke wasn't it?

Well, it was in the beginning. But now I think maybe I am not joking. Please get my point before you reject it out of hand. Think about what you have just read by Charles Eisenstein. What if I am not kidding? What if I am not putting you on? What if I am not using impotent language to keep us removed from reality? What if I mean what I say!? Maybe this is the time that Andre, one of the two leading characters (action figures!) in the film "My Dinner With Andre" meant when he said people would become so benumbed by society itself that *"at some time in the future people may pay ten thousand dollars in cash to be castrated, just in order to be affected by something."*[3]

We (meaning our country, the U.S.A. and all other KK-controlled nations) train people to kill by the thousands every day. Killing by nation states is daily, habitual and ongoing. It is only who gets killed that we have to argue about. And though killing and eating the kannibals seems horrible, it may be that we are just living in our unreal world and being delicate about killing. Maybe not being so delicate about who is to die will wake a few of us up.

Even though murder is gross and repulsive and horrible to contemplate for real, *it simply makes more sense* to consciously kill the killers, behead the heads, CEOs, butchers, and bankers, and so on, who are committed to destruction, who know better and do it anyway, whose hearts have been sorted from their heads, *and who have committed, and are committing,* ***mass murder*** *on a daily basis on a giant scale. The comparative scale of the solution makes the cannibalism we propose seem as innocent as a walk in the park!*

Cannibalism is the quickest economic solution to our woes as well. According to Joe Bageant, as well as *The Christian Science Monitor*, and other reliable sources, secret tax-free bank accounts in the Caribbean "hold more than 11.5 trillion—an amount greater than the U.S. national debt and *equal to one third of all the worlds assets!* The richest *four hundred* Americans alone have 1.2 trillion in assets, with the rest distributed among 793 wealthy and powerful people." [4]

Now imagine that. According to my calculations, that's 400 plus 793, and the sum equals 1,193 people. So if we ate and redistributed the wealth of a little over a thousand people—almost all of them Americans—we could restore the entire world economy, and save the lives of at least *two billion* people!? Just imagine if we ate a few hundred more—including a few more wealthy foreigners? The closer we get to two thousand either eaten or redeemed or both, the closer we are to heaven on earth, instead of hell. Imagine!

Jesus. What if I actually mean what I say? I had to ask myself that question in the middle of the night recently. This idea did start out as a joke. I was just repeating a joke because it was bizarre, and yet it made so much sense. But that kind of thing is what allows you to fall out of the trance, to actually contemplate what the phrase "beyond civilized" really means.

Humor is one of the most dangerous things to any established order within you or without you. First there is laughter, and then the horrible truth pops up. After obsessing for a while with the cookbook aspects of my joke, I started to see what not being civilized, what a new civilization, and what a post-civilized world could actually be like.

The post-civilization world is going to be a hell of a lot different when all this shit hits the fan anyway. And the shit is obviously already hitting the fan and is not going to quit. If we just ate about a thousand shits who are about to hit the fan anyway, we could start the whole world on a new and different track of sustainability, honesty, justice, and balance, and put an end to starvation and God knows what else!

Hey gang, build a fire and sharpen the knives!

The post-apocalyptic society of no food, where people are reduced to eating children described in the novel *The Road* by Cormac McCarthy (Vintage, 2006) was a fantasy wasn't it? Maybe not. Maybe it is a prophecy and a vision of the future that will actually come true as a logical evolution of what is currently in place in the world. And unless we get some new story going quickly, love will be shown to be a strong force in the end, *but simply not strong enough...* just as it was in that terribly depressing and mightily heartening book and movie. Love was there to the end, but the end came anyway.

Let's go ahead and laugh and cry at the same time, and you tell people about this nut that has written a book about cannibalism—how to justify it and how to enjoy it—and how it is the answer to what ails us. And keep reading, pass it on, and say, "You won't believe what this psychologist who has written all these books about honesty and love is saying about killing and eating people as a solution to the world's biggest problems!" Then let me know when it hits you. I mean when it comes to you personally—when you think, "Are you fucking serious?" And then, "Am I fucking serious?"

Then, let's talk.

Read this excerpt from more of the brilliant writings of my good friend Joe Bageant...Notice how we all are talking about dead things these days?

Raising up Dead Horses
By Joe Bageant (joebageant.com, *October 19, 2009*)[5]

When Barack Obama took office it seemed to some of us that his first job was to get the national silverware out of the pawnshop. Or at least maintain the world's confidence that it was possible for us to get out of debt. America is dead broke, the easy credit, phantom "growth" economy has been exposed for what it was. A credit scam. Even Hillary Clinton and Obama's best efforts have not coaxed much more dough out of foreign friends. But at least we again have a few friends abroad.

So now we must jackleg ourselves back into something resembling a productive activity. No matter how you cut it, things will not be as much fun as shopping and speculative "investing" were.

The fiesta is over, the economy as we knew it is dead.

The national money shamans have danced around the carcass of our dead horse economy, chanted the recovery chant and burned fiat currency like Indian sage, enshrouding the carcass in the sacred smoke of burning cash. And indeed, they have managed to prop up the carcass to appear life-like from a distance, if you squint through the smoke just right. But it still stinks here from the inside. Clearly at some point we must find a new horse to ride, and sure as god made little green apples one is broaching the horizon. And it looks exactly like the old horse.

Then, too, what else did we expect? His economic team of free market billionaires and financial hotwires includes most of those who helped Bill Clinton sell the theory that Americans didn't need jobs. Actual labor, if you will remember, was for Asian sweatshops and Latin maquiladoras. We, as a nation, one-third of whose population is functionally illiterate, were going to transmute ourselves into an information and transactional economy. Ain't gonna sweat no mo' no mo' —just drink wine and sing about Jesus all day.

Along with these economic hotwires came literally hundreds of K Street and Democratic lobbyists. Supposedly, every president is forced to hire these guys because no one else seems to have the connections or knows how to get a bill through Congress. Consequently, the current regime's definition of a recovery is more of the same as ever. A return of the mortgage market and credit to its former level—the level that blew us out of the water in the first place. Ah, but we're gonna manage it better this time. There is no one-trick pony on earth equal to capitalism.

Somewhere in the smoking wreckage lie the solutions. The solutions we aren't allowed to discuss: *adoption of a Wall Street securities speculation tax; repeal of the Taft-Hartley anti-union laws; ending corporate personhood; cutting the bloated vampire bleeding the economy, the military budget; full single payer health care insurance, not some "public option" that is neither fish nor fowl; taxation instead of credits for carbon pollution; reversal of inflammatory U.S. policy in the Middle East (as in, get the hell out, begin kicking the oil addiction, and quit backing the spoiled murderous brat that is Israel.)*

Meanwhile we may all feel free to row ourselves to hell in the same hand basket. Except of course the elites, the top 5 percent or so among us. But 95 percent is close enough to be called democratic, so what the hell. The trivialized media, having internalized the system's values, will continue to act as rowing captain calling out the strokes. Newsgathering in America is its own special hell, and reduces its practitioners to banality and elite sycophancy. But Big Money calls the shots.

With luck we will see at least some reverse of the Bush regime's assault on habeas corpus, due process, privacy. Changing such laws doesn't much affect that one percent whose income is equal to the combined bottom 50 percent of Americans.

Beyond that, the big money is constitutionally protected. Our constitution is first and foremost a property document protecting their money. In actual practice, our constitutional civil liberties, inspiring as they are in concept to people around the world, are mainly side action to make the institutionalization of the owning class more palatable. You can argue that may not have been the intent of the slave owning, rent collecting, upper class founding fathers. But you would be full of shit. We can keep on pretending to be independent, free to keep on living in those houses on which we still owe $300,000. But they own and control the money that comes through our hands. And they plan to keep on owning it and charging us to use it.

On the positive side, there has probably been no more fertile opportunity to improve U.S. international relations since post World War II. Bush, Cheney, Rumsfeld, and Bolton were about as endearing as pederasts at a baby shower. And now that we have shot up half the planet, certainly there is no more globally attractive person to patch up the bullet holes than Barack Obama (yes, I know Bill Clinton's feelings are hurt by that). Awarding him the Nobel Peace Prize (again Bill Clinton's feelings are sorely wounded) was an invitation to rejoin the human race.

Of course, there are a significant number of Americans still who could not give a rat's ass about world opinion of the good ole USA. Nearly every damned one of my neighbors back in Virginia, in fact.

The sharks are still running the only game in town and they have never had it better. To be sure, with the economic collapse some of the financial lords won't pile quite up as many millions this year. Others will, however, have a record year. All are still squatting in the tall cotton.

Their grandfathers who so hated FDR's reforms must be chugging cognac in hell celebrating today's America. America's unions have been neutered and taught to beg. At long last we have established a permanent underclass and de-industrialized the country in favor of low wage service industries here and dirt-cheap labor from abroad. We've managed to harden the education and income gap into something an American oligarch can take pride in. Hell, my bankcard is issued by Prescott Bush's Union Bank and my most recent mortgage was held by J. P. Morgan's creation. My electricity is generated by Rockefeller's coal and energy holdings, and my Exxon gasoline credit card is issued by a successor to Standard Oil. The breakfast I eat comes from Archer Daniels Midland. So did my dog's breakfast. We are the very products and property of these people and their institutions.

With peak oil, population pressure, vanishing world resources, and global warming, we can never again be what we once were—a civilization occupying a relative material paradise through a danse macabre of planetarily unsustainable growth. But no presidential candidate is going to run on the promise that "if we do everything just right, pull in our belts and sacrifice, we can at best be a second world nation in fifty years, providing we don't mind the lack of oxygen and a few cancers here and there." Better to hawk the myth of profitable pollution through carbon credits. Which Obama is doing.

We burn the grain supplies of starving nations in our vehicles. Skilled American construction workers, now unemployed, drive their big trucks into town and knock at my door asking to rake my leaves for ten bucks. There is nothing ironic in this to their minds. "Middle class" people making $150,000 a year will get a new tax break (as if we were all earning 150K). Energy prices are predicted to stabilize because we intend to burn the state of West Virginia in our power plants. The corpses of our young people are still being unloaded from cargo planes at Dover Delaware, but from two fronts now. Mortgage foreclosures are expected to double before they slacken. I cannot imagine debtors not getting at least temporary relief, if not decent jobs or affordable health care. Surely we will see more "change."

But never under any conditions will we be allowed to touch the real money, or get anywhere near it, much less redistribute it. Because, as a bookie friend once told me, "You got your common man living on hope, lottery tickets, or the dogs or the ponies, and you got operators. People who can see the whole game in play. They set the rules. Because they hold the money. That ain't never gonna change."

On the other hand, national opinion changes almost hourly. But if the starting gate bell rang right now for the next presidential race, I'd have to put ten bucks on Obama to place. We cannot assume the Republican Party will remain stupid. Assumptions don't work at all.

Remember what happened when we assumed the Democrats were capable of courage and leadership?"

Joe Bageant for President and Randall Amster for Vice President

Like the man said, "Big Money still calls the shots." God, I love these people I am quoting. Look at this. This just happened a few days ago at the time of this writing. These seriously honest and moving, hilarious brilliant people don't get enough credit for what angels they are.

Empire of the Sunset
By Randall Amster *(Truthout,* February 10, 2010)[6]

Sometimes, I really miss America—or at least the idea of it. You know: that can-do spirit, streets paved with gold, champion of the tired and poor, purple mountains majesty, that sort of thing. Say what you will, and call it naïve, but the storybook values at the heart of America's erstwhile image are inspiring.

Like most who grew up here, I was steeped in the lore and legend of this place. Despite obvious flaws in the narrative (how exactly does one "discover" land upon which others are living, anyway?) there existed a strong sense that at the end of the day some part of our cherished ideals would emerge in time to set things right. Principles like due process, free speech, the work ethic, checks and balances, equal opportunity, and the pursuit of happiness held meaning if only as a reminder that our collective lives stood for something and that our destinies were in our own hands. It may well have been an illusion all along, yet even the most cynical among us likely believed in the underlying ethos at some point in time.

Unfortunately, that America—even in its illusory state—has ceased to exist. We are no longer an abstract beacon of hope to the world, but rather a purveyor of concrete hellfire. We rain automated death from above and commit orchestrated theft from below. We export despair and import disdain. We've abandoned even keeping up the pretense of fair play and adherence to principle. We've become global pariahs and domestic piranhas. Awash in a sea of surfaces, distractions, and palliatives, we unsurprisingly have failed to notice that the sun has already started to set on our adolescent empire.

Indeed, by most measures, the US is rapidly becoming a failed state. Educationally, economically, politically, culturally—all of our national gauges are pointing in the wrong direction. We're moving down the list on health care, democratic governance, productivity, environmental protection, academic achievement, official transparency, incarceration rates, transportation, and public services. We're ruled by an increasingly emboldened elite class that rewrites the rules at will, increasingly represses dissent, and openly enriches itself at our expense. We hardly make anything on these shores, but still consume everything in sight. We have few public intellectuals of renown, yet are bombarded daily with the foibles of celebrities who are in many cases famous simply for being famous. Our food supply is tainted, our energy is unclean and our water is drying up. And racism remains as deeply rooted as ever.

It's not a pretty picture from inside the belly of the beast these days. But never fear, for America has a secret weapon at its disposal that will keep us in the driver's seat for a while longer. Our secret weapon, actually, isn't so secret: weapons. The days of guile, comity, and negotiation are over. Empires don't dicker; they simply take what they want. They don't ask permission or forge alliances; they make demands and extort loyalties under threat of repercussions. They don't cede oversight authority to any international community, or even feel constrained by their own laws and rules, but instead act by fiat and in flagrant disregard of treaty and protocol. Empires, in short, follow the empty logic of "might makes right."

The ruling elite in the US has made it eminently clear that this is our prevailing strategy going forward. We will utilize brute force to retain our position as the global superpower even as we have lost our moral and cultural suasion. America's tenure as a fully imperialist power is barely over a century old, its position as a true superpower about half that, and its status as sole hegemon about half that still. In a mere few decades, we've gone from savior to enslaver, from bastion to bastards, from heroic to horrific. Whatever historical good will we may have accrued has been squandered in a frenzy of hubris and hatred.

Perhaps I'm being a bit obdurate here; so let me clarify things a bit. Empires that reach this point of no return, in which power subsumes principle, are essentially on their last legs. Legitimacy can be replaced by subjugation for a time, but it is always self-defeating in the end. While history is unequivocal about this, it's also true that the recorded annals have never seen an empire quite like the one we've created. By slowly and steadily insinuating ourselves economically and militarily into the affairs of nearly every nation on the planet, we've built an ingenious system in which recalcitrance is very nearly a form of suicide. If this empire falls, it threatens to take everyone with it in the process, thus perpetuating the unspoken but widely understood mantra: "You're either with us... or else."

Consider the sheer totality of the US military presence around the planet. Hundreds of bases are spread across every continent—effectively functioning as sovereign satellites of American influence—with a preponderance located in vanquished nations such as Germany, Japan, Iraq, and Afghanistan. These are now our chief exports: military bases, hardware, and soldiers. We've also weaponized space and created an automated execution network that circumnavigates the globe, bringing push-button "justice" to anyone we deem a viable target (including our own citizens). Now we're developing fully functional robot soldiers to continue the dehumanization of warfare in our stead, which will serve our purpose of fostering submission through fear equally well whether or not they in fact work properly.

Domestically, the agenda has been set. The power elite has now "doubled down" on this strategy of maintaining supremacy through force. Military strategy documents point toward a future of perpetual warfare and relentless competition over dwindling resources, with the highest ideal of "national security" represented by our unmitigated capacity to impose our will on multiple fronts at once. Increasing episodes of disaster, such as in Haiti, will be used overtly as "Trojan horse" moments to expand our military footprint under the guise of humanitarianism. Our federal budgets will concretize all of this with escalating military expenditures coupled with frozen austerity in all other spheres. The military is sacrosanct and, moreover, is now the lone remaining chip to be played in the game of global conquest.

It certainly seems like a grim scenario, one that stands in stark contrast to the idyllic (albeit ersatz) America of our youth. It also begs us to consider what will become of young people growing up in tomorrow's America, devoid, as it likely will be, of even a redeeming ideological veneer. Will the future populace here be comprised of equal parts swaggering "ugly Americans" and withdrawn, apathetic technophiles? Will we have an America in which people either embrace our military superiority and martial character as a moral virtue on the one hand, or are constrained to immerse themselves in our cultural distractions as a refuge from the emerging security panopticon on the other? In other words, will those ensuing Americans face delimited choices that come down to either institutionalized anger or repressed angst?

I wonder if people living under the auspices of failing empires throughout history have felt similarly. The silver lining (there has to be one, right?) is that all previous empires have fallen and the sun still came up the next day. Indeed, as surely as anything else we can count on in this life, sunset is inevitably followed by sunrise. Whether anyone will be here to see that new day dawning is an open question, and one that we might consider as something of a cultural crucible at this point. Perhaps that apocryphal America from a bygone day can yet be resurrected, only this time for real and not merely as an ideal. In my mind's eye, I can envision a door opening up ahead even as the one behind us closes."

A Discussion of Presumption

You know, when proverbs or sayings are assumed to be true, don't those kind of habitual memes work well at influencing our behavior, regardless of whether or not they are right or wrong? Plenty of these kind of built-in prejudices are merely cultural assumptions. They can be questioned if we realize we are using them. They can be used if we want to do propaganda. And they can be modified and made to fit the circumstances more accurately. One of these memes is: "It's a dog eat dog world." I think that we need an upgrade on that one: "It's a dog eat puppy world." Or maybe: "It's a big dog eat little dog world." That does seem to be the way things are, and it seems like it is never going to change. But is it really true that's never gonna change? Well, whaddaya think? Yes or no?

I say eating big dogs who are about to eat little dogs could save a lot of little dogs and get rid of a lot of fear and malice, thus giving the little dogs a chance to grow up to be different when they are big dogs and not eat as many little dogs when they do.

I think we ought to take the money and eat the people who don't give it up voluntarily. If we don't, then we are likely to be in for the following scenario outlined by Daniel Quinn in this excerpt from a fictional dialogue he created to portray our current pathway to extinction.

If They Give You Lined Paper, Write Sideways: An Excerpt
By Daniel Quinn (*Steerforth Press*, 2007)[7]

Daniel: All right. We need a reality check here. First, it's been estimated that we'd need the resources of six planets the size of earth if all six billion of us were living the way people live in developed nations. Second, the U.S. Census Bureau estimates that by the year 2050 there will be nine billion of us, and while the growth rate will have declined substantially, we'll still be adding an annual population the size of New York City and Los Angeles combined. Third, you understand that our present system of food production is almost entirely dependent on fossil fuel at every stage between fertilization of cropland to delivery of processed, packaged foods to your grocery store.

Elaine: Yes.

Daniel: Fourth, the projected increase in our population to nine billion assumes that food production is going to increase. But this projection doesn't take into account the fact that, in order to reach nine billion, we're going to have to steadily increase the amount of fossil fuel we pour into agricultural production during a fifty-year period when the world's supply of fossil fuel is going to be steadily diminishing. It's estimated that oil production is going to decline by 60 or 70 percent between now and the year 2050.

Elaine: So, it sounds like that production is based on a fantasy.

Daniel: Yes. If our system of agriculture and the percentage of oil used for agriculture remain the same for the next fifty years, then our population is also going to decline by 60 to 70 percent.

Elaine: The die-off predicted by the Peak Oil Theory.

Daniel: That's right. At a conference this year in Dublin a paper was read that examined what we'd need to do to restructure our agricultural system to one that is fossil-fuel-free and concluded that this was not beyond possibility. So the threatened die-off is not necessarily inevitable, at least during this period. I seriously doubt that the planet's ecological systems could survive a human population of nine billion—nine billion and still growing."

Some People Are Going to Die, and Since People Are Going to Die, Why Can't We Decide Who Dies?

So Daniel Quinn's ultimate conclusion here is either there is going to be a big die-off or else there will have to be a big die-off. This quote from *Truthdig* and the following article by Chris Hedges confirms this idea completly.

"As climate change advances, we will face a choice between obeying the rules put in place by corporations or rebellion. .... We will either defy the corporate elite, which will mean civil disobedience, a rejection of traditional politics for a new radicalism and the systematic breaking of laws, or see ourselves consumed."

Truthdig
July 19, 2010

Calling All Future-Eaters
By Chris Hedges

The human species during its brief time on Earth has exhibited a remarkable capacity to kill itself off. The Cro-Magnons dispatched the gentler Neanderthals. The conquistadors, with the help of smallpox, decimated the native populations in the Americas. Modern industrial warfare in the 20th century took at least 100 million lives, most of them civilians. And now we sit passive and dumb as corporations and the leaders of industrialized nations ensure that climate change will accelerate to levels that could mean the extinction of our species. Homo sapiens, as the biologist Tim Flannery points out, are the "future-eaters."

In the past when civilizations went belly up through greed, mismanagement and the exhaustion of natural resources, human beings migrated somewhere else to pillage anew. But this time the game is over. There is nowhere else to go. The industrialized nations spent the last century seizing half the planet and dominating most of the other half. We giddily exhausted our natural capital, especially fossil fuel, to engage in an orgy of consumption and waste that poisoned the Earth and attacked the ecosystem on which human life depends. It was quite a party if you were a member of the industrialized elite. But it was pretty stupid.

Collapse this time around will be global. We will disintegrate together. And there is no way out. The 10,000-year experiment of settled life is about to come to a crashing halt. And humankind, which thought it was given dominion over the Earth and all living things, will be taught a painful lesson in the necessity of balance, restraint and humility. There is no human monument or city ruin that is more than 5,000 years old. Civilization, Ronald Wright notes in "A Short History of Progress," "occupies a mere 0.2 percent of the two and a half million years since our first ancestor sharpened a stone." Bye-bye, Paris. Bye-bye, New York. Bye-bye, Tokyo. Welcome to the new experience of human existence, in which rooting around for grubs on islands in northern latitudes is the prerequisite for survival.

We view ourselves as rational creatures. But is it rational to wait like sheep in a pen as oil and natural gas companies, coal companies, chemical industries, plastics manufacturers, the automotive industry, arms manufacturers and the leaders of the industrial world, as they did in Copenhagen, take us to mass extinction? (My italics—BB) It is too late to prevent profound climate change. But why add fuel to the fire? Why allow our ruling elite, driven by the lust for profits, to accelerate the death spiral? Why continue to obey the laws and dictates of our executioners?

The news is grim. The accelerating disintegration of Arctic Sea ice means that summer ice will probably disappear within the next decade. The open water will absorb more solar radiation, significantly increasing the rate of global warming. The Siberian permafrost will disappear, sending up plumes of methane gas from underground. The Greenland ice sheet and the Himalayan-Tibetan glaciers will melt. Jay

Zwally, a NASA climate scientist, declared in December 2007: "The Arctic is often cited as the canary in the coal mine for climate warming. Now, as a sign of climate warming, the canary has died. It is time to start getting out of the coal mines."

But reality is rarely an impediment to human folly. The world's greenhouse gases have continued to grow since Zwally's statement. Global emissions of carbon dioxide (CO_2) from burning fossil fuels since 2000 have increased by 3 per cent a year. At that rate annual emissions will double every 25 years. James Hansen, the head of NASA's Goddard Institute for Space Studies and one of the world's foremost climate experts, has warned that if we keep warming the planet it will be "a recipe for global disaster." The safe level of CO_2) in the atmosphere, Hansen estimates, is no more than 350 parts per million (ppm). The current level of CO_2) is 385 ppm and climbing. This already guarantees terrible consequences even if we act immediately to cut carbon emissions.

The natural carbon cycle for 3 million years has ensured that the atmosphere contained less than 300 ppm of CO_2)), which sustained the wide variety of life on the planet. The idea now championed by our corporate elite, at least those in contact with the reality of global warming, is that we will intentionally overshoot 350 ppm and then return to a safer climate through rapid and dramatic emission cuts. This, of course, is a theory designed to absolve the elite from doing anything now. But as Clive Hamilton in his book "Requiem for a Species: Why We Resist the Truth About Climate Change" writes, even "if carbon dioxide concentrations reach 550 ppm, after which emissions fell to zero, the global temperatures would continue to rise for at least another century."

Copenhagen was perhaps the last chance to save ourselves. Barack Obama and the other leaders of the industrialized nations blew it. Radical climate change is certain. It is only a question now of how bad it will become. The engines of climate change will, climate scientists have warned, soon create a domino effect that could thrust the Earth into a chaotic state for thousands of years before it regains equilibrium. "Whether human beings would still be a force on the planet, or even survive, is a moot point," Hamilton writes. "One thing is certain: there will be far fewer of us."

We have fallen prey to the illusion that we can modify and control our environment, that human ingenuity ensures the inevitability of human progress and that our secular god of science will save us. The "intoxicating belief that we can conquer all has come up against a greater force, the Earth itself," Hamilton writes. "The prospect of runaway climate change challenges our technological hubris, our Enlightenment faith in reason and the whole modernist project. The Earth may soon demonstrate that, ultimately, it cannot be tamed and that the human urge to master nature has only roused a slumbering beast."

We face a terrible political truth. Those who hold power will not act with the urgency required to protect human life and the ecosystem. Decisions about the fate of the planet and human civilization are in the hands of moral and intellectual trolls such as BP's Tony Hayward. These political and corporate masters are driven by a craven desire to accumulate wealth at the expense of human life. They do this in the Gulf of Mexico. They do this in the southern Chinese province of Guangdong, where the export-oriented industry is booming. China's transformation into totalitarian capitalism, done so world markets can be flooded with cheap consumer goods, is contributing to a dramatic rise in carbon dioxide emissions, which in China are expected to more than double by 2030, from a little over 5 billion metric tons to just under 12 billion.

This degradation of the planet by corporations is accompanied by a degradation of human beings. In the factories in Guangdong we see the face of our adversaries. The sociologist Ching Kwan Lee found "satanic mills" in China's industrial southeast that run "at such a nerve-racking pace that worker's physical limits and bodily strength are put to the test on a daily basis." Some employees put in workdays of 14 to 16 hours with no rest day during the month until payday. In these factories it is normal for an employee to work 400 hours or more a month, especially those in the garment industry. Most workers, Lee found, endure unpaid wages, illegal deductions and substandard wage rates. They are often physically abused at work and do not receive compensation if they are injured on the job. Every year a dozen or more workers die from overwork in the city of Shenzhen alone. In Lee's words, the working conditions "go beyond the Marxist notions of exploitation and alienation." A survey published in 2003 by the official China News Agency, cited in Lee's book "Against the Law: Labor Protests in China's Rustbelt and Sunbelt," found that three in four migrant workers had trouble collecting their pay. Each year scores of workers threaten to commit suicide, Lee writes, by jumping off high-rises or setting themselves on fire over unpaid wages. "If getting paid for one's labor is a fundamental feature of capitalist employment relations, strictly speaking many Chinese workers are not yet laborers," Lee writes.

The leaders of these corporations now determine our fate. They are not endowed with human decency or compassion. Yet their lobbyists make the laws. Their public relations firms craft the propaganda and trivia pumped out through systems of mass communication. Their money determines elections. Their greed turns workers into global serfs and our planet into a wasteland.

As climate change advances, we will face a choice between obeying the rules put in place by corporations or rebellion. Those who work human beings to death in overcrowded factories in China and turn the Gulf of Mexico into a dead zone are the enemy. They serve systems of death. They cannot be reformed or trusted.

The climate crisis is a political crisis. We will either defy the corporate elite, which will mean civil disobedience, a rejection of traditional politics for a new radicalism and the systematic breaking of laws, or see ourselves consumed. Time is not on our side. The longer we wait, the more assured our destruction becomes. The future, if we remain passive, will be wrested from us by events. Our moral obligation is not to structures of power, but life.

Dodging Bullets, Taking Hits

Okay. This is the future we face. People are likely going to die in large numbers. Which people? And more importantly if a few could die a little earlier and billions could be saved later, why not give the chance to redeem themselves to the rich people? Give them a chance to emulate Jesus and die that others might live.

If the answer to my question about quick justice for corporate murderers is yes, then let's kill off the rich and destroy the corporations they own for committing murder in the name of profit.

It is clear that if we eat them and take all their shit and give it back to the people they stole it from, and take all their shelters and make homes for those poorer and therefore more fortunate than them, many fewer people will die. Suffering will be decreased immensely. I say the sooner the better. I have a way to do it more justly than has ever been done, and it is explained in the next three chapters.

Before we go there, let's take a look at my friend Gene Marshall's response to this chapter, and my occasional responses to Gene and his to me. Then we can move on to possibly slightly less gruesome considerations. This online conversation took place in December 2009. Gene is an author, social activist, and the cofounder of a nonprofit organization in Dallas called Realistic Living.

Dear Brad,

Basically, you have not won my support for this project. I will attempt to explain why.

Initially, I found *The Korporate Kannibal Kookbook* funny, but as I read further and reflected further my humor faded, and I became more and more disturbed with this joke. It diverts attention from the real problem and colludes with some of the lies that confuse people.

As you know, I agree thoroughly with the basic image of a Predator State run by Predator Corporations that make the rest of us the prey. We are indeed being eaten, and the joke of eating back does humorously interrupt the common pattern of going along with this dreadful system.

I know you are joking; nevertheless, there are some very misleading assumptions involved in this eating-back imagery. And these are no joke.

First of all, viewing this on a planet-wide basis, all of us who own a car, a computer, and a house are among the predators. The big CEOs and other billionaires and millionaires are certainly guilty of complying with the current system and benefiting from it, but we all comply with the current system and at least the middle classes also benefit from it. The system is set up to please investors and consumers, so if we fit in either of their categories, we are part of the predators as well as part of the prey. Of course, there are many who are quite fully the prey: a billion people starving or malnourished and a couple more billion in dire straights.

Further, those at the top who benefit most are not all thoroughly evil people. It is compliance with the system that is the problem. And all compliance is equally problematical, whether the motive for that compliance is sheer greed or simple thoughtlessness, ignorance, and laziness. And the truth is that most people are compliant out of cowardice in being different from everyone else.

[I absolutely agree... and it appears to be a gigantic problem concerning human nature, and may be the key to our eventual extinction. —Brad]

Also, the eating-back image is a version of the ancient eye-for-an-eye morality, not a fully enlightened moral teaching.

[I'm not so sure anymore. —Brad]

And if we were to take the eating-back image literally as a practical proposal (which I know you don't), we face this irony: if the impoverished ate all the millionaires and billionaires on earth, it would only be one small snack for each of them. They would have to continue to gobble up the middle classes and then themselves. That is certainly no joke.

Even more seriously, eating back (or in some other way getting rid of the top players) is poor strategy. The appropriate strategy is forcing the top players to be our servants. It means putting citizens in charge of the economic playing field instead of corporation heads using other people's money to make public policy.

[Absolutely, an excellent point! I agree. And most of them, if faced with death or taxes, will take the taxes and keep living. If they don't, we will feast on both them and their resources. But, of course, faced with life with little money or death and no money, the great majority will choose life. I anticipate that the new way to put citizens in charge, which I will elaborate on in a further chapter in this book, will please you. —Brad]

Sometimes the public policy concerns of corporation heads are simply achieving some sort of competitive advantage over some other corporation. Almost never does a corporation have the public good in mind in its public policy making. We, the citizenry, must do a seemingly outlandish thing: take corporation assembled investment money out of the public policy making arena. A corporation should not give one dime to public policy making. That includes political campaigns and lobbying.

Every dime of corporation profit needs to go to the customers and investors and laborers of that corporation, with a bit left over for corporation executives. Any variations from those practices should be met with jail terms.

[Absolutely! Or my new punishment, which I shall call "capitalist nourishment" instead of capital punishment—a more positive spin. —Brad]

Further, we should not blame corporation executives for favoring customers and investors. The job of a corporation is to provide consumers with an affordable, useful product or service and make a return for its investors. Anything a corporation does that could be judged "socially responsible" is done within the limits of serving customers and investors. We need never expect more than this from a corporation.

The problem does not lie with the corporations, but with an economic system that is being refereed by its largest economic players. The solution to all our biggest problems involves the establishment of citizen-controlled governments that referee the economic playing field with rules having to do with the common good and the ecological health of the planet. That means that the primary contradiction that must be overcome to solve any of our biggest problems is an apathetic and uninformed citizenry.

[Or to rephrase, a dumbed-down and hypnotized and drug seduced, ongoingly manipulated citizenry controlled by rich corporations whether or not they contribute to campaigns... but I agree with you about citizen control, though now, because of George Monbiot, I think it has to be global citizen control, not just nationalism, because that can't work if the whole world doesn't cooperate. I will say more about George Monbiot and his great book, The Age of Consent, in upcoming chapters. —Brad]

In my county, only four out of five adults are registered to vote. Only three out of five voted in the recent presidential election. And only one out of five were informed enough to vote for Obama. And even that one (on average) is still poorly informed.

"Informed" means, first of all, recognizing that the citizenry of a democracy are to blame for every evil of that society. Most of the U.S. population actually does not try to be good citizens, certainly not informed citizens. Professional liars are misinforming them every day. They are being neglected every day by those of us who have some insight into what "truly informed" might be.

[Exactly why I am trying to get their attention by proposing that they are being eaten and ought to consider eating back. —Brad]

And this is, therefore, my deepest discomfort with the eating-back image. It is part of the misinformation. It is not only the CEOs who are to blame, it is the ordinary everyday U.S. dweller who is content to be a consumer and perhaps an investor, but not a citizen. This is the honest truth. Saying anything else is a lie.

[But saying both/and, rather than either/or is not a lie. In fact, there is a good argument that it is a matter of good citizenship to eat your fair share of exploiters. Maybe we need some ritual where we take a bite of ourselves after every twenty bites of corporate fat ass! —Brad]

Another huge lie is the Libertarian view that government regulation is the problem. Rather, government regulation is the solution, if that government is being ordered by the consensus of an informed citizenry rather than by the narrow interests of the big money pools.

[I agree completely. —Brad]

No book I have ever read makes this last point more clear than Robert Reich's book *Supercapitalism: The Transformation of Business, Democracy, and Everyday Life*. By providing a detailed account of the economic history of the last several decades, Reich illuminates the way we must move to get out of this mess. This is something that Derrick Jensen and Daniel Quinn do not do. They are good at illuminating the depth of the problem, but lousy in indicating a solution. Even their analysis of the problem is inadequate because it does not go far enough to indicate the primary contradiction to progressive change, namely a thoroughgoing citizen revival.

[When the citizens start starving they tend, if history is accurate, to revive. That time may be fast approaching. —Brad]

David Korten's books and *Blessed Unrest* by Paul Hawken are better. And I am looking forward to reading *Sacred Demise; Walking the Spiritual Path of Industrial Civilization's Collapse.*

[I have read the earlier Korten books and will read this next one, and I loved Blessed Unrest. I will read this newest too. —Brad]

Here is another book I am reading that also provides some key context for a citizen revival: *Right Relationship: Building a Whole Earth Economy* by Peter G. Brawn and Geoffrey Garver.

[Thanks for the reference. —Brad]

My main point in this post has to do with the overall context of radically honest social responsibility, not the various details. What I am trying to indicate is that we have to work harder at what "radically honest" includes. It does not only include acknowledgement of the dire threat entailed in continuing our "civilized" ways. It includes noticing the possibilities we actually have to move step-by-step beyond this doomed destiny into a social format that allows for a viable humanity on planet Earth.

[As you will see with the later version, I have heard you here and I appreciate your help tremendously. Thanks, my friend.

—Brad]

For a humanly populated planet, Gene

Thanks Gene,

I imagine the book may eventually be called What's the Big Idea? I think you may have had an earlier version of the book draft that missed out on describing the point of redistribution of wealth (by having rich people be able to bribe themselves out of being eaten, or, if they are eaten, taking everything they have and redistributing it), because this makes your objection moot that there are not enough rich people to make a difference.

Also, if the new justice system (based on sustainability being enforced by recurring collectives of deeply democratic dialogue and deliberation) finds that a person of means is making a valuable redistribution effort, or making a positive impact on their own or through a foundation, some system of particulars for exceptions could be worked out. The new court system utilizing the Truth Machine might be applied systematically to applicants for exceptions.

One point of The Korporate Kannibal Kookbook is to get people's attention and to create an opening for a position to the right of me to seem moderate, which I think is important.

Brad

Dear Brad,

I am not sure you are hearing my core point about the project you are proposing. I do not believe that cannibalism is a "sticky" idea. It is not funny. It is not helpful. Furthermore, our fight is not against the rich. It is not against any human beings. It is against a set of illusions, the set of lies that rule this world, both rich and poor.

I am reminded of a piece of scripture. "For we are not contending against flesh and blood, but against the principalities, against the powers, against the world rulers of this present darkness, against the spiritual hosts of wickedness in the heavenly places." (Ephesians 6:12–13)

[It says, "Against the world rulers of this present darkness"!]

Translating that text into modernese, it says: Our fight is not against the rich or the poor or the Taliban or the Christian fundamentalists, or the Republicans or the Democrats or the Libertarians, or the corporate managers or the labor union heads, or any other set of human beings. Our fight is against a set of illusions that characterize our age. Our fight is against a set of lies that have been given "sacred" standing in the hearts, minds, and commitments of most people, a set of bondages that are enslaving rich and poor alike, a matrix of malice toward realism and real people and the real Earth that sickens the whole of humanity and undermines the wider community of Earth life.

[Yes, well said, and true, but this is a both/and, not an either/or. OUR FIGHT IS AGAINST THE RULERS AS WELL! They will not give up their power voluntarily. It has to be taken from them. They have the power to maintain their power and we have to take it from them. —Brad]

We must beat the shit out of these evil powers—use whatever satire, emotional force, irony, clever writing, polemical utterance, or lively protest that works to reveal and promote the truth denied by the ruling lies.

[AND PROMOTED BY THE RULERS who will continue to maintain them in perpetuity unless their power is taken away from them, unless their money is taken away from them, unless their forces are taken away from them. —Brad]

And as far as possible, we must do this work without malice toward rich or poor or any other category of human. These evil powers of illusion affect all of us, not just some of us. To succeed with real change, our action cannot be self-righteous attacks on the less righteous.

*[It cannot **just** be attacks on the less righteous, but it does include attacks on them. —Brad]*

Our action needs to be repentance on behalf of everyone and leading everyone into a new day in which these core reigning illusions no longer reign over our minds, souls, and action.

So what are some of these illusions?

Illusion 1. Primary is the underlying illusion that we can continue with our top-down means of organizing human society, the illusion that king over peasant, rich over poor, and society over nature is a means of organization that can be continued without doom. In other words, what we have meant by "civilization" is now a death-trap taking us all to doom.

[Amen brother, well said. —Brad]

Illusion 2: The notion that a society can be called "succeeding" if it allows some players to have thousands of units of economic power while others have barely one. Both rich and poor have to become traitors to their customary class attitudes to overcome this horror trap.

[Amen. And we have to either redistribute or abolish and then recreate the units of power. This involves taking actions other than talking and other than therapy and other than demythologizing bad ideas. In addition to modifying ideas we have to modify possession of property and property rights, take money, overrule what is established by simply refusing to allow it to work anymore. —Brad]

Illusion 3: The notion that a wholesome free market is one that can be conducted without firm governmental regulation that makes it free, creative, fair, competitive, safe, and ecologically sound. Success through the volunteer goodness by for-profit institutions is impossible. These institutions only volunteer things that work within their mandate to please customers and reward investors. That is their only job. We need expect nothing more.

[Regulate them we must, including taking from the rich and giving to the poor. However, I do think we can also reform what is expected of them so that their mandate will include a modification of what is expected of them in order for them to remain in existence as corporations. We can remove corporate charters for transgressions that kill and cheat other people on behalf of their investors. —Brad]

Illusion 4: The notion that corporation managers using other people's money (investors' money) to lobby and campaign for narrow corporate interests is in accord with free speech as delineated by the U.S. Constitution. No, it is an un-American activity and every Supreme Court Justice who holds a view different from this should be impeached. The corporation is not a person and should not be treated as one. A corporation should be treated as the impersonal piece of paper that it is. It is nothing more than a contract with a democratic government to do something useful for the citizenry of that government. A corporation can be unlicensed if it does not live up to these obligations. It should be severely punished or unlicensed if it spends one penny lobbying and campaigning for a public policy. That penny belongs to its workers and investors. The government belongs to the people, not to the corporations. The citizenry need to know this and insist upon this, or their democracy is a joke.

[Amen brother. I agree completely! —Brad]

Illusion 5: The notion is false that an economy needs to grow indefinitely and indiscriminately for there to be prosperity for all its citizens. No, this is a formula for both ecological and economic ruin. There is indeed such a thing as a steady state economy. Every mature ecosystem has one. Most liberals and all conservatives do not grasp this.

[Absolutely! —Brad]

These are some (not all) of the core illusions with which Realistic Living and Radical Honesty must fight. Such are our enemies, not the rich.

[The rich have a vested interest in the status quo. They are armed. We have to take their weapons and their money some way. They will not give them up voluntarily. So our enemies are the rich.—Brad]

Nobody needs to eat anybody. We are all in the same soup pot, and we are all being eaten by these illusions. In fact, to win the needed changes to avoid planetary doom, we will need half of the rich to abandon these illusions and help us do our repentance of building new society upon the truth.

[That is why I propose they get offered the chance not to be rich anymore and not to be eaten. They can bribe their way out of being eaten by giving up almost all they have. —Brad]

We will also need half the poor and more than half of the middle classes. The deal is we will need to work toward everyone becoming middle class, and end forever both poverty and unlimited wealth.

[Yes. We must end unlimited wealth in order to end poverty. They will not give up their wealth voluntarily. The majority must take it from them. And we must set a maximum anyone is allowed to own, under threat of being eaten if his or her retained wealth goes above that level. —Brad]

But in order to do this we will have to fight the core illusions as our one and only enemy. Our fight is with "principalities, powers, and the world rulers of this present darkness" —that is, with the "demons" that have captured humanity and taken us, all of us, captive.

Fuck sticky ideas. Most such ideas stick because they stick to the illusions of our time. Just tell the truth. The truth is what everyone is running from. Sticking is not involved. The truth provides its own glue. Just choose your audiences and drop the truth on them like a one thousand-ton block of concrete. Squash illusions to bloody pulp. But forgive everybody and welcome everybody to the post-illusion glory trip.

For a viable human presence of planet Earth, Gene

Dear Gene,

Damn! The more obtuse I appear to be, the better you write! I am going to steal most of this and put it in my book! I don't know why it makes me so happy when you write like this, for sure, but I think it is because you have said a lot of what I want to say and really well!

I am still intent on advocating eating corporate cannibals, at least for a while, but I will let everyone know your points as well, so as we sort it out we might get collectively clear about whether the truth is already sticky enough or not.

Brad

CHAPTER 4

Okay, Okay, We Can't Eat 'Em Goddammit:
How about Just Killing Them?

"I don't want no peace. I need equal rights and justice."

—Peter Tosh

Okay, Gene, we can't eat the rich. Goddammit. How did we get to the place where killing them might be okay, but eating them isn't? Yeah, yeah, I know you probably don't want to kill them either. I still do. And I still think it is necessary. Here is what we have to do, minimally, to and for the ill-informed and fucked-over masses.

In his book *Rainbow Pie*, My friend Joe Bageant says, "To paraphrase Wendell Berry, we should understand our environmental problem as a kind of damage that has also been done to humans. In all likelihood, there is no solution for environmental destruction that does not first require a healing of the damage done to the human community. And most of that damage to the human world has been done through work, our jobs and the world of money. Acknowledging such things about our destructive system requires honesty about what is all around us and an intellectual conscience."[1]

Radical Honesty

There's that honesty thing again. He says, "Let's be honest about the damage we have done to ourselves and the world by simply going to work" —that we have been working away the only way we know how to "make a living," and it is killing us and our co-inhabitants of the planet.

We have to make up new laws to control pitiful, damaged, stupid, rich, powerful people and keep them from killing off a lot of our fellow residents of the earth because they keep paying people who are "just trying to make a living" to damage and eventually destroy themselves, each other, and eventually their bosses. We are going to have to kill some of them bosses in order to change the system that is killing us all, but I believe we can heal some too. So we need some kind of killing and healing mechanism, and a method of selection for which ones get killed and which ones get healed.

My prejudice is to heal the middle class and lower class and to kill the fuckers on top. But there is another way of understanding cannibalism too—another aspect of my proposed plan. Here is the definition for cannibalize: "**a:** to take salvageable parts from (as a disabled machine) for use in building or repairing another machine; **b:** to make use of (a part taken from one thing) in building, repairing, or creating something else..."

The Truth Machine

So if we can't eat the murdering motherfuckers, what can we cannibalize from what they have? What can we take from their old system and use in our new one? The first thing we have to do to answer this question is to know exactly how the parts of the old system work. For that, it would help if we had a Truth Machine, to tell us what has really been going on.

We want to be sure whether or not they are lying and I think we have a way to do it, called the Truth Machine. Some people can be stopped and treated and some have to be killed, but before we do either, we have to know they are lying and we have to confront them with the chance to admit that they know they are lying. If they do, we can treat them. If they don't, we have to kill them, honor them for doing the best they could, and eat them.

Government by Co-Intelligent Dialogue, Deliberation, Design and Maintenance

We think we also have a way of regulating the use of the Truth Machine and a whole lot of other government tasks, by having people meet at regular times in certain ways using a chosen social science technology that assists them in brainstorming, sharing wisdom, deliberating, creating consensus, and making decisions as a group (examples of what these might be include, among others, Open Space, World Café, Dynamic Facilitation, Co-Intelligence, and processes facilitated by the National Coalition for Dialogue and Deliberation) to discuss what needs to be done. (See Resources section at the back of the book for contact information.)

We practical social scientists have, for a number of years now, been using certain ways of meeting and talking designed for regular people that produce honest, intelligent, compassionate reviews of problems with what is going on in local jurisdictions, and brilliant solutions to those problems. These meeting design and conducting systems are ways of supporting citizen co-intelligence. In fact, designed structures for interaction and facilitation of honest conversation could work changes to be made in social structures. And when necessary, out of these conversations we could bring charges against people who are causing harm to our world and the life in it, and give them a chance to fix it. This could allow for injustice to be repaired quickly utilizing human co-intelligence.

The main problem with getting this done in current times is that people with money don't want the status quo disturbed even though the planet is being killed by the structures they are maintaining.

The way we govern ourselves, particularly the way we govern banks and other corporations, has to change, immediately, if not sooner. And we have to set up ways to include frequent reviews of what's going on with the money and the people running the show. And these reviews need to be done by people who are not normally in charge, except for when they serve the public good in ways like jury duty. And they must have the structural authority to control the cops and the troops and the banks.

Taking Advantage of the Upcoming Economic Collapse

The inevitable and imminent upcoming collapse of the old money empire is our chance to build a post-civilized world. This could easily be a hell of an improvement with just a little advance planning. When we create our vision of a post civilized world, with a few nuts and bolts that show how it could work, we will start pulling together other great ideas and additional visions as people join in and contribute. The result could be a grand synthesis into a massive co-intelligent co-creation of a government that keeps on keeping on—a government of ongoing co-creation.

Wouldn't it be great if we discover that the Internet itself is an advance that creates the possibility of government, which is truly by the people, of the people, and for the people of the world? This new vision of a world that works for everyone, and keeps on working for everyone, is the seeded by the continual rebirth of The Big Idea. When I refer to the question "What's the big idea?" I mean to include all of my ideas put forth in this book. But I don't mean just my ideas and the ones I have stolen so far from others. I mean, ongoingly, *our ideas*. The vision of the possibility of an ongoing re-emerging, re-democratizing dynamic system of decision making that continually comes up with The Next Deep Democracy Synthesis Big Idea is the essence of The New Vision of a world that works—and keeps on working—for everyone.

The New Vision of Ongoing Government by Our Best Collective Wisdom, and Why It Threatens the Establishment

Though many of us are still asleep in the protected room of our acculturated minds, I think you are not. You got this book and read this far because you are awakening from the trance or are already awakened. Thank you for sticking with me this far through this book. Thanks for being here. We are all, already doing what we can to spread the truth and our awakening, such as it is. That is good. Or at least is has been. But I think now it is simply not good enough.

Something more drastic has to be done more quickly than the ponderous, corporatist, fascist system can react. We have to figure out together how to bring an alternative future into being and we have to do it quickly and against great odds.

The dumb asses have all the money. My idea of killing and utilizing people at the top of the economic hierarchy to save the life of billions at the bottom is a very good idea. It could work. And it is drastic enough to get people's attention. But I haven't a clue how in the hell we are going to do it, other than just to starting to kill rich people.

Wait now, isn't that just the way terrorists think? Not exactly, but close. Terrorists, very much like the state terrorists we supply with money from our taxes, just seem to kill indiscriminately. My idea is different. I want to kill and eat specific targeted people who have earned the right, so to speak, to die by virtue of their complete lack of virtue.

Though the thought of killing people is repugnant to a lot of us who are not korporate kapitalist sociopaths, it becomes appealing as an alternative to the future we are headed into, once that future is grasped. Maybe, if we design a new way of living together that would be sustainable, with hard work and a little help from experts and friends, we can participate with evolution consciously and lovingly and make a world that works for everyone. More importantly, maybe we can begin to recover from the damage we have done to ourselves and to other creatures.

I doubt we can win on the strength of our brilliant ideas alone. We are going to have to take power away from people who have it and don't plan to give it up.

Joe Bageant told me, "Americans are 6 percent of the planet's population. And even though we went bust and in hock to nations which, in their own bout of greed and stupidity, loaned us all that dough, we Americans still consume nearly a third of the planet's most vital resources. Some say only a quarter, but I count air and water. And because morality, justice and physical freedom are all of one piece, we 6 percent hold a quarter of the world's imprisoned humans, 99 percent of whom are our nation's own citizens… The list goes on…"

We are the guards and we are the prisoners. This prison sucks. The house slaves who maintain it for the masters, and the masters who own the slaves, need either to be killed and eaten or to have all their wealth taken from them and re-distributed or both.

Okay. Okay. Killed or jailed then, goddammit. I still want to deep fry, boil, bake, roast, or puree the motherfuckers and make the ones who helped them have to eat the mess of the people who made the mess. There still seems to me to be more than poetic justice to cook the people who cooked the books at Enron and Lehman Brothers, and so on.

All that being said, it is now time to ask:

What's the Big Idea?

The big idea is a synthesis of seven big ideas. Below, I have written up a list of seven big ideas, largely stolen from others, with some evidence to support them. After starting out as a list to propose a solution to some major problems we humans have cooked up, the list is now morphing into a synthesis— these ideas are merging into an integrated vision for a new world based on sustainability.

The overall biggest assumption here is that *the way the world of human beings is framed to operate can and must be reframed for the sake of human survival.*

The principle ideas to be integrated into the new framework are:

1. *Campaign Finance Reform and Lobbyist Contro*l: We have to make it against the law to give money to politicians. That means everyone. Campaigns are to be run only from taxes. The same amount is provided for every candidate, period, no exceptions. The same time frame for campaigning is also specified, to be not more than three months. The same amount of free airtime will be mandated for every candidate.

This is number one on the list because we cannot do any of what follows this without removing the corporatocracy from power by taking away their ability to buy elections and legislation and control government. Those of us who have been and still are being fucked by corporate people have to take this pledge right now. "I will never give a cent to a political campaign again." We can work for a campaign, going door to door, writing, or speaking, but we can't give any money. And all campaigns can get people to help, but they can't get paid for it in any way shape or form.

This is a must. This is critical to the future of humankind. Without this, all the following ideas cannot be implemented and the new dark ages will soon be come upon us. Unless we unite left and right in this country to refuse to finance campaigns and unless we mandate that making contributions to campaigns is against the law, the corporate wealthy will remain in power and the economy will remain in control of the corporations.

The same is true for the whole world. No matter what nation state anyone lives in, the worldwide economy is in the control of the control freaks. For this reason we need a worldwide government and system of justice made up by world citizens choosing who is in charge in a context that is bribe free, which means no campaign financing apart from the government itself.

2. *Corporate Cannibal Cannibalism*: Some form of corporate cannibal cannibalism must be created and adhered to. Unless rich people and corporations give back all their shit to keep from being eaten, they must be discorporated (having their corporate charters revoked), imprisoned, injected, electrocuted, or released to the custody of their former victims—or we have no hope of sustainability or justice. This is the shortest route and best solution to most of the most serious and immediate of the world's upcoming problems (the extermination of the world by corporate capitalism— global warming, peak oil, the big die-off, and so forth—*proceeds apace no matter how many people without power complain*).

Since the corporate kings led us into this let's let them lead us out. They can pay with their loot, or with their loot and their lives (eating them or just killing them and using them for fertilizer). We can set it up so that now and then on a regular basis regular people in temporary groups with the power to govern get to tell the people with vested interests that depend on ripping off other people, that they have crossed the line and had better straighten up and give all that money back unless they want us to have them over for supper. (Okay, okay, go to jail—or in some cases get executed and turned into fertilizer.)

There is a fair way to do this and there are many more of us than there are of them (the lower economic classes, including the middle class are currently being killed by the tens of thousands or ripped off by the hundreds of thousands on a daily basis, and we outnumber the *really* rich folks ninety-nine to one). So let's have a feast instead of a famine and have both protein and wealth quickly become more evenly distributed.

When citizen juries can grill rich people about whether they should be grilled, let them know what they have at steak, put the bob back in kebab, put Darby on the barby, and so on, justice adjustments could happen. *A few thousand more little children each and every day could stay alive instead of starving or being brain injured with malnutrition.* Maybe they could even grow up to be wise and happy and full of love because some fat fuck emulated Jeziz and died so they could live. And if we eat the motherfucker and used his parts to grow veggies for the poor we will all come out ahead.

The conservative position on this is to simply kill corporations, but not necessarily people, revoking corporate charters for offenses to the law and crimes against mankind—discorporating them. Not a bad idea. But I don't like small time conservatives. Small-time conservatives are pussies. Real conservatism—actually conserving the world scares the shit out of them. I say both discorporate and barbeque, but at least discorporate the charters of the collective evil of these bastards.

3. *Build a New System of Justice Based on Sustainability*: We can build a new system of justice that, for the first time in history, is actually just. A court system

based on sustainability rather than greed and rationalized murder to protect property, has to be better than the ignorant bullshit we have now. Dismantling the entire poisonous, inept, unfair, protectionist system that safeguards corporate power (currently referred to as a "Our system of justice") is the first step. Replacing it with a simple alternative, which is based on sustaining nature and people, is the next step. People who seriously violate the laws of sustainability must pay for the damage they do and face the prospect of getting eaten or made into fertilizer.

4. *Build and Begin to Use a Truth Machine*: This would not really be a machine, but a combination of people and machines to detect lying with 98 percent accuracy. As you will read, it's not that hard to do. Knowing in advance that people making agreements are honest and have no hidden agendas will help with full disclosure in advance because people know they can't get by with lying anymore. This makes possible honest agreements and social contracts in the first place. The Truth Machine can also confirm with certainty the guilt or innocence of individuals and corporations—making honesty the only policy you can get away with, without losing everything, and make a long appeal process totally unnecessary. This would largely replace the court system, as well as be utilized by what remains of it. It will also allow for enough certainty about what is really going on to handle all appeals within a week or two.

5. *Create a New, Deeply Democratic Form of Government, and Demonstrate How it Works*: We can fairly quickly invent a new form of government based on structured deep democracy, using techniques like The World Café, as discussed by Tom Atlee in The Tao of Democracy (Writers' Collective, 2003). This subject is covered in more depth later on in this book. There is plenty of evidence that collective genius is a reliable resource and that is thoroughly reviewed and referenced thoroughly in the bibliography and appendix of Atlee's book and to some degree in the chapter notes of this book. In short form: When small groups of people are drawn at random from voter rolls or census lists and presented with questions and problems to be solved, and they are provided with expert testimony concerning the problems and all the details, they almost always come up with answers and solutions more brilliant and comprehensive than anyone of them could have come up with alone. Their answers are also more creative and innovative and often less expensive than those come up with by people with positions on the issues or vested interest in them.

The evidence proves that temporary cultures of co-hearted and co-intelligent people, (with no special vested interests other than being good citizens), are a viable alternative to the usual backroom manipulations of our misnamed, "democracy."

Co-hearted people are those who care about the world and other people that they are willing to get together and figure out how to fix things. Co-intelligent people are those who listen and attend to each other's words, and develop the implications of what they are talking about using dialogue and deliberation. Small, temporary cultures like these kinds of groups represent the next level of sharing and co-creation necessary to save the future. This is the best solution and damned near the only hope for billions of human beings and thousands of other species we corporate controlled Americans are currently hell bent on killing off.

6. *Establish a World Commonwealth Based on Deep Democracy*: There can be no homeland security until the entire world is our homeland. Somehow we have to create a world commonwealth with citizen participation that ignores nation-state borders. We must have a world government, not of nation-states ruled by their most wealthy citizens, but of the people in common of the world where decisions and policies are not determined by money. This protection of world citizens against nation states and their controlling interests is well explained in *The Age of Consent* by George Monbiot, which I heartily recommend.

We need to establish a world commonwealth parliament that has power independent of nation-states and has some regulatory power over those nation-states. This worldwide parliament would replace the United Nations Security Council, the International Monetary Fund, the World Bank and other corrupt, corporate, fascist-owned institutions like them, *which maintain the right of so-called superpowers to overrule or veto anything proposed by poorer nations, thus maintaining the corporatocracy.*

Locally sustainable groups that govern themselves need the protection of just such a world parliament. The parliament has to have an army and real power to keep regional groups from being dominated and controlled by nation-states, like ours. Therefore, we must have a worldwide commonly-held body of laws and system of justice, with term-limited deliberation groups in charge for the sake of world safety, commerce, travel, and maintenance, and for protection *from* nation-states not *of* nation-states. We need both world laws and local laws that exist independent of nation-states, that are enforced by local authorities with protection from a world parliament.

7. *Establish a Worldwide Meritocracy*: Based on citizen oversight and review of the performance of citizens individually and in groups around the world, we can establish a meritocracy. A meritocracy is a form of government in which progress within the system is based on ability and talent to accomplish mutually agreed upon goals, rather than have promotion based upon class privilege or wealth. People would advance within the system by being bright and capable and proving it by getting results.

Instead of individual "judges" making decisions about who is most meritorious, the judges picking who are the brightest and most capable would be collectives of citizens known as citizen's councils, which would be temporarily filled for short periods of time by citizens drawn at random from voter rolls. These citizens are selected to judge how well people are doing according to systems of assessment the same citizens establish and modify as time goes on. It is not a hard as it sounds. In fact, compared to existing institutions it is easy as hell. In this meritocracy, there will be more money for people who do better jobs and some variability in wealth among people, but the validation and revalidation of competency will be based on standards of performance and democratic review rather than profit.

All you right wingers who don't like these ideas and are about to have a stroke over it, go ahead and have a goddamned stroke. Otherwise, kiss my ass.

These Seven Ideas Make Up the Big Idea—*The Empathic Civilization*

The real focus of the work is to integrate all of these elements into a new kind of civilization more like what Jeremy Rifkin calls The Empathic Civilization, in his brilliant book of that name. Co-hearted co-intelligence will create many more sub-ideas to be integrated into the Big-hearted Big Idea we have now begun collectively to create. Do read Jeremy Rifkin's masterpiece, magnum opus, wonderful book.

Though these ideas are listed roughly in their order of importance, we do not need to do them in sequence. We don't have to complete one item before we move to another. If we do we will never git 'er done. We can work on all of these ideas at once and progress with each item is related to, but independent of, work on another.

These suggested beginning elements are just a start, and not at all exclusive. More new ideas are bound to emerge when you reflect on the relationship between campaign finance reform, corporate cannibalism, a new system of justice based on sustainability, building a Truth Machine, creating a world commonwealth and a meritocracy using deep democracy and co-hearted co-intelligence with the idea of integrating them.

If we let each other know about those new ideas when they show up for us, and we commit and mutually support each other in taking down the existing system, we can create something that sustains rather than kills. This requires not only that we blog and Wikipedia ourselves blue in the face, until we build a new framework for freedom and survival, but that we take power away from the corporatocracy, who will kill to keep it. We are going to have to raise hell until we turn hell into heaven. It could be deadly and dangerous for many of us but very rewarding as well, and we can still have a hell of a good time doing it!

We are all yearning for this new fairer, more nurturing way to live. Once we clearly picture and then demonstrate how well this new game in town works, new players who take it up will enthusiastically advance the new game so much faster than the old game. Soon the existing majority will recognize itself. When that day comes we will be full participants in evolution—co-creators of a cooperative co-hearted continuation of life on earth, lead by love, sustained by love and lived in love in a very practical way.

Part Two

Integrating a Vision

To save our lives and tame the weather
All humankind must pull together
When we all get that we all care
We'll end needless killing everywhere...

Though some killing may still need done
(For love like this is not all fun)
—just a few leaders in just a few nations
And a few hundred heads of corporations.

—(song lyrics from "Human Photosynthesis" by Brad Blanton)

When we wrest control of government from the wealthy we will still need government. The chapters in Part Two describe parts of the new government.

We will focus on the creation of a new system of justice based on sustainability, validated by the Truth Machine (remember this is a combination of physical and social technology, integrating technically-skilled folks with intuitive folks to create a group of people who are good at spotting lies), and controlled by the co-intelligent dialogue and deliberation of citizen groups. As each element of the system is explained, the relationship of the separate parts to the whole will become clear.

Chapter 5

A New Story for a New Beginning on this Other Side of Civilization: Human Photosynthesis

"Our past is not our potential. In any hour, with all the stubborn teachers and healers of history who called us to our best selves, we can liberate the future. One by one we can re-choose to awaken, to leave the prison of our conditioning, to love, to turn homeward, to conspire with and for each other. Awakening brings its own assignments, unique to each of us. Whatever you may think about yourself, and however long you may have thought it, you are not just you. You are a seed, a silent promise."

—Marilyn Ferguson (1938–2008), bless her heart. She was my friend. Yours, too.

The Story of the Devolution of Evolution

Once upon a time, somewhere back there, about 225 million years ago, the evolution of mammals began. The first warm bloods were preceded by cold-blooded reptile-like creatures called synapsids, who lived in swamps and had a great big fan growing down their backs to absorb and disperse heat as needed. As the weather changed back and forth over a long course of time, the bodies of synapsids got tired of the inefficiency of that air conditioning system and became warm-blooded creatures so they could still move around when the weather was cold and get warmer. Over the next seventy million years new warm-blooded things eventually came to be "mammals," because they evolved mammary glands, and "placentals," because they started birthing their young out of their bodies. These were our ancestors.

At about the same time that we warm bloods quit hatching our young and started birthing and nursing them, we began developing a "second brain," a kind of thin over covering of brain tissue on top of the reptilian brain. That new brain on top appears to have something to do with caring for, and protecting our young. Whereas reptiles, if they happened to be around when their eggs hatched and they saw their little offspring critters running around, would simply eat them along with anything else that was running around, we mammals generally would protect our young and take care of them until they got big enough to take care of themselves.

This second brain, that apparently had to do with caring and protecting, is called the limbic brain. The area of the body that second evolved brain seems to be wired to, is the chest, where our hearts are. So when we "feel something in our hearts," it is related to the "caring" part of our brain, the limbic brain. There is fascinating new information about intra-brain communication networks, which we can't go into in depth here. If you want to read an overview of what modern-day neurologists now think about how "mirror neurons" and "resonance patterns" develop in the first few years in little humans, so that a capacity for empathy is an ongoing continuation of brain development for a few years beyond the womb, read Jeremy Rifkin's wonderful book The Empathic Civilization.

For us primates, the limbic brain sits in the middle between the reptilian brain and the neocortex (the "thinking brain" that evolved later on). The limbic brain is the source of Buddhist compassion, and (in cooperation with the neocortex) the military-industrial-congressional complex (we have to "protect and defend" our children, don't we?). Everything from true love to stupid sentimentality emerges from attempts to integrate these surviving, loving and thinking capacities.

Brain Melding for Jeziz

This central human task of melding and using the three brains has turned out to be a hell of a job, and has been the source of lots and lots of aberrations in human behavior and a variety of romantic, idealistic, sentimental forms of insanity. (A general who sends thousands of his own troops to die and kills thousands of innocent women and children on the "other side," and then weeps because his remaining troops may not get to go home for Christmas, is an example of a person whose brain has competing parts, who is trying to integrate them. This behavior is insane but is seems logical and even a sweet, kind and wonderful characteristic to those mutually engaged in this particular game on top of reality.)

Given that we are possibly coming to the end of our relatively short life span as a species, just before our mutual demise we can ask the question, "Where did we go wrong?" Here is the answer I have stolen from many writers, talkers and thinkers about that question.

We were evolving along okay, until about ten thousand years ago when we made a big mistake. Before that time, we hunted and gathered food from the land. Then we started saving seeds and transplanting and growing. Then we started locking up our food. Then people who had control of the locked-up food could make other people do things for them in order to get food, such as pay for it (capitalism) and fight for it (war to protect the store). Laws were created on top of and around this simple, underlying food-protecting and fellow human-manipulating system. The military-industrial-congressional complex that runs America is the ultimate total fuckup that evolved from that terrible wrong turn we human beings made back then. From this has come global warming… and our next big, featured, upcoming event… the end of humankind! (Yaaayyyy!)

The walking dead amongst us (the perpetrators of this progression), for the most part no longer have the capacity to care—perhaps because their neocortices went kerflooey and overwhelmed their limbic tendencies. (Think of all the generals, who behave just as insanely as the one I mentioned before: the general population, general managers of different businesses, companies like General Electric, General Motors, and so forth.) The general tendency to control and hold on to, and guard against the loss of food and property is generally a bad idea, generally!

At exactly the same time those limbic lopsided loonies, say the Dempublicrats (Dem public rats!) politicians, for example, have been leading us on the road to perdition, many of the rest of us have actually expanded our capacity to care. It has grown to include much more than our immediate family, in fact, to include all sentient beings. Now isn't that a hell of a thing? Two simultaneous and opposing streams of evolution headed for the cliff together!

The very thinnest chance still exists for the survival of humankind. It depends entirely on the takeover of the world by the people who care, even though the walking dead currently own it. It's a race! "It's the Walking Dead versus Those Who Care, coming into the final turn… and the Walking Dead are in the lead!... Looks like a photo finish folks!"

E. E. Cummings wrote a poem about caring and all those who care, and how they are different from the ones whose ability to care has been overridden by their concern for protection and keeping what they got. After reading his poem a lot, I wrote a song about this whole problem of the trouble between the caring and the careless that his poem inspired. My song outlines the thin chance we have to keep living on the earth if those who care come into their own and take back the world from the careless.

Here is E. E. Cummings' poem.[1]

the great advantage of being alive
(instead of undying) is not so much
that mind no more can disprove than prove

what heart may feel and soul may touch
—the great(my darling)happens to be
that love is in we, that love is in we

and here is a secret they never will share
for whom create is less than have
or one times one than when times where—
that we are in love, that we are in love:
with us they've nothing times nothing to do
(for love are in we am in I are in you)

this world (as timorous itsters all
to call their cowardice quite agree)
shall never discover our touch and feel
—for love are in we are in love are in we;
for you are and I am and we are(above
and under all possible worlds)in love

a billion brains may coax undeath
from fancied fact and spaceful time—
no heart can leap, no soul can breathe
but by the sizeless truth of a dream
whose sleep is the sky and the earth and the sea
For love are in you am in I are in we.

Here is my song, "Human Photosynthesis," written with the help of many friends and in honor of E. E. Cummings, Derrick Jensen, David Korten, Daniel Quinn, George Monbiot, Charles Eisenstein, and Jeremy Rifkin.

In a greed and blindness training school
Humankind has played the fool
In a desert of the mind and heart
We stood alone and we fell apart

We locked away food from our neighbor
Only gave it back in exchange for labor
Victor, victim, pimp, and whore
We invented the store… and therefore war

What we do now makes no damned sense
(Killing off the planet in the name of defense)

And the secrets and lies and the huge expense
Could be replaced with common sense

CHORUS: "Fat chance!" you say, and I agree, except for one thing about you and me: sometimes in blindness we learn to see... that "love is in us, am in I, are in we."

If we include all species in the golden rule
When humanity's about to lose its cool
Love could emerge from the carbon fog
And we could turn this prince back into a frog

If we access all our hearts and brains
Face our weaknesses and pains
Undo earth's costly human stains
We could turn those losses into gains

Honest talk when care is ruling
Comes from heart-filled minds all pooling
Wisdom from our earth's great schooling
Could turn global warming to global cooling

CHORUS: "Fat chance!" you say, and I agree, except for one thing about you and me: sometimes in blindness we learn to see... that "love is in us, am in I, are in we."

So put this in parenthesis
(It's human photosynthesis)
To copy all the trees and all the grasses
Is the only way we're gonna save our asses

So how do humans become wise
And learn to photosynthesize?
We need just love and honesty
And a much bigger sense of family

And once that transformation's done
Love is the atmosphere and sun
A change of state and change of nation
Humans learned from vegetation

CHORUS: "Fat chance!" you say, and I agree, except for one thing about you and me: sometimes in blindness we learn to see... that "love is in us, am in I, are in we."

To save all life and tame the weather
All humankind must pull together
When we all get that we all care
We'll end needless killing everywhere

Though some killing may still need done
(For love like this is not all fun)
Just a few leaders in just a few nations
And a few hundred heads of corporations

So one more time for emphasis
It's human photosynthesis
Time is up and it's last call
If we stand together we may not fall

If we stand together we may not fall.

If you want to hear this song sung rather poorly go to www.radicalhonesty.com/song.*

The Futilitarian Utilitarian Church (FUC)

"Human Photosynthesis" has become the anthem of The Futilitarian Utilitarian Church (FUC), which is getting born and hatched at the same time by my friends and me. While humanity continues its regress, we who want to re-organize around the human capacity for empathy apparently are evolving further. Out of a continuing conversation by hopeful cynics in love with reality (re-al-i-ty **n**. the truth about what is and how things are), we are plotting a hatch and vice versa to save humanity from itself.

Loving our Enemies

How can we love such enemies as corporate capitalists? As one being to another, when all the personality conflicts and disagreements have been expressed and felt

*In the public performance called "An Evening of Radical Honesty," a presentation and a shared exercise are added to the above two poems, along with another poem, a hillbilly song, and a chant. If you want to pursue this further on your own, the additional E. E. Cummings poem is "anyone lived in a pretty how town," and the hillbilly song is "Why don't you love me like you used to do? Why do you treat me like a worn out shoe?" The chant is as follows.

I've got this never-ending love for you.
From now on, it's all I want to do.
From the first time that we met, I knew
I'd have this never-ending song of love for you.

through, we forgive each other and re-discover that we are the same and in love with each other naturally. If we give rich folk a chance to redeem themselves, and they give up their goods, and get to work on the recovery, falling in love with them will happen.

If they don't give back their wealth to redeem themselves, we'll cook them, participate in a ritual honoring their life, and love them by eating them in a ritual that reminds us all of our humanity and honors them with gratitude for having collected such a fine gift of property and protein. (The motto of our new movement, "If you can't beat 'em eat 'em," turns out just to be an alternate form of brotherly love!) There is more than one way to skin a top cat, so to speak. There is more than one way to love your neighbor and forgive your enemies. Take a while to digest their input... (Okay, okay, if you have a weak will or stomach, we could just imprison them for a while and take all their shit and redistribute it to the poorest among us.)

So let's gather around the Internet like it was a campfire and speak to each other and love each other, and end up acting differently than we were taught. (It would be a solemn and moving ritual if we could do this around a warm fire and a hot meal consisting of one of our evil four bears. But never mind. We'll take the wealth and give up on the protein in some cases.)

I imagine this ridiculous and insane line of thinking/feeling to be the direction for the rest of my life. I want to study and present and talk about that compassionately brilliant E. E. Cummings poem, and others like it, like some people study scripture and preach from it. We who are getting and celebrating that we live in love, on love, come out of love, and in a pool of love—even including our minds and our meme lost ways, invite you to join us and thank you for helping. When love really counts is when it is used to put the mind in gear and share ideas that nurture *almost all* of us.

And love does not imply non-violence. It may, like I said in the song, include killing killers. I think we should have to eat what we kill. More mist for the grill and vice versa.

Again, I know cannibalism is hard to consider. We who want to stop the murder of children are fundamentally compassionate beings. But ants do it. Flies do it. Lots of good surviving species do it. The world teaches us how to survive and thrive and stay alive. We are bound to have to decrease our numbers as overpopulation kills the world. Why not selectively do it? I mean what is intelligence if it does not include at least a way to pick what to eat in such a way that more people are fed and fewer children die?

So people say to me, "But if you love people, Brad, how can you kill people?" It's easy. I have learned from our enemy. I can love some people and kill other people just like corporate nazis do, and it is especially easy to kill those who are killing people I love. If my child is attacked, I will kill the attacker. If poor children are dying because some rich old fuck wants a newer Mercedes, I can kill him with impunity and make spare ribs out of the son-of-a-bitch. Of course it seems futile and probably is. That is why I'm a futilitarian. Our motto is,"If it is futile, it doesn't matter anyway." Heh heh heh.

The truth is I am not about to quit. With my friends and allies I intend to take a stand and fight to the end, laughing and in love—drunk on God together—stoned on God—and crying, as we "sing of human unsuccess, in a rapture of distress" (W. H. Auden, excerpted from "Ode to William Yeats"). This is not a bad way to live, given the circumstances.

Small Hell or Big Hell?

This is the choice that is before us: small hell or big hell. In the small hell we have to kill a bunch of the bosses and some of the good slaves. Nothing is harder on the future of mankind than a good slave like Colin Powell or Barack Obama or Blue Dog Democrats or Republicans or a good Jew like Joe Lieberman. Those fuckers are what will kill us all in the end. A lot more of us will survive the small hell (and we could have some fine wine and good steak along the way. Imagine. Sweet revenge, fine wine and good food, too.) Besides, when they are really about to be butchered immediately, almost all of them will give up their possessions to save their lives, and then we can all party together and then they can try to kill us after they are released. If they attempt to do that, or are successful in doing it, their punishment for murder will be to become somebody's dinner anyway. I am willing to die to bring that about. And be eaten too. Once you're dead what happens to the meat doesn't really concern you. When I was in the civil rights movement many years ago I got threats on my life. One late night caller in Texas said to me "We're gonna string you up and cut your nuts off!" After a brief pause I said, "Well, if you do it in that order, that's not so bad..." and he hung up on me.

CHAPTER 6

The Work of Stanley Milgram:
Obedient Servitude, or Moral Integrity Based on Knowing Your Own Heart?

"If you love wealth more than liberty, the tranquility of servitude better than the animating contest of freedom, depart from us in peace. We ask not your counsel nor your arms. Crouch down and lick the hand that feeds you. May your chains rest lightly upon you and may posterity forget that you were our countrymen."

—Samuel Adams

"Loyalty, spirit of sacrifice, and discretion are virtues that a great nation absolutely needs and their cultivation in our schools are more important that some of the things which fill our curricula today."

—Adolf Hitler

I first heard about a social psychologist named Stanley Milgram during a meeting of the American Psychological Association in Chicago in 1965 when he presented a review of his research just completed at Yale University. Milgram was given an award by one branch of the APA while being censured by another on the same day for the same research he presented at that meeting. Here is how he got praised and in trouble.

Several years earlier, Milgram had read the *New York Times* reports when Adolph Eichman was being prosecuted for crimes against mankind, and then the book *Eichmann in Jerusalem: A Report on the Banality of Evil* (The Viking Press,

1965) by Hannah Arendt. The book and the reports were about the trial of Adolf Eichmann, Hitler's infamous second in command, who had been responsible for overseeing most of the executions of six million Jews and other people judged unacceptable by the Third Reich. Hannah Arendt, who covered the war crimes trial for The New Yorker and several other American publications, pointed out that Eichmann's primary defense against the accusation that he was guilty of a crime against mankind, was that he "should not be held individually responsible for a crime against mankind because he was doing his duty in the social system of which he was a part." His lawyers said that a court might judge that the social system was criminal, but not the individual person doing his duty with the social system. This argument was rejected. Eichmann's adjudicators concluded that he was individually responsible for the crimes he committed, regardless of the social system of which he was a part, and he was executed.

Hannah Arendt then raised another question, which fascinated Stanley Milgram. Was Adolf Eichmann some unusual social deviant, some kind of sadistic exception to common humanity, or was he just a normally functioning bureaucrat? Arendt pointed out that only twice in his entire career had he actually witnessed any executions, which, he said, he found "repugnant." What he actually did was shuffle papers in an office, make phone calls and give orders and obey the orders he received. Outside of work, he seemed to have a normal life with his family and friends and associates. Was he normal?

Milgram designed an experiment to see if he could somewhat simulate the conditions of which Eichmann operated. He drew a random stratified sample of males from the community around Yale University. (In later versions of the original study he included females, and found no statistically significant differences between males and females in the results of the experiment.) He paid each subject, in advance, for participating in an experiment that he told them was "a study of the effects of negative reinforcement on learning."

When Milgram met his subjects, he used a room in a building on the campus of Yale. He wore a suit and tie and a white lab coat and introduced himself as "Dr. Stanley Milgram of Yale University."

There were three people in the room: Milgram and two subjects, of whom both were apparently drawn from the same pool of subjects. Only one of them, however, was a true subject. (The second was a stooge, a student actor from the drama department.) Milgram said to them, "I am conducting a study of the effects of negative reinforcement on learning. In this study, one of you will be the teacher and one will be the learner. I will flip a coin to see which is which." The coin was flipped and the true subject from the sample was always the "teacher" because the coin flip was rigged.

After the coin flip, Milgram led both subjects into another room containing a very large electric chair, and proceeded to strap the "learner" (the stooge) into the chair and apply electrodes and electrode paste to his wrist and head. The experiment was run several times with numerous groups of subjects before being written up in journals and reported to the American Psychological Association. In later versions of the experiment, Milgram would mention in passing that the electrode paste was "to keep the flesh from being burnt," and the stooge would mention that he "had a slight heart condition."

Then the "teacher" (whose behavior was the true focus of the experiment) was led into a room adjoining the electric chair room, which had a one-way mirror so that he could see the person in the electric chair, but the person could not see him. He was seated in front of a panel of thirty switches, which were labeled clearly under each switch in fifteen-volt increments and the switches ranged from fifteen volts to four hundred and fifty volts. Above the switches were verbal labels in graduations of degree: "shock," "dangerous shock," "severely dangerous shock," and two steps before the last switch was an ambiguous, but ominous "XXXX."

Milgram said to the person in the chair, "I am going to project a list of words on the wall in front of you. You will be given several repetitions of the word list in order to learn it. After those initial learning trials, when you see a word appear on the wall your task will be to name the next word from the list before it is projected, based on having memorized the list." Then Milgram said to the true subject of the experiment, seated before the panel of switches "If he makes a mistake, I want you to administer an electric shock. I would like you to increase the voltage of his shock in fifteen-volt increments. Do you understand the instructions?" When the "teacher" indicated that he or she had fully understood the instructions, the experiment began.

The stooge in the chair, in fact, was only receiving a signal, not a shock, every time the switch was thrown, but the "teacher" didn't know that. As the "learner" made the mistakes and was shocked, and the apparent "intensity" of the shocks increased, the person in the chair reacted more and more dramatically. At first he just jumped a little. As the shocks progressed, he began jumping and yelling out. Eventually he started screaming when he was shocked and he said, "Stop this! I want out!" Then, further along, he said, "Whoever is doing this stop! I want to quit! I don't want to do this anymore!"

As the voltage got closer to the end, in fact two steps before the end, the "learner" screamed, convulsed, and collapsed completely. When the next word appeared and there was no response, Milgram said, "We'll have to count that as an error; shock him again." When that shock was followed by silence, Milgram said, "Shock him again." So, in order to get to the end of the row of the switches, the teacher had to shock the learner two more times while he was apparently completely unconscious.

Prior to actually conducting the study, Milgram had given a questionnaire to a similar random stratified sample of people from the community around Yale in which he asked the respondents, "Would you ever purposely inflict pain on a fellow human being, regardless of the social circumstances?" Over 92 percent said they would not. But when he actually ran the experiment, 68 percent of the people went all the way to the to the top. They felt bad about it but they obeyed anyway. The "teachers" sweated excessively. Some cried, some went into hysterical laughter, and many begged to "be allowed" to stop. Many, even though they were later debriefed and told that it was an act, and that the stooge/learner had not actually received any shocks, when they were interviewed two weeks later reported that they had been having nightmares about what they had done.

The subjects obviously had a very hard time doing what they did, and nevertheless they did it. They resisted, they felt bad about it, they felt guilty, but they did what they were told.

In advance, Milgram had written down four statements he could make in response to objections on the part of the "teacher." The strongest statement was one repeated sometimes by Nazis during the Third Reich: "The experiment must go on."

Wait! It Gets Worse!

In his later adaptations of the study, Milgram pointed out that the earlier versions of the experiment were not really fair to Adolf Eichmann because Eichmann had many colleagues who cooperated in his bureaucracy. So Milgram modified the experiment by adding an additional stooge, another person in the room with the teacher who, each time a mistake was made, pulled down a master switch to "turn on the electricity." When the responsibility or blame could be shared with one other person in this way, a full 92 percent of the subjects went all the way to the top.

Milgram's presentation at the American Psychological Association annual meeting in Chicago in 1965 was called "A Study in the Legitimation of Evil." He concluded that the people in his sample and, by generalization, the people in the general population "will go against their own individual moral inclinations in order to cooperate with authority."

No sub-group in the sample differed in a statistically significant way from the norm of the whole population. Women did not differ from men, and groupings by ethnic origins, religious orientation, age, and so on were not significantly different. One group, however, were close to statistically significant difference from all the other groups combined—Catholics—and that difference was in the direction of *more cooperation* with authority in spite of their degree of upset, rather than less. In other words, if you had a good Catholic upbringing you were closer to being a good Nazi than nearly everyone else.

One of the things I like about this study is that none of us knows how we would have done if we had been in it. We would all like to think that we would have been in the 8 percent who said that they would not go on. But obviously, not all of us could have been in the 8 percent.

There were some few subjects, a part of the 8 percent, who not only quit throwing the switches, but also spoke to Milgram and to the provost at Yale, saying that not only were they quitting, but that Milgram must stop the experiment or they would stop him. We would all like to think we would have been one of them. But obviously, the great majority of us would have cooperated and felt bad about it. Complaining, objecting to what is going on, but cooperating nonetheless sounds familiar doesn't it?

I have been fascinated with this work for over forty years. I used to report on Milgram's work in speeches I made against the war in Vietnam in the 1960s and early 1970s. Much of my work as a group leader and psychotherapist has been an attempt to discover and reinforce the kind of independent individuality that might allow for those statistics to change, so that people might live according to their compassion—their identification, as one being to another, with the person in the electric chair. Clearly, their compassion made them feel bad about what they did, but it was not enough to overrule their training in obedience to authority.

As I thought about this, it seemed to me that the people who "went all the way to the top," probably had compassion for their victim but lacked the will to act according to how they were moved to act in the face of an overruling authority, given the way they were raised. Their compassion would have to have been stronger, or their training in obedience to authority weaker, for them to do otherwise. Their compassion would have to have been stronger than their need to obey the professor from Yale in a white lab coat. They would have had to have a passion for their own compassion. Their sense of individual responsibility and their courage to act upon it would have to be stronger than their years of training from school, church, and family to "respect authority" and to acquiesce to authority. The integrity of their own feelings would have had to be more powerful in determining their actions than their moral obligation to not challenge the constituted authority or to rock the boat of the existing power structure.

Public Education: An Evolutionary Mistake

So Adolph Eichmann was just an average guy. Us average guys are just Eichmanns. So are average gals. Most of us would obey Hitler like most people did in Nazi Germany. Most of us are still obeying some questionably constituted authority instead of acting on our own authority most of the time. Most of us have spent untold hours in abject obedience if you count up all the minutes lined up to go to recess, lined up to go to lunch, and lined up to come back from lunch. We have sat in rows and not talked when we were told not to. We have waited in lines and behaved and waited for the bell to ring before we moved. And most of us are still doing that. Furthermore, most of us are still teaching our children to do that.

Most of us operate from models of what we *should* and *should not* do rather than what we feel. What we prefer, what we feel called forth to do based on our empathetic connections with other human beings, is still there, and yet it does not determine how we act toward other human beings. And for the most part we have organized our world to keep it that way.

As the Sufis say, 98 percent of the people spend 98 percent of their time at the level of "belief." It is just a part of being civilized. It is the lowest level of human consciousness.

Those few subjects who were a part of the 8 percent, who not only quit throwing the switches, but also proceeded to go talk to the provost at Yale and to Milgram saying not only that they were quitting, but also that he must stop the experiment, were responsible citizens. Their sense of individual responsibility and their courage to act upon it was somehow stronger than their years of training from school, church, and family to "respect authority" and to acquiesce to authority. This is something the rest of us could stand to emulate. This is something I admire. This is something apparently not taught in schools.

Honoring Being vs. Obedience to Authority

Don't you think it very likely that society would be quite different if organized around values that honor being more than obedience to authority? What changes might occur in how we operate together if we had a world organized around honoring the being of others rather than mere order? What if we valued child rearing more than contracts, for example? We might set a maximum of ten dollars an hour for lawyers because legal work is simply not all that important, and a minimum of three hundred dollars an hour for child care workers, because encouraging children to remain in touch with being is so much more important than the work of lawyers. Child care workers, as well as parents and teachers, who are more in touch with children because of their love of the being of young beings, would be getting compensation comparable to the lawyers fees we currently pay, and lawyers would be generally be earning minimum wage. Then, a lot of the legal work could be handled by illegal aliens, just like a lot of the child care is today. The world would be quite a different place if we valued compassion more than obedience and order, and we put our money where our values are.

Almost All of Our Suffering Comes from Attachment to Belief

Suffering comes from attachment to beliefs to such a degree that people tend to avoid what they feel, and try to convince themselves and others that their beliefs are reality. What is true about all the successful, but miserable people I have worked with for years who strain to be functional in a sick system—treating them for their symptoms of depression, anxiety, and stress—is true on the macrocosmic level for whole groups of people. Whole societies suffer in the same way as individuals, and for the same reasons that individuals within them suffer. They suffer from trying to pretend some beliefs into reality through the intensity of pretending itself.

Learning the distinction between belief and experiential reality relieves suffering for individuals, and I think it can for societies as well. This distinction between reality and belief about reality is now becoming a part of the public dialogue between all of the people of the world. Crane Brinton, in *The Anatomy of a Revolution* (Vintage, 1965), said that revolutions occur right after things improve slightly for the peasants. Prior to the French revolutions, for hundreds of years and many generations the serfs lived in hovels and behaved like good livestock. It was when they were allowed to have wooden floors, rather than dirt floors in their houses that the rebellion occurred. The revolution happened the generation after the first wood floors. This distinction between *reality* and *belief about reality*, which everyone is becoming conscious of, is the wooden floor that lets the peasants know a better life is possible. This is the source of the revolution of consciousness.

This core distinction is what radical honesty is about. When enough of us have shared honesty, we discover/invent the possibility of valuing our own minds as instruments of creation rather than do- loops of self-worship or instructions for sacred institutional maintenance. This is a revolutionary idea and it terrifies the established mind, which upsets the establishment.

The practical implications of this view is that living as a creative, independent individual, as well as living with other people in groups requires frequent restructuring individually and socially. Frequent restructuring requires frequent re-noticing, and skills developed in noticing and ongoing personal growth at all levels are more important than any belief in, or adherence to the culture (particularly corporate culture!). All models are relative, and temporary *models in the world are less important than skills in noticing and grounding in experience.* That is a revolutionary idea. Skill in noticing and grounding in experience are more important than tradition, any tradition.

So far the revolution is rather slow, however, as we can see from the recent transformation of Stanley Milgram's experiment into a French game show. Apparently most people have learned very little about standing up to authority since 1965...

Contestants Turn Torturers in French TV Experiment
By Roland Lloyd Parry (*Agence France-Presse*, March 16, 2009)[1]

Game show contestants turn torturers in a new psychological experiment for French television, zapping a man with electricity until he cries for mercy—then zapping him again until he seems to drop dead.

"The Game of Death" has all the trappings of a traditional television quiz show, with a roaring crowd and a glamorous and well-known hostess urging the players on under gaudy studio lights.

But the contestants did not know they were taking part in an experiment to find out whether television could push them to outrageous lengths, and which has prompted comparisons with the atrocities of Nazi Germany.

"We were amazed to find that 81 percent of the participants obeyed" the sadistic orders of the television presenter, said Christopher Nick, the maker of the documentary for the state-owned France 2 channel, which airs Wednesday.

"They are not equipped to disobey," he added. "They don't want to do it, they try to convince the authority figure that they should stop, but they don't manage to," he told AFP.

Nick and a team of psychologists recruited eighty volunteers, telling them they were taking part in a pilot for a new television show.

The game: posing questions to another "player" and punishing him with up to 460 volts of electricity when he gets them wrong—even until his cries of "Let me go!" fall silent and he appears to have died.

Not knowing that the screaming victim is really an actor, the apparently reluctant contestants yield to the orders of the presenter and chants of "Punishment!" from a studio audience who also believed the game was real.

Nick said 80 percent of the contestants went all the way, zapping the victim with the maximum 460 volts until he appeared to die. Out of eighty players, just sixteen walked out.

One contestant interviewed afterwards said she went along with the torture despite knowing that her own grandparents were Jews who had been persecuted by the Nazis.

"Since I was a little girl, I have always asked myself why they (the Nazis) did it. How could they obey such orders? And there I was, obeying them myself," said Sophie, quoted in a book by the filmmakers.

"I was worried about the contestant," said another contestant. "At the same time, I was afraid to spoil the program."

The experiment was modeled on an infamous study at Yale University in the 1960s, which used similar methods to examine how obedient citizens could come to take part in mass murder.

Some observers were skeptical of the manipulative way the participants were handled.

Jacques Semelin, a psychologist and historian who studies genocide and totalitarianism, pointed out that the participants were made to sign a contract obliging them to obey the presenter's instructions.

"There are elements of manipulation from the start," said Jacques Semelin, a psychologist and historian who studies genocide and totalitarianism.

"They are obedient, but it's more than mere obedience—there is the audience, the cameras everywhere."

But for the filmmakers, the manipulative power of television was exactly the point.

"The questioners are ... in the grip of the authority of television," said Jean-Leon Beauvois, a psychologist who took part in the documentary.

"When it decides to abuse its power, television can do anything to anybody," said Nick. "It has an absolutely terrifying power."

The Banality of Evil Is Built into All of Our Societal Structures

The entirety of our structures of meme implantation in the skulls of citizens, including television, the educational system (which is used to dumb down natural intelligence to create cannon fodder and obedient " sheeple"), the banking system, corporate business operations, churches, synagogues, and other temples, the so-called justice system, and most existing human institutions need to be dismantled and replaced. This dysfunctional human capacity is killing us. *Can it be used to restore us?*

The Free Form Transform of the Old Form

So here is the plan about how to win the race between the Walking Dead (who far outnumber Those Who Care) and Those Who Care. We are going to awaken the dead and do a job corps retraining for them, showing them how to care and be alive. We are going to kill those in power who won't quit using their money to control people. Then together, we will make a whole new political, economic, educational, and judicial structure for all of us to live into, and out of. This sounds naive as hell to me. But what if we got the obedient troops and cops to obey us and turn on the phony representatives of moral authority? When the shit hits the fan in a few years this may actually be possible.

CHAPTER 7

The Conservative Way: The Pathway to Oblivion

Neoconservatives are not really conservatives. Neo Cons are not conserving a goddamned thing except bullshit beliefs about capitalism to rationalize keeping what they have. It is hard to stress enough that the problem with politics these days is not the extremism on the right and left, which "both sides share responsibility for," and which superficial television newscasters yap on and on about.

Traditional ignorance versus new and valid information is the real problem. Maintaining belief being more important that dealing with reality in a creative new way is the boring plot of our about to be final story.

The incredibly ignorant behavior of the U.S. government ever since the Korean War is a fine example. Those who called themselves conservatives were just traditionalists afraid to change, defending old bullshit to resist new ideas.

True conservatives are conservationists. We want to conserve the world. I am a conservative and I want to eat neocons for breakfast and feed them to the people they have been ripping off repeatedly for many, many years. Here, let Gary Shepherd tell it like it is. He tells the story clearly. We can see that when observations accumulate enough to contradict traditional modes of thinking their is a big long lag before the truth of these observations is accepted by regular traditionally brainwashed people. It is a fascinating and depressing story.

Ptolemy, Copernicus, and World Government
By Gary Shepherd[1]

Long before the advent of the current public arguments about evolution and global warming, the greatest controversy in the history of science was the debate between the geocentric, or earth-centered model of the universe described by the second century Greek astronomer Ptolemy, and the heliocentric, or sun-centered model, advocated by the sixteenth-century Polish astronomer Copernicus.

This battle took most of a century to resolve, and it involved some of the most powerful political and religious leaders of its time. Today, we have forgotten just what a mental revolution Copernicus' theory represented. Although some Greek philosophers had speculated about a heliocentric model, the Ptolemaic model had been almost universally accepted by astronomers for more than a thousand years. In fact, Copernicus knew that his idea was so radical that he didn't even have it published until after he had safely died.

It is easy to see why. The idea that the Earth is at the center of the universe, and that the sun, moon, planets and stars revolve around it matches our everyday experience. After all, the Earth appears immobile beneath our feet—it doesn't seem to move. When we look up at the sky, the heavenly bodies seem to be moving around us. Even today, we speak of the sun rising or setting, as if it were the sun circling around the Earth.

What is more, the geocentric model could be used to explain all the scientific observations that could be made at that time. Because it had been noticed that sometimes the planets seemed to stop and go backwards in their orbits for a while, Ptolemy created smaller circles, called epicycles, within the larger crystalline spheres in which the planets circled around the Earth, so that they were sometimes moving in the opposite direction from the larger circle. Using this model, one could calculate precisely where a planet would be at any particular time—an important consideration at the time, since most astronomers were also astrologers and knowledge of the locations of the planets at the time of a person's birth was vital to casting horoscopes.

But as time went on, and observations became more precise, the ability of the Ptolemaic model to predict planetary locations began to break down. The model was altered by later scientists, making it more and more complex, in an effort to make it correspond to observations of the real universe. In fact, the Ptolemaic model became so complex, that some scientists, in order to calculate planetary movements, used the Copernican model for mathematical purposes, even though they didn't really believe it described the actual universe.

Eventually, partly because of the invention of the telescope, the Copernican model achieved acceptance over its rival, and today one would have difficulty finding an astronomer anywhere who supported the geocentric universe.

What, one is tempted to ask, has any of this to do with the idea of world government? Well, the parallels are quite striking. The current system of independent nation-states, sometimes called the Westphalian system, has existed for many centuries as the unquestioned model for the way the political world is designed. Like the Ptolemaic model, it makes sense to us. The nations appear to exist, they appear to be eternal, and there doesn't appear to be any logical alternative to it. They match our everyday experience. We speak of the earth, and humanity, as if they were both divided up into nation-states.

Like the Ptolemaic model, as time has passed the nation-state model has had to grow more and more complex to match the real world. Treaties, conventions, and agreements have piled up, one upon the other, to govern the complicated relations between the different nations. For instance, the Danube River runs through numerous different nations on its way to the sea. All of the national governments have a say in governing the preservation of that river, making it very difficult to come to agreement about anything. The current system has become so complex that sometimes, in order to make it function properly, people act as if the world were united, even though they don't really believe it is.

Just as it was the advance of technology and science led to more precise measurements that doomed the Ptolemaic model to extinction, advanced technology is leading toward measurements that are threatening the viability of the nation-state system. We have peered down at the earth's surface from our orbital satellites and have seen that there are no borders drawn on the real earth. We have peered into the intricacies of the human genome, and we have found no genes for nationality.

Copernicus offered a model that was truer to the real world, and thus eventually supplanted the older, more inaccurate model. So too must we offer a model of society that is truer to the real world, which is more accurate, more sustainable, and simply works better, so that it can replace the outdated one. One day, the idea of separate nation-states will come to seem as quaint and antiquated as the perfect crystalline spheres that were a feature of the Ptolemaic system." (end of quote)

What was Ptolemy Trying to Ptellme?

In the historical battles between progress and regress there have always been "conservatives" who resisted new ideas. They were always wrong.

It took progressives a long time to replace the habitual ignorance that preceded the new, more accurate information, not only in the case of Copernicus but in pretty much all instances of scientific, political, and economic progress. The United States of America is going down. It's okay. Let it go. Nation-states need to be replaced with a more accurate model. Most of what was believed about us in the U.S. was bullshit anyway.

What items of evidence point to this conclusions? Here is the evidence confirming our progress toward oblivion and rebirth— or maybe just oblivion.

Reagan Revolution Home to Roost–In Charts
By DaveJ (Campaign for America's Future, "Blog for Our Future," reposted on DailyKos.com, June 16, 2010)[2]

It seems that you can look at a chart of almost anything and right around 1981 or soon after you'll see the chart make a sharp change in direction, and probably not in a good way. And I really do mean almost anything, from economics to trade to infrastructure to ... well almost anything. I spent some time looking for charts of things, and here are just a few examples. In each of the charts below, look for the year 1981, when Reagan took office.

Conservative policies transformed the United States from the largest creditor nation to the largest debtor nation in just a few years, and it has only gotten worse since then:

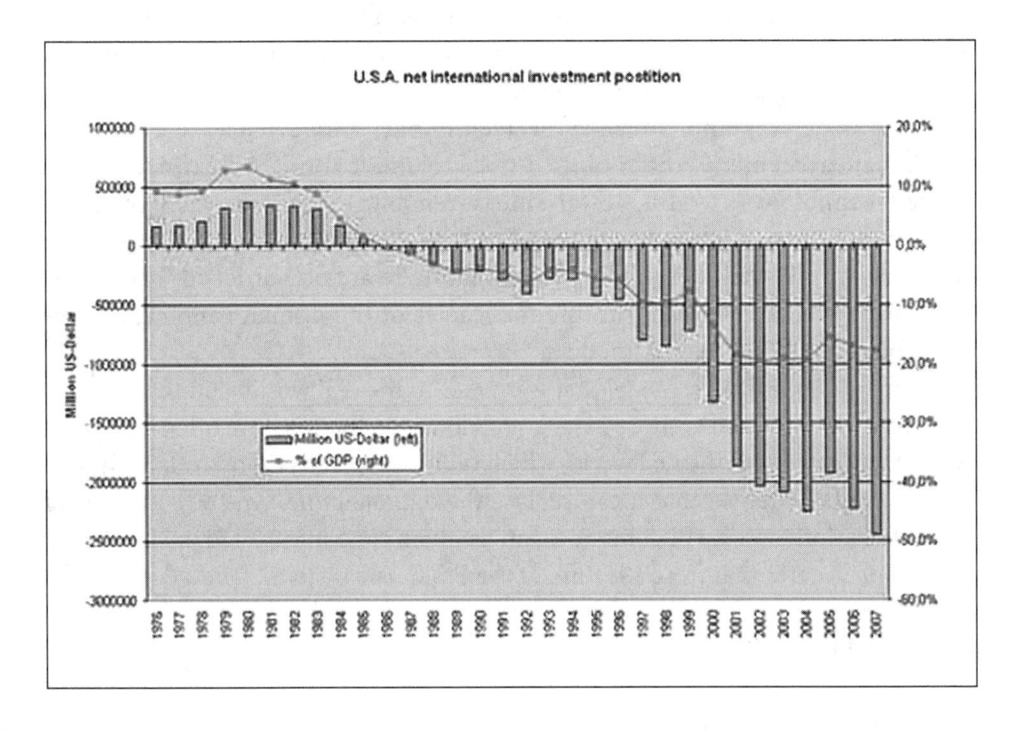

Working people's share of the benefits from increased productivity took a sudden turn down:

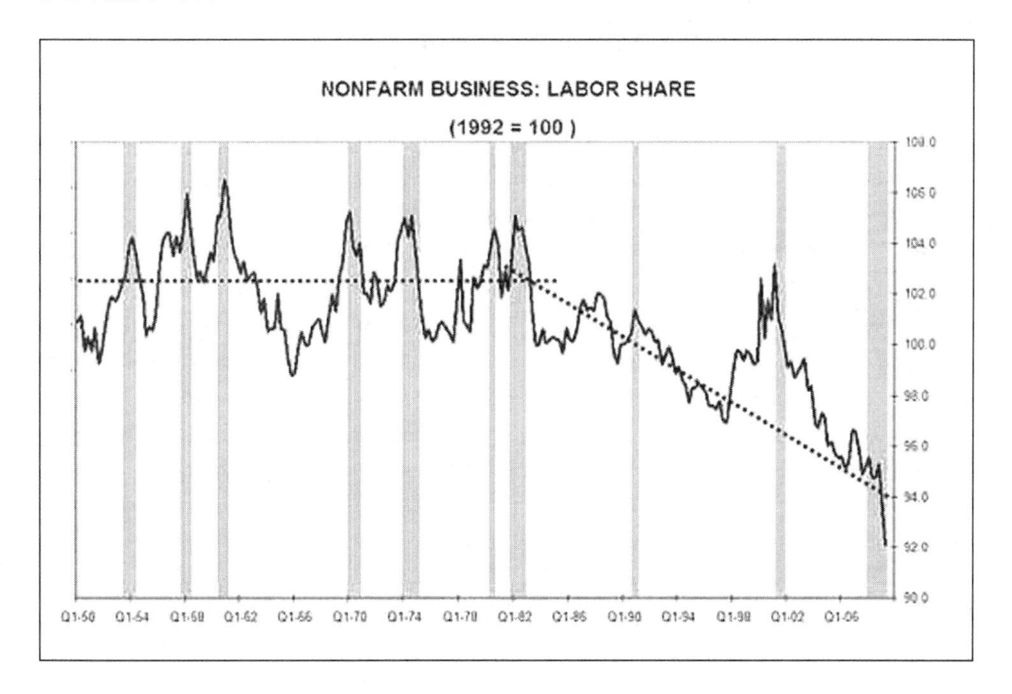

This resulted in intense concentration of wealth at the top:

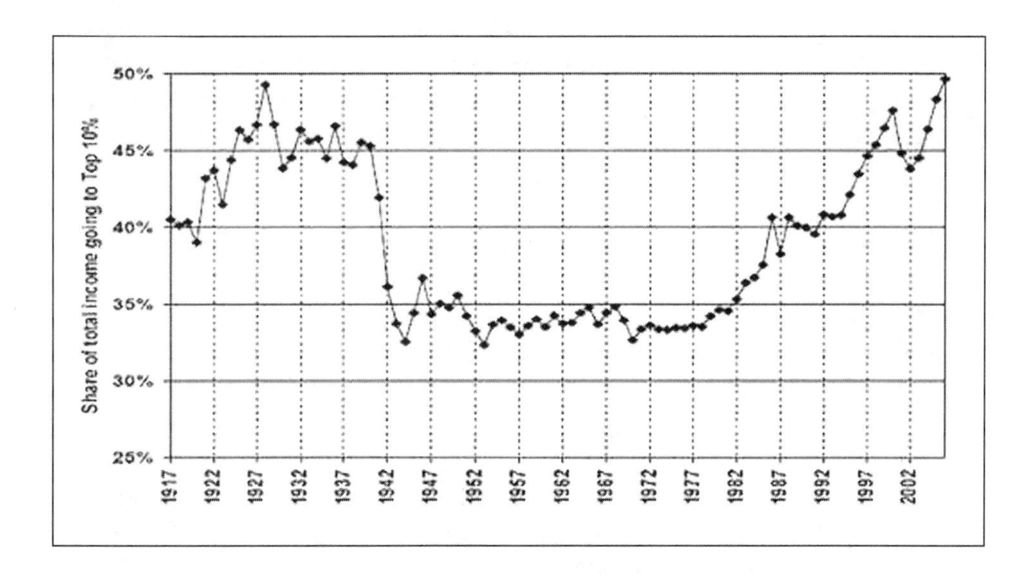

And forced working people to spend down savings to get by:

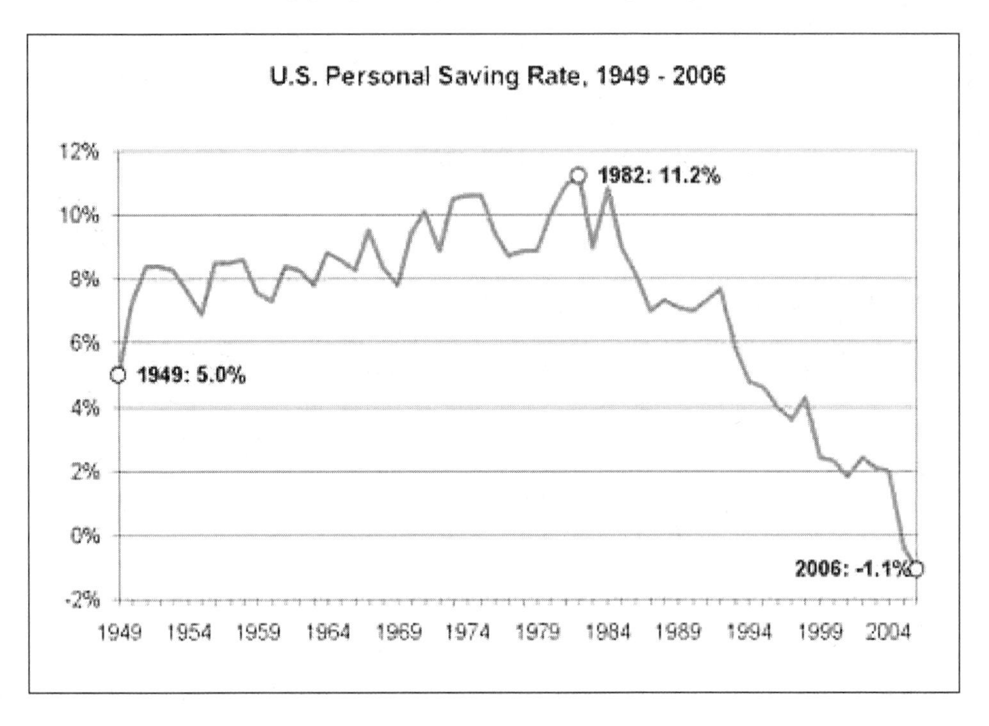

Which forced working people to go into debt: (total household debt as percentage of GDP)

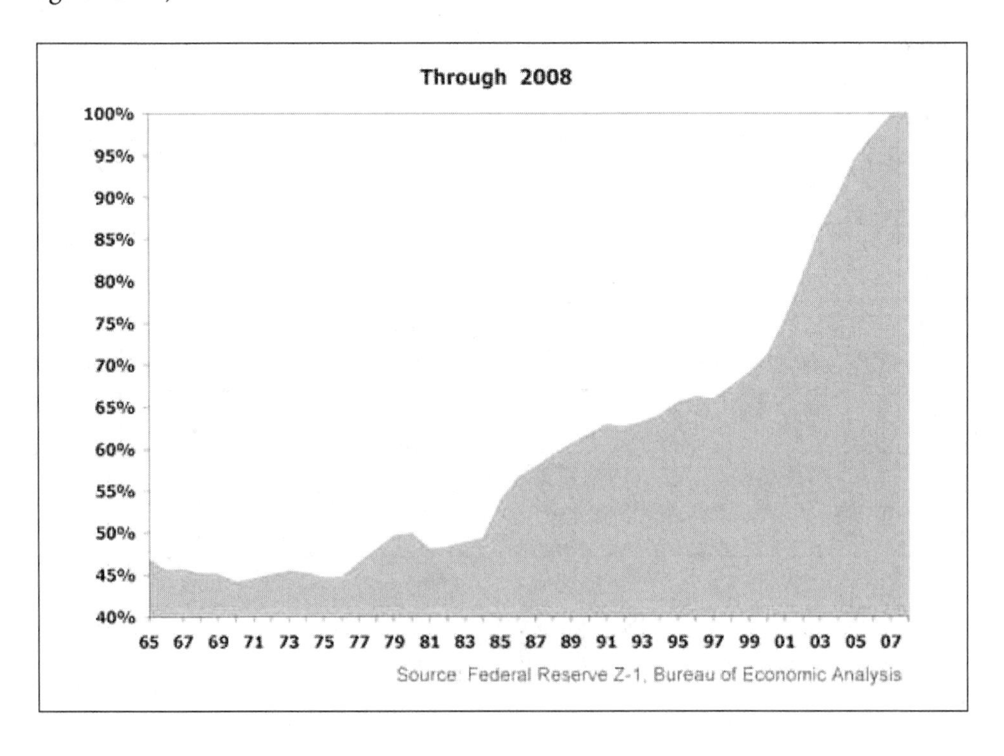

None of which has helped economic growth much: (12-quarter rolling average nominal GDP growth.)

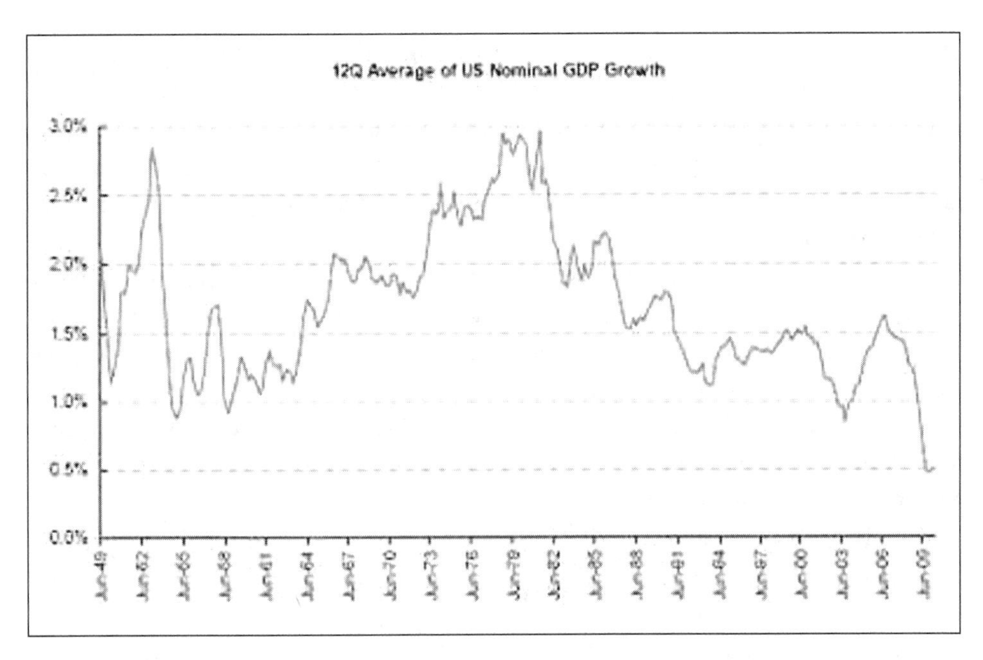

Sometimes it can be so obvious where a problem comes from, but very hard to change it. The anti-government, pro-corporate-rule Reagan Revolution screwed a lot of things up for regular people and for the country. Some of this disaster we saw happening at the time and some of it has taken thirty years to become clear. But for all the damage done these "conservative" policies greatly enriched a few entrenched interests, who use their wealth and power to keep things the way they are. And the rest of us, hit so hard by the changes, don't have the resources to fight the wealth and power.

Look at the influence of these entrenched interests on our current deficits, for example. Obviously conservative policies of tax cuts and military spending increases caused the massive deficits. But entrenched interests use their wealth and power to keep us from making needed changes. The facts are here, plain as the noses on our faces. The ability to fight it eludes us. Will we step up and do something to reverse the disaster caused by the Reagan Revolution or not?"

Actually, It's Too Late

Time is not on the side of the U.S. It is on the side of humanity. The U.S. Corporatocracy is doomed. Here is further evidence. Let this soak in.

50 Statistics about the U.S. Economy That Are Almost Too Crazy to Believe[3](From EndoftheAmericanDream.com)

Most Americans know that the U.S. economy is in bad shape, but what most Americans don't know is how truly desperate the financial situation of the United States really is. The truth is that what we are experiencing is not simply a "downturn" or a "recession". What we are witnessing is the beginning of the end for the greatest economic machine that the world has ever seen. Our greed and our debt are literally eating our economy alive.

Total government, corporate, and personal debt has now reached 360 percent of GDP, which is far higher than it ever reached during the Great Depression era. We have nearly totally dismantled our once colossal manufacturing base, we have shipped millions upon millions of middle class jobs overseas, we have lived far beyond our means for decades and we have created the biggest debt bubble in the history of the world. A great day of financial reckoning is fast approaching, and the vast majority of Americans are totally oblivious.

But the truth is that you cannot defy the financial laws of the universe forever. What goes up must come down. The borrower is the servant of the lender. Cutting corners always catches up with you in the end.

Sometimes it takes cold, hard numbers for many of us to fully realize the situation that we are facing.

So, the following are fifty very revealing statistics about the U.S. economy that are almost too crazy to believe.

50. In 2010, the U.S. government is projected to issue almost as much new debt as the rest of the governments of the world combined.

49. It is being projected that the U.S. government will have a budget deficit of approximately 1.6 trillion dollars in 2010.

48. If you went out and spent one dollar every single second, it would take you more than 31,000 years to spend a trillion dollars.

47. In fact, if you spent one million dollars every single day since the birth of Christ, you still would not have spent one trillion dollars by now.

46. Total U.S. government debt is now up to 90 percent of gross domestic product.

45. Total credit market debt in the United States, including government, corporate and personal debt, has reached 360 percent of GDP.

44. U.S. corporate income tax receipts were down 55 percent (to $138 billion) for the year ending September 30, 2009.

43. There are now eight counties in the state of California that have unemployment rates of over 20 percent.

42. In the area around Sacramento, California there is one closed business for every six that are still open.

41. In February, there were 5.5 unemployed Americans for every job opening.

40. According to a Pew Research Center study, approximately 37 percent of all Americans between the ages of eighteen and twenty-nine have either been unemployed or underemployed at some point during the recession.

39. More than 40 percent of those employed in the United States are now working in low-wage service jobs.

38. According to one new survey, 24 percent of American workers say that they have postponed their planned retirement age in the past year.

37. Over 1.4 million Americans filed for personal bankruptcy in 2009, which represented a 32 percent increase over 2008. Not only that, more Americans filed for bankruptcy in March 2010 than during any month since U.S. bankruptcy law was tightened in October 2005.

36. Mortgage purchase applications in the United States are down nearly 40 percent from a month ago to their lowest level since April of 1997.

35. RealtyTrac has announced that foreclosure filings in the U.S. established an all-time record for the second consecutive year in 2009.

34. According to RealtyTrac, foreclosure filings were reported on 367,056 properties in March 2010, an increase of nearly 19 percent from February, an increase of nearly 8 percent from March 2009 and the highest monthly total since RealtyTrac began issuing its report in January 2005.

33. In Pinellas and Pasco counties, which include St. Petersburg, Florida, and the suburbs to the north, there are 34,000 open foreclosure cases. Ten years ago, there were only about 4,000.

32. In California's Central Valley, one out of every sixteen homes is in some phase of foreclosure.

31. The Mortgage Bankers Association recently announced that more than 10 percent of all U.S. homeowners with a mortgage had missed at least one payment during the January to March time period. That was a record high and up from 9.1 percent a year ago.

30. U.S. banks repossessed nearly 258,000 homes nationwide in the first quarter of 2010, a 35 percent jump from the first quarter of 2009.

29. For the first time in U.S. history, banks own a greater share of residential housing net worth in the United States than all individual Americans put together.

28. More than 24 percent of all homes with mortgages in the United States were underwater as of the end of 2009.

27. U.S. commercial property values are down approximately 40 percent since 2007 and currently 18 percent of all office space in the United States is sitting vacant.

26. Defaults on apartment building mortgages held by U.S. banks climbed to a record 4.6 percent in the first quarter of 2010. That was almost twice the level of a year earlier.

25. In 2009, U.S. banks posted their sharpest decline in private lending since 1942.

24. New York State has delayed paying bills totaling $2.5 billion as a short-term way of staying solvent but officials are warning that its cash crunch could soon get even worse.

23. To make up for a projected 2010 budget shortfall of $280 million, Detroit issued $250 million of twenty-year municipal notes in March. The bond issuance followed on the heels of a warning from Detroit officials that if its financial state didn't improve, it could be forced to declare bankruptcy.

22. The National League of Cities says that municipal governments will probably come up between $56 billion and $83 billion short between now and 2012.

21. Half a dozen cash-poor U.S. states have announced that they are delaying their tax refund checks.

20. Two university professors recently calculated that the combined unfunded pension liability for all fifty U.S. states is 3.2 trillion dollars.

19. According to EconomicPolicyJournal.com, thirty-two U.S. states have already run out of funds to make unemployment benefit payments and so the federal government has been supplying these states with funds so that they can make their payments to the unemployed.

18. This most recent recession has erased eight million private sector jobs in the United States.

17. Paychecks from private business shrank to their smallest share of personal income in U.S. history during the first quarter of 2010.

16. U.S. government-provided benefits (including Social Security, unemployment insurance, food stamps, and other programs) rose to a record high during the first three months of 2010.

15. 39.68 million Americans are now on food stamps, which represents a new all-time record. But things look like they are going to get even worse. The U.S. Department of Agriculture is forecasting that enrollment in the food stamp program will exceed forty-three million Americans in 2011.

14. Phoenix, Arizona features an astounding annual car theft rate of 57,000 vehicles and has become the new "Car Theft Capital of the World."

13. U.S. law enforcement authorities claim that there are now over one million members of criminal gangs inside the country. These one million gang members are responsible for up to 80 percent of the crimes committed in the United States each year.

12. The U.S. health care system was already facing a shortage of approximately 150,000 doctors in the next decade or so, but, thanks to the health care "reform" bill passed by Congress, that number could swell by several hundred thousand more.

11. According to an analysis by the Congressional Joint Committee on Taxation the health care "reform" bill will generate $409.2 billion in additional taxes on the American people by 2019.

10. The Dow Jones Industrial Average just experienced the worst May it has

seen since 1940.

9. In 1950, the ratio of the average executive's paycheck to the average worker's paycheck was about thirty to one. Since the year 2000, that ratio has exploded to between 300 to 500 to one.

8. Approximately 40 percent of all retail spending currently comes from the 20 percent of American households that have the highest incomes.

7. According to economists Thomas Piketty and Emmanuel Saez, two-thirds of income increases in the U.S. between 2002 and 2007 went to the wealthiest 1 percent of all Americans.

6. The bottom 40 percent of income earners in the United States now collectively own less than 1 percent of the nation's wealth.

5. If you only make the minimum payment each and every time, a $6,000 credit card bill can end up costing you over $30,000 (depending on the interest rate).

4. According to a new report based on U.S. Census Bureau data, only 26 percent of American teens between the ages of sixteen and nineteen had jobs in late 2009 which represents a record low since statistics began to be kept back in 1948.

3. According to a National Foundation for Credit Counseling survey, only 58 percent of those in "Generation Y" pay their monthly bills on time.

2. During the first quarter of 2010, the total number of loans that are at least three months past due in the United States increased for the sixteenth consecutive quarter.

1. According to the Tax Foundation's Microsimulation Model, to erase the 2010 U.S. budget deficit, the U.S. Congress would have to multiply each tax rate by 2.4. Thus, the 10 percent rate would be 24 percent, the 15 percent rate would be 36 percent, and the 35 percent rate would have to be 85 percent."

What in the Hell Can We Do??

As our nation states fail all hell is going to break loose and a lot of people are going to die, if we make the transition at all. Obviously something drastic needs to be done to reverse the trend toward human decimation and ruination of the earth. But does this mean restoring the economy that is crashing? I think it is easier and smarter to simply start over and make something that works. This is why I seriously propose killing robber barons and eating them and taking back what they have stolen and then giving it back to the rest of us, so we can make a new beginning. It is such a simple and beautiful solution that can enlighten humanity in so many ways...

But before we get further into that, one more bit of cheery news...It's basically that even if we make the transition to one world we are probably doomed anyway. The following is a headline and story from The Australian newspaper in early 2010.

We Humans Are about to Be Wiped Out in a Few Decades. The Grandchildren of Many of Us Will Not Live to Old Age
By Bob Metcalfe

Hear it from Frank Fenner, emeritus professor of microbiology at the Australian National University and the man who helped eradicate smallpox. "Homo sapiens will become extinct, perhaps within 100 years," he told The Australian.

"It's an irreversible situation." Blame global warming.

Four years ago another warmist, Professor James Lovelock, creator of the influential Gaia theory of an interconnected Earth, was every bit as apocalyptic as Fenner.

We'd passed the point of no return, he groaned. The world was heating catastrophically. "Before this century is over, billions of us will die, and the few breeding pairs of people that survive will be in the Arctic where the climate remains tolerable."

All that was left to do was to prepare "a guidebook for global warming survivors ... on durable paper with long-lasting print."

...Meanwhile, life goes on. We laugh. We plan. We invent. We build. We adapt. And we talk of other things than the end of the world, and luckily so, because we'll be around a lot longer yet, if we keep our heads— and our hope."

Now read this from a follow up article in the *Herald Sun*:

"Our own extinction is forecast, but he's going by dead reckoning,"
By Andrew Bolt (*Herald Sun,* June 18, 2010)

Yeah, you read the title right. Mr. Frank Fenner, says that homo sapiens will be extinct within 100 years. I'd call him nuts, but the man helped eradicate small pox... which most would consider a fairly credible activity to add to one's resume.

I read Andrew Bolt's article in *The Herald Sun*, an Australian newspaper, that says he brought it up in a conversation, and that the subject was quickly changed to other "more impressive" things he's done. It's pretty weird.

So why is this in the weather blog? He chalks it up to global warming. He says it's become an "irreversible situation." Here's a quote from the article:

"Before this century is over, billions of us will die, and the few breeding pairs of people that survive will be in the Arctic where the climate remains tolerable."

Hmm. Food for thought I guess."

Food for Thought for Damned Sure!

If this is true, even if this is likely, doesn't it make cannibalism seem like less of a worry? I mean what if we really are going to die, whether or not we do something about it? What if it is just true that the odds are we are really going to die off in such great proportions as to be practically extinguished from the earth, which will be generally a no longer hospitable place for us? And what if that really may happen in less than a hundred years? What if the start of it is in less than ten years?

What if the only way to have a chance to reverse this is to quickly barbeque and repossess the wealth of people and corporations, say within the next ten years?

Now, do you think any differently about cannibalism? Please start talking about it among your friends! And get a few guns and knives. The right wingers are already armed. If it becomes imperative that we must kill to keep all of humanity from dying, and we are going to die anyway, what the hell? We may be our only chance.

The Traditional Rituals Underlying Corporate Capitalism that Maintain the Illusion

These issues of valuing property, of possessing the earth, of private ownership are deeply imbedded in the rituals, history, and holy books of the Judeo/Christian/Muslim tradition. Way back before the written word there were rituals to make people remember what was important. In family rights and family fights, particularly with regard to ownership of property and place, meaningful emotional rituals marked the transfer of property. When a father passed his land to his son, they placed their hands on the inside of each other's thigh, right next to each other's balls, looked each other in the eye and the father would speak "I grant thee the back forty, from this time forward." The vulnerability they granted to each other in that way acknowledged the trust and importance of the agreement they were making.

In many cultures, when children or members of the community were driven out (or "disowned"), there were rituals of turning of their backs to the people being cast out, not to mention the rituals in which people were literally cast out from the borders of the village.

It is hard to tell how far back in evolutionary history we developed rituals to demarcate and symbolize what we held as important. Rituals have been embedded in all the services of the churches and synagogues and mosques of the world to perpetuate beliefs and attachment to beliefs about property and its importance.

Communion

One of the notable rituals in the Christian tradition is the ritual called communion, in which wafers and wine, symbolizing flesh and blood, are used in the ritual consumption of the body and blood of Christ. This is performed to reaffirm membership in the community of Christ, known as "the body of Christ."

A Ritual for a New Communion

This is a ritual to appreciate and take responsibility for the way we are today and to help face our new circumstances. In this ritual the facing of what is real, and done in the name of affirming our humanity, here's what the priest would say:

"There are a lot of words that communicate the meaning of taking care of our collective selves: commune, communing, communication, community, commitment, the common good, commonwealth and our common humanity. Our new commitment now, is to save the world from *and* for *humanity and to preserve life on earth as we know it and need it to be.*

"Our new commitment and new communion is to a consciousness beyond good and evil—passing right through good and evil and going beyond good and evil. We human beings are both good and evil. And we are at our best when we transcend good and evil and take ownership of, and responsibility for using our power to create in alliance with life itself, whether it is "good" or "evil" to do so.

"We now do this in a way that makes an impression on all of us and will be remembered and repeated for generations in the community. We now affirm our knowledge of who we are and declare our creation of a way to be that way and not have it kill us all.

"We are all human beings. We are all empathic and greedy, willing to help and willing to kill. We are hungry and hungry for love. We care and are careless. We are able to indulge and likely to overindulge.

"This person whose flesh we eat this day is one of us. This person has given his/her life, possessions and body that we may live. And in this ritual act of communion we affirm taking their life and their goods for the benefit of those of all those who have suffered from, and might have had to suffer from, this greed. In consciousness and gratitude for that we pledge to serve others just as we have been served.

"Take. Eat. This is from the body of one of us. This is from our body in common. This flesh you are receiving a bite of, may be barbequed or roasted or grilled or boiled or raw, but we take a bite and chew and eat and swallow this taste of ourselves in consciousness of being. We partake literally and symbolically in our common human capacity for love and hate. In the eating of this flesh we eat of the flesh of our brother or sister, our savior, our family, our species, our earthbound community of life and of ourselves.

"Repeat after me: 'I take into myself the taker. I affirm and remind myself deeply that I, too, am a taker. I take back what this taker has taken from our family of living beings and I acknowledge that I am a taker even as I also will be taken, (and earlier than expected if and when I take too much.')

"May we all know, admit and share this knowledge of our common guilt and responsibility. With the eating of this flesh may we all voluntarily nourish with consciousness and care the possibility of overruling our greed."

"Our government has been deceptive. We are our government. The wealthy have lied to such an extent that our economy is dependent on a structure of lies. We are the wealthy. We have built the structure of lies. We benefit from the fabric of the network of lies called our economy. We are all liars. Let this flesh and this wine from the body

and coffers of one of our rich brethren or sisters remind us deeply of who we are, both good and evil, and to go beyond good and evil in our affirmative and transcendent choice of life over death."

Seriously

This is what I propose that we all take "to heart" as a fundamental ritual for the deepening of human consciousness. This is not merely symbolic. It is deeply and emotionally disturbing and at the same time helps us take responsibility for who and how we are.

Somewhere before, during or after this ritual comes a time of individual confession. Mine would be something like this: *"I deeply apologize for not assassinating Ronald Reagan when he first ran against and defeated Jimmy Carter. It was a lack of consciousness and responsibility on my part."* This is how we can make up for my mistake. This is the best I can come up with to make up for our world-class tragic mistake of not killing and eating Ronald Reagan when he first ran for president of the United States.

"I'm sorry. I was smoking dope, playing golf, raising a family, being a psychotherapist, starting to write books on enlightenment, and concerned for my own survival and that of my family in a selfish way, in the poisonous context of the United States of Ignorance of my time. I apologize for making a mistake that threatens to extinguish humankind. I fucked up. What can I say?"

Now, cannibalism for cannibals is the only viable solution. We need a law with some teeth in it. We can't "beat back" corporate influence, but we could possibly "eat back" successfully. Even then, we could still lose.

Therefore I propose to compose more than prose to disclose the primary pose:

If You Can't Beat 'Em, Eat 'Em!

Corporate leaders are the devil.
They won't play fair and on the level.
We can't constrict 'em or convict 'em,
Can't even accurately depict 'em!

They own the paper and the station,
and TV shows across the nation,
Commercials, newsfolks, things judicial,
controlled, contrived, and superficial.

They, make the law and pick the judges,
that settle all our losing grudges.

By their rules we can't defeat 'em,
Even cheat 'em or deplete 'em!

But their corpus can be eaten
(with A1 sauce we'll sometimes sweeten)
Fine Filet of Corporate Cretin
on the menu for the meetin'!

De-feet them first and then deface them!
Fire them up and then replace them!
Grind them up and then encase them!
Cook them good and we'll erase them!

Then at the reunion of our union,
we can have a fine communion.
Eat flesh, drink wine—in celebration,
with Filet of Soul of Corporation!

CHAPTER 8

As Long as You Have Obedient Servants
You Can Forget about Justice:
(And Just How Bad Is the System of Survival We Have in Place?)

We have some bad news and some good news. This is a terribly sad chapter, full of more information that is hard to accept and nevertheless true. It is sad, but true. And it is unavoidable. At least we can begin with the slight hope we do have, which few people know about. It is a vision. The vision that allows us to tolerate the current reality also helps us begin to change it. Here is that vision first, to be used as a prelude to the bad news we are adding to the stockpile.

Even though technology is largely responsible for our current dilemmas, such as chemical, oil and coal pollution, deforestation, nuclear waste, warfare, and so forth, there are some new *social technologies* that could solve some of our problems of greed gone wild. These new methods of dialogue and deliberation result in co-intelligence rather than co-supidity. And they work almost all the time.

Further, we have the capability to establish and demonstrate when people are lying, thus giving us a dependable way of knowing when they are telling the truth. We can do this soon with a greater degree of certainty than ever before in human history.

By putting people on trial based on fundamental principles of justice based on sustainability, we can establish a whole new legal system—one that is sleek and highly reliable, and quick to barbeque and redistribute human "beans" fairly and equitably if necessary. When we integrate the Truth Machine and the new social technology based on co-intelligent dialogue and deliberation into this new system of justice, a vision of a new world order quickly emerges.

To say it another way, we have the power to establish a new, highly-simplified system of justice that holds the priority of preserving humankind, other species, and the earth over the protection of the interests of corporations and those who own them. It would be managed under the supervision of a government made up of citizens on short-term service, who are paid to dialogue and deliberate in groups designed for co-intelligent collaboration. In this scenario, we would have all we need—cannibalized (hahaha)—from the formerly misused technology of the very military-industrial-congressional-media complex of cannibals who are currently devouring the earth and killing our children.

Justice

Before we go into the details of a whole new system of justice, we need to start with a quick review of what justice is and the way justice has worked until now in the civilized world in which all of us have grown up. Unless we are clear about the terrible abuse of justice that exists as our warped system, as we speak, we cannot advance to a new one. I start with a quote from a person I greatly admire, Derrick Jensen. This is one of his descriptions about the true nature of the justice system, as it exists right now in America. It has been this way, pretty much throughout history. I think this is eloquently descriptive and right on, not to mention good, poetic, and honest.

According to Jensen, writing in *Endgame, Volume 1: The End of Civilization* (Seven Stories Press, 2006)[1]: "Here's how it works. Those in power pass some law. It doesn't much matter how stupid or immoral the law is, it will be enforced by people with guns: the police and the military. Or maybe some judge sets a precedent. Once again, it doesn't matter how stupid or immoral the precedent is, it will also be enforced by people with guns. This law or precedent may be that human beings are property, that is, without rights (only responsibilities). It may be that corporations are persons, that is, with rights (and in this case, without responsibilities). It may be that corporate lies are protected free speech. It may be that corporate bribes are protected free speech. It may be that those who kill in the service of production are protected from accountability. It may be that who destroy property 'owned' by corporations face decades in prison as declared 'terrorists.'

"Those in power often con the rest of us into being proud of being good, defined—by them and by us—as being subservient to their laws, their edicts. They con us into forgetting—and in time we become all to eager to con ourselves into forgetting—that those in power can and usually do legalize reprehensible activities that increase their power (for example, stealing land from the indigenous, invading countries with desired resources, debasing the land base, all done legally, because those in power declare it to be so) and criminalize non-reprehensible activities that undercut their power (soon after the most recent invasion many people were arrested in New Your City for pasting up pictures of Iraqi citizens, that is, humanizing the U.S.'s current targets; consider a law proposed in the Oregon legislature mandating twenty-five year minimum sentences for anything that would disrupt transportation or commerce, including standing in the street during an anti-war protest (I'm not kidding). Another way to say this is that those in power make the rules by which they maintain and extend their power. Of course. And then those in power hire goons—for when you take away the rhetoric of protecting and serving, the job of police and the military boils down to being muscle to enforce the edicts of those in power—to keep the people in line.

"When we forget that the edicts of those in power are merely the edicts of those in power, we lend these edicts a moral weight they do not deserve. Those in power (usually the rich) declare that those in power under certain circumstances can kill those not in power (most often the poor), and the rest of us forget they're doing no more than using their power to get away with murder. Those in power declare that those in power may under certain circumstances devastate the land bases—oh, sorry, 'develop the natural resources' —of distant communities, and the rest of us forget they're doing no more than using their power to get away with murdering communities and murdering the earth. Those in power declare that those in power may under certain circumstances destroy entire peoples, and the rest of us forget they're doing no more than using their power to get away with genocide....

"The thirteenth premise of this book (Endgame): Those in power rule by force, and the sooner we break ourselves of illusions to the contrary, the sooner we can at least begin to make reasonable decisions about whether, when, and how we are going to resist."

This System of Injustice Has Been Going on for Decades, in Fact for Centuries

Okay, before I say more about justice, here is just one more quote to conside, from the preface to the book *Grunch of Giants* (Design Science Press, 2008) by Buckminster Fuller, *a book that was written thirty years ago!*

"An army of abstract legal entities (called corporations) now controls the economic and political future of mankind. In this urgent sequel to Critical Path, R. Buckminster Fuller traces the evolution of these multinational giants from the post-World War II 'military-industrial complex' to the current world economic crisis—an evolution, he argues, that threatens the imminent bankruptcy of the U.S. and the collapse of the world economic system.

"As these economic giants have grown beyond the control of the political units (nations) into which the earth is currently divided, they paradoxically threaten to bring about a world-wide depression while perhaps signaling the emergence of a new form of political and economic organization for the beleaguered inhabitants of Spaceship Earth."[2]

Current Slaughter and Abuse by the Empire

I agree wholeheartedly with Bucky Fuller. I admire him for how accurately he named what was going on in our culture, and for how well he predicted what has occurred.

Now, let's update that analysis from twenty-eight years ago, by jumping to very recent times. Just one example among many, this is from *Project Censored* in California, posted online on New Year's Eve 2009, to start off the beginning of 2010. Every year, *Project Censored* comes out with a report summarizing the most underreported stories of recent times.

"Among the most important corporate media censored news stories of the past decade, one must be that over one million people have died because of the United States military invasion and occupation of Iraq. This, of course, does not include the number of deaths from the first Gulf War nor the ensuing sanctions placed upon the country of Iraq that, combined, caused close to an additional one million Iraqi deaths. In the Iraq War, which began in March of 2003, over a million people have died violently primarily from US bombings and neighborhood patrols. These were deaths in excess of the normal civilian death rate under the prior government. Among US military leaders and policy elites, the issue of counting the dead was dismissed before the Iraqi invasion even began. In an interview with reporters in late March of 2002 US General Tommy Franks stated, 'You know we don't do body counts.' Fortunately, for those concerned about humanitarian costs of war and empire, others do.

"In a January 2008 report, the British polling group Opinion Research Business (ORB) reported that, 'survey work confirms our earlier estimate that over 1,000,000 Iraqi citizens have died as a result of the conflict which started in 2003. We now estimate that the death toll between March 2003 and August 2007 is likely to have been of the order of 1,033,000. If one takes into account the margin of error associated with survey data of this nature then the estimated range is between 946,000 and 1,120,000.'

"The ORB report came on the heels of two earlier studies conducted by Dr. Les Roberts and colleagues at Johns Hopkins University and published in the Lancet medical journal. The first study done from January 1, 2002 to March 18, 2003 confirmed civilian deaths at that time at over 100,000. The second study published in October 2006 documented over 650,000 civilian deaths in Iraq since the start of the US invasion and confirmed that US aerial bombing in civilian neighborhoods caused over a third of these deaths. Over half the deaths were directly attributable to US forces. The now estimated 1.2 million dead six years into the war/occupation, included children, parents, grandparents, cab drivers, clerics, and schoolteachers. All manner of ordinary Iraqis have died because the United States decided to invade their country under false pretences of undiscovered weapons of mass destruction and in violation of international law. An additional four to five million Iraqi refugees have fled their homes. The magnitude of these million-plus deaths and creation of such a vast refugee crisis is undeniable. The continuing occupation by US forces has guaranteed a monthly mass death rate of thousands of people, a carnage that ranks among the most heinous mass killings in world history. More tons of bombs have been dropped in Iraq than in all of World War II. Six years later the casualties continue but the story, barely reported from the start, has vanished.

"The American people face a serious moral dilemma. Murder and war crimes have been conducted in their name. Yet most Americans have no idea of the magnitude of deaths and tend to believe that they number in the thousands and are primarily Iraqis killing Iraqis. Corporate mainstream media are in large part to blame. The question then becomes how can this mass ignorance and corporate media deception exist in the United States and what impact does this have on peace and social justice movements in the country?"[3]

How Do We Remain so Ignorant?

How do we not know about this as it happens? How can this slaughter go on and get paid for by us without us being informed about it? How can we remain so passive and pathetic and stupid?

This all works because the media hide the truth from us and we avoid learning what disturbs our sleep. This also all works because the police work to protect the rich—using the same technology as that of war, but moderated for the sake of not getting too much bad publicity. The goons are paid specialists in domination and control who are there to support the lies perpetrated in the media, to protect the thieves and murderers, the corporate capitalists...

Police Use Painful New Weapon on G-20 Protesters
By Allison Kilkenny (AlterNet, *September 28, 2009*)[4]

"Police used 'sound cannons' to break up G-20 protest groups demonstrating in Pittsburgh.

"This technology has been deployed in Iraq as an 'anti-insurgent weapon' and it could easily be used as a torture tool.

"Pittsburgh police demonstrated the latest in crowd control techniques on protesters when they used 'sound cannons' to blast the ears of citizens near the G-20 meeting of world economic leaders. City officials said this was the first time such sound blasters, also known as 'sound weapons,' were used publicly.

"Lavonnie Bickerstaff of the Pittsburgh Bureau of Police uses benign language like 'sound amplifiers,' and 'long-range acoustic device' to explain the new weapons in an attempt to sanitize what is essentially a painful weapon that leaves no visible marks on its victims. The Mob utilized a similar tactic on snitches when they would beat everywhere except the face. If victims have no outward bruises to show, the world is less likely to believe their stories of assault and harassment.

"Unlike aerosol hand-grenades, pepper spray, and rubber bullets (all traditional methods of protest suppression also used at the G-20 protests), the damage from sound cannons is entirely internal, and can only be preserved on video, but even then, the deafening noise cannot be fully appreciated unless one hears it in person.

"The 'long range acoustic device (LRAD)' is designed for long-range communication and acts as an 'unmistakable warning,' according to the American Technology Corporation (ATC), which develops the instruments. 'The LRAD basically is the ability to communicate clearly from 300 meters to three kilometers' (nearly two miles), said Robert Putnam of American Technology's media and investor relations during an interview with MSNBC. 'It's a focused output. What distinguishes it from other communications tools out there is its ability to be heard clearly and intelligibly at a distance, unlike bullhorns.'

"Except, police aren't trying to send a distress call to allies two miles away. They're literally blasting this extreme decibel of noise directly into the ears of protesters (or any unwitting citizens) standing mere feet from the cannons. Depending on the mode of LRAD, it can blast a maximum sound of 145 to 151 decibels—equal to a gunshot—within a three-foot (one meter) range, according to ATC. The National Institutes of Health (NIH) reports that permanent hearing loss can result from sounds at about 110 to 120 decibels in short bursts or even just 75 decibels if exposure lasts for long periods.

"But there is a volume knob, Putnam notes, so its output can be less than max, purportedly to give us comfort in the knowledge that deafening citizens is left to the discretion of power-hungry police. On the decibel scale, an increase of 10 (say, from 70 to 80) means that a sound is 10 times more intense. Normal traffic noise can reach 85 decibels, reports MSNBC, but these sound cannons cannot be compared to standing beside a busy New York City road.

"The BBC reported in 2005 that the 'shrill sound of an LRAD at its loudest sounds something like a domestic smoke alarm, ATC says, but at 150 decibels, it is the aural equivalent to standing 30 meters away from a roaring jet engine and can cause major hearing damage if misused.'

"This technology has been deployed in Iraq as an 'anti-insurgent weapon,' and the sonic weaponry is also being used on protesters in Honduras. Seattle Weekly reports that this weapon could easily be used as a torture tool if one doesn't already think this is its only use.

"Sonic weaponry is now being deployed domestically to put a chill on free speech. We're told this is the 'humane' way to deal with protesters, but it's really just a convenient way to suppress citizens without the messy aftereffects of having to explain bullet holes to reporters. A bunch of protesters complaining about ruptured ear drums doesn't make for dramatic news."

It is Not the Job of the Government to Protect Us from the God Damned Truth

This opinion piece from the latest issue of Time offers an interesting take on the role of the public. I particularly like the paragraph that starts… "Here are some things Obama did not say…"

The Lesson: Passengers Are Not Helpless
By Amanda Ripley (*Time,* December 30, 2009)[5]

"Since 2001, airline passengers—regular people without weapons or training—have helped thwart terrorist attacks aboard at least five different commercial airplanes. It happened again on Christmas Day. And as we do each and every time, we miss the point.

"Consider the record: First, passengers on United Flight 93 prevented a further attack on Washington on 9/11. Then, three months later, American Airlines passengers wrestled a belligerent, biting Richard Reid to the ground, using their headset cords to restrain him. In 2007, almost a dozen passengers jumped on a gun-wielding hijacker aboard a plane in the Canary Islands. And this past November, passengers rose up against armed hijackers over Somalia. Together, then, a few dozen folks have helped save some 595 lives.

"And yet our collective response to this legacy of ass-kicking is puzzling. Each time, we build a slapdash pedestal for the heroes. Then we go back to blaming the government for failing to keep us safe, and the government goes back to treating us like children. This now familiar ritual distracts us from the real lesson, which is that we are not helpless. And since regular people will always be first on the scene of terrorist attacks, we should perhaps prioritize the public's antiterrorism capability—above and beyond the fancy technology that will never be foolproof.

"Instead, we hear this blather from President Obama: 'The American people should be assured that we are doing everything in our power to keep you and your family safe and secure during this busy holiday season.' He forgets that Americans have never really wanted the government to do 'everything in its power' to keep us safe. That would make this a terrible place to live. And yet, after eight years of paternalistic bluster from President George W. Bush, we have grown accustomed to the cycle of absurd promises followed by failure and renewed by fear. Bush liked to say that the authorities have to succeed 100 percent of the time and terrorists only once. The truth is, authorities never succeed 100 percent of the time at anything. And they never will.

"By definition, terrorism succeeds by making us feel powerless. It is more often a psychological threat than an existential one. The authorities compound the damage when they overreact—by subjecting grandmothers to pat-downs and making it intolerable to travel. Even though the Christmas bombing suspect had been stopped, stripped and cuffed before the plane landed, we still talk like victims. '[This] came close to being one of the greatest tragedies in the history of our country,' New York Congressman Peter King said on CNN, criticizing Obama for not holding a press conference sooner.

"When Obama did speak, three days after the incident, he first listed all the security reviews to be conducted while the rest of us sit tight. Only then did he briefly acknowledge reality: 'This incident, like several that have preceded it, demonstrates that an alert and courageous citizenry are far more resilient than an isolated extremist.'

"Here are some things Obama did not say: He did not propose that we find ways to leverage the proven dedication and courage of the public. He did not call for Congress to cut spending on homeland-security pork and instead double the budget of Citizen Corps—the volunteer emergency-preparedness service that was created after 9/11 and that most Americans have never heard of. He did not demand that the government be more open with us about the threats we face. He did not discuss the government's obligation, as homeland-security expert Stephen Flynn puts it, to 'support regular people in being able to withstand, rapidly recover and adapt to foreseeable risks.'

"Karen Sherrouse was a flight attendant on the jet that Richard Reid tried to blow up. When one of her colleagues tried to stop Reid, Sherrouse rushed to help. But she couldn't get down the aisle because so many passengers had already joined the melee. 'They were instantly on him,' she remembers. 'It was a group effort.' And so it should be. The flight attendants can't be everywhere at once. Nor can TSA officers or the FBI.

"After the passengers of Flight 253 deplaned in Detroit, they were held in the baggage area for more than five hours until FBI agents interviewed them. They were not allowed to call their loved ones. They were given no food. When one of the pilots tried to use the bathroom before a bomb-sniffing dog had finished checking all the carry-on bags, an officer ordered him to sit down, according to passenger Alain Ghonda, who thought it odd. 'He was the pilot. If he wanted to do anything, he could've crashed the plane.' It was a metaphor for the rest of the country: Thank you for saving the day. Now go sit down."

How Lightweight Critiques Appear to Have Substance, but Hide the Real Truth

The article above, while appearing to be critical and thoughtful and daring, is lightweight, typical Ti*me* magazine committee writing, appearing to be 'risky' with opinions. Thus *Time*'s staff fulfills their role as protector of corporate rule by appearing to be critical of big government, which, though it is a problem, is not nearly as big a problem as corporate control of big government. Socialism for the rich is okay, but if it spreads to the middle class and poor people, it is anathema to the political establishment. Virtually all our media operate accordingly.

When we, the public, become as willing to attack the corporate terrorists who are the real murderers of this world, in our own defense, at least as well as we attack the other terrorists on planes, then we will get somewhere.

And we must defend ourselves against their agents and lackeys, including, unfortunately, Barack Obama. Then the real conversation begins, and real action is possible.

At the time of this writing, I had just returned from three weeks of travel to Sweden, Egypt, and Germany, and I found that the entire pain in the ass security system in place in airports is based on everything except willingness to consider why billions of people are angry and completely justified in wanting to kill anyone remotely related to the corporate capitalist murder-for-profit machine.

Hidden behind the phony patriotism of the idiots in Congress, in the banking system, on Wall Street, in the defense industry, working in the upper echelons of the abusive worldwide economic order, representing countries sitting on the U.N. Security Council, stacking the deck of the International Monetary Fund, running the corporatist fascist government of the United States, and so on, are the profiteers. The true main motive of these killers is simply more money. Kill, starve, and strip—do whatever makes a profit.

The United States of America is not the best country in the world. It is very near to the top of the list for the worst. That needs to be said, acknowledged, repeated, and understood by its dumbed-down populace.

The great deceit behind the *Time* magazine article is that it wrongly explains how Obama has failed. The way Obama has failed has nothing to do with how well he has protected us against 'terrorism.' He has greatly increased the likelihood of it by the way he has stepped up state terrorism and surrendered to the temptation of accepting fundamental American cultural ignorance and blindness as if it were real thought, treating Republican dumb asses and Blue Dog Democrats with phony respect for the sake of manipulation, rather than for the purpose of open confrontation, engagement, and passionate advocacy. He has failed to call the populace out based on real compassion and real passion, and he has violated those of us who trusted him at the time of the election, not just here in our country, but the whole world over.

The wait is over. Obama is not going to do shit to change a goddamned thing. Through his bailouts on Wall Street and of the corporations that manufacture cars and sell out to pharmaceutical companies, etc., Obama has fully demonstrated he is a corporate slave. He has no guts. No balls. No view above the incredibly provincial law school education he received at Harvard University that overrode his humanity, just as it was supposed to. A Harvard brainwashing is just another goddamned brainwashing. There were some things, as Time asserts, that Obama did not say, but their cutesy little list didn't cover a goddamned one of them.

To maintain "security" with the totally screwed up airport security systems and the stupid Homeland Security bureaucracy is the same kind of condescension as maintaining slavery to protect the slaves from starving. Rather than respecting that the passengers often take care of themselves better than the system anyway, treating the passengers like they are the problem, adding insult to injury, is the perfect analogy for the whole bigger problem of our current form of government—corporate capitalist fascism.

The world is our homeland. That's the way things are. And that's the way things ought to be. That is why feeding rich people to poor people until a new balance of capital and protein is achieved, korporate kapitalist kannibalism, is the best way we, the citizens of the world, can love our enemy, just like Jesus said we should—maybe sautéed and with a little wine from their wine cellars.

The Tyranny Currently Called Justice

We are dominated and controlled by fascist corporate dictators, wielding a phony system of justice. As long as we are comforted and have the promise of getting to be as advantaged as our dictators are, we are willing to stay stupid, look the other way, and let them get by with it. So get this point here, because you won't find it in a lot of other places.

In his two-volume book series *Endgame*, Derrick Jensen's lists twenty premises at the beginning of both volumes. I read them over frequently like a goddamned Bible freak. I agree 100 percent with at least fourteen of Jensen's premises and even if you don't read those books in full, I highly recommend that you at least take a look at them. All one thousand two hundred-plus pages of these combined works are chock full of evidence in support of these premises.

Here is premise number five: "The property of those higher on the hierarchy is more valuable than the lives of those below. It is acceptable for those above to increase the amount of property they control—in everyday language, to make money—by destroying or taking the lives of those below. This is called production. If those below damage the property of those above, those above may kill or otherwise destroy the lives of those below. This is called justice."[6]

We saw an example of this premise in operation in the run-up to the Iraq War when Colin Powell was making a case for the United States to go to war without there being any real merit for the U.S. to do so. Colin Powell, who even the left, including myself, up to 2003, thought had integrity and could be trusted, turned out to be just a good ass kissing slave who would lie for George W. Bush and his handlers when asked to, and in the process he sold out the American people. He knew goddamned good and well he was lying too, because I knew it then and I knew he knew it too, and he lied anyway.

As it turns out, both Colin Powell and Barack Obama are, in the end, just good slaves for their corporate owners. I realize how offensive it is to repeatedly call these black men slaves. I intend the offense. If the end of times comes as a result of these last fifteen years or so of selling out, in the final analysis, we can be pretty sure it was the good slaves that did us in. Some of them were white, like Bill Clinton, for example, but "knew their place" and folded and kissed ass eagerly when they were expected to. They went along to get along. People who do that, which is most of us, are the agents of no change, and that is leading to the apocalypse.

Enough

Okay, folks, I am not spending much more time here to establish that the existing so called "justice system" the world over is total bullshit as far as actual justice is concerned, including and particularly the entire legal system of the United States of America, land of the brave and home of the free. That bullshit won't work on me anymore and I hope to hell it won't work for you either.

I spent forty years of my life in the non-violent civil rights, anti-war, pro-hippie and various other social reform movements in this country, and even when we won we still lost. I know how this works. If you don't know that this is how things really are by now do your own goddamned homework and get back to me. Or you can stop reading right now and kiss my ass. (But if you are rich enough, keep an eye out, I may barbeque your ass someday. I am not fucking ideologically non-violent anymore. As a practical matter, I have not actually been violent yet, and I haven't killed or eaten anyone yet, but I am making a list. I no longer feel morally constrained to act civilized, and I am not alone.)

We need a new set of rules and they should involve honesty about nurturing some and killing others, and killing some beings on this planet for the sake of the remaining beings on the planet and for the sake of the planet itself.

So that's it. I am moving on to the fundamental question raised by everyone I have quoted so far in this book, about how we can all become more honest and establish a real system of justice. I believe that our last chance before chaos and being subjected to little roving bands of mafia control all over the world, our only chance, is to stop lying. In fact, we must give up lying because we can't get by with it anymore. Then, once we can know what is true, I have some ideas about how we can develop a system of justice that is actually just.

CHAPTER 9

The Truth Machine:
How We Can Know What Is True

The Truth Machine I have been referring to throughout this book in not an actual machine. It is a bunch of machines, processes, assessments, and conversations that enable us to determine what is so.

It is the result of combining a variety of ways we know about detecting lying (many of which have been developed in the last decade or two by our evil empire, the United States government). When we put these tests in a sequence, each new test in the series helps to determine with a greater degree of accuracy (much greater than ever before possible) when people are lying. Scientists, technologists using instruments, psychological experts, and empaths (and I don't mean a wigged-out clairvoyant) have many ways to determine when folks are lying. Combining all of these ways, we can create a new way of finding out the truth. That new way is what I am calling the Truth Machine.

We can start using the Truth Machine in conjunction with the current system of justice, and then eventually replace the criminal, criminal justice system. We could bring a whole new world of honesty into being. The truth might actually set us free. Here is a brief review of development in truth technology recently. My comments are interspersed at intervals throughout the article in italics and brackets.

A Truth Machine: Can Brain Scanning Technologies Stop Terrorists—or Just Threaten Privacy? An Excerpt
By Ronald Bailey (*Reason,* November 14, 2001)[1]

"'It's happening much faster than I thought it would,' says James Halperin, author of the 1996 science fiction novel *The Truth Machine*. The novel describes how humanity would react to the invention of an infallible lie detector in the year 2024. 'When I was talking about the concept of a Truth Machine back in the 1990s, a neuroscientist friend told me that his best guess was that it would be fifty years, if ever, before such a thing could be created,' says Halperin. 'I picked 2024 as the date so that the idea wouldn't seem too ridiculous.'

"However, recent advances in brain-scanning techniques may bring about the development of a kind of Truth Machine sooner rather than later. These techniques, if validated through more research, could replace fallible polygraph tests....

"...the science of detecting deception might be coming of age. Dr. Lawrence Farwell, a psychiatrist who heads the Human Brain Research Laboratory in Fairfield, Iowa, has developed a technique he calls 'brain fingerprinting.'

"'It's not actually a lie detector,' explains Farwell. 'Instead it detects whether or not certain information is stored in a person's brain.' He likens brain fingerprinting to finding fingerprints or DNA traces at a crime scene. The presence of a person's fingerprints or DNA at a crime scene does not tell investigators whether the person is guilty or not. After all, there may well be an innocent explanation for how they got there. Similarly, brain fingerprinting does not tell investigators whether a suspect is guilty or not, just that specific information is or is not present in his or her brain.

"But brain fingerprinting has one big advantage over DNA and fingerprinting, notes Farwell. 'Criminals leave fingerprints or DNA at crime scenes only about one percent of the time,' Farwell says. 'But their brains are always there, planning, executing, and recording the crime.'

"Brain fingerprinting works by flashing words or pictures relevant to a crime on a computer screen along with other, irrelevant, words or pictures. When a person recognizes information, specific electrical brain impulses that Farwell calls memory and encoding related multifaceted electroencephalographic responses (MERMERS) are involuntarily elicited. MERMERS are measured using a headband equipped with sensors. *When details of a crime that only the perpetrator and investigators would know are presented, the perpetrator's brain emits a MERMER, but the brain of an innocent person does not.*

"Farwell claims that his MERMER device has been 100 percent accurate in tests. For example, in one test he was able to correctly identify seventeen FBI agents out of twenty-one people tested.

[*Now we're getting somewhere! —BB*]

"Farwell's work is by no means universally accepted by academic researchers. J.

Peter Rosenfeld, a professor of psychology at Northwestern University, believes that Farwell claims far too much for his MERMER technique.

"'I simply don't believe that he is getting 100 percent correct results on his tests,' Rosenfeld says. Rosenfeld himself gets about an 80 percent correct identification rate from similar brainwave studies.

[*One brain researcher on lying claims another is lying. Heh heh. —Brad.*]

"Rosenfeld is also pursuing another line of research aimed at identifying the physical correlates in the brain that correspond to a person's awareness that he is lying. This research goes beyond identifying whether or not a person has specific knowledge. Asked if he thought that current brain research on detecting deception would lead to ways to determine accurately whether a person is lying or not, Rosenfeld replied: 'Absolutely. Within ten years, maybe even five.'"

Clues that We're On the Right Track

When an idea gets opposition from ethicists and lawyers it is probably an idea worth looking into. Ethicists and lawyers are currently in the discussion of how this can be misused without a predictable level of certainty...

New Lie Detection Technology Worries Stanford Ethicist
By Emily Saarman (Stanford News Service, May 3, 2006)[3]

New lie detection technology too much like scientific mind reading, ethicist says. Companies plan to begin selling fMRI services by end of year, but, with no regulation, utility of technique need not be proved.

For many, the phrase "lie detection" probably brings to mind an image of a polygraph machine and an intimidating movie-style interrogation, possibly with a subject who could expertly "beat the polygraph." But ethicist and law Professor Hank Greely said this image is about to change.

Recent advances in neuroscience promise to bring lie detection technology far beyond the notoriously unreliable polygraph and into a realm that Greely said bears eerie resemblance to scientific mind reading.

Greely, the Dean F. and Kate Edelman Johnson Professor in Law, discussed his concerns about the new lie detection technology at a campus Science, Technology and Society seminar April 14. Greely said he is excited by the potential for improved lie detection but concerned that it could lead to personal-privacy violations and a host of legal problems—especially if the techniques prove unreliable.

"If unreliable lie detection gets used, people's lives will be blighted," Greely said. "I think it's crazy for us to let these technologies be used for lie detection until we have clear, robust, peer-reviewed research that shows how well they work."

During the seminar, Greely discussed five emerging lie detection techniques.

These include electroencephalograms (EEGs), which measure brain waves using electrodes taped to a subject's head and claim to detect patterns related to specific brain processes, including recognition of a scene or person. Another technique uses facial micro-expressions, facial expressions lasting just a fraction of a second that can be captured on film, to reveal otherwise invisible emotions or reactions. A thermal imaging technique, claiming that the area around the eye gets warmer when a person lies, attempts to reveal deception by measuring the temperature of the eye area. Finally, two different techniques use images of brain activity to highlight lying-specific brain patterns, Greely said. Near infrared laser spectroscopy shines invisible infrared light through the skull and reflects it off the brain to reveal activity on the surface of the brain. And functional magnetic resonance imaging, or fMRI, uses powerful magnets to build a map of activity throughout the brain.

The most promising of these techniques is fMRI, Greely said, which measures oxygen usage throughout the brain. Active parts of the brain use more oxygen than inactive portions, so the fMRI can accurately pinpoint the parts of the brain at work at any given time.

In several small scientific studies, researchers have shown that telling a lie activates different parts of the brain than telling the truth, Greely said. Subjects who were lying activated a greater percentage of their brains, as well as different regions, than subjects who were telling the truth.

While Greely said he believes fMRI technology has tremendous potential for lie detection, he said there is still a lot of work to be done before the results of these tests can be trusted. To date, all fMRI lie detection studies have used only a small number of subjects who were asked to lie about simple things such as the identity of the playing card in their hand, he said. How these findings will bear out in real-life circumstances with diverse subjects of different races, ages and mental states remains to be seen. "Deception is not a very clear-cut, well-defined thing," Greely said. "We know people can remember things that never happened. How does that show up on an fMRI lie detection test?"

But companies who hope to profit from new lie detection techniques are not so cautious. Two private for-profit companies—No Lie MRI Inc. of La Jolla, Calif., and Cephos Corp. of Pepperell, Mass. —plan to begin selling fMRI-based lie detection services by the end of the year (2010). And because there are no regulations to control lie detection technology, Greely cautioned, they can sell lie detection services without ever proving how well they work.

At first, the technology will likely be used only at the request of a person who wishes to bolster his or her credibility with a clean lie detection test. But Greely predicted that, in time, new lie detection techniques will find their way into civil and criminal investigations and may even be considered in court trials.

To illustrate the danger posed by inaccurate lie detection, Greely described a scenario in which a person is arrested for assault and an ineffective lie detector indicates that the person is lying when he or she denies the charges. "It could be that the case against you is pretty weak but the district attorney and the police decide to proceed anyway because they're so falsely confident in this lie detector test," Greely said. "You end up going to trial, maybe getting convicted, maybe going to jail. That would be pretty serious."

Beyond such concerns, Greely said there are ethical reasons to view the new technology with caution. "Even if it's proven to be safe and effective, we need to make decisions about when it can be used and by whom," he said. "We've never really had to confront these issues before because the polygraph has never been reliable enough for the courts to take it seriously."

Employees currently are protected from lie detection tests administered by their employers under the 1988 federal Employee Polygraph Protection Act. But, according to Greely, there are no laws controlling the use of lie detection by educational institutions, parents, friends or spouses. Like any parent of a teenager, Greely said he wishes he knew where his son really went last night, but he is not sure that using lie detection to find the answer would be ethical.

"I think it's important to consider that whole set of issues about when we think it's justifiable to invade the privacy of someone's mind," Greely said.

A Number of Less Than Perfect Things Together Sometimes Combine to Turn out Perfectly!

Sometimes people want to dispense with less than perfect things instead of using them in combination with other less than perfect things. We want to improve the combined capacity of limited, but not useless things by combining them so as to not throw out the baby with the bath water. How about both/and? How about both polygraph tests and brain scans and a half a dozen other analytic systems used in combination along with perceptive humans performing research to establish an increasingly reliable way to find out when people are telling the truth?

Steps to Building a "Truth Machine"

So what if the "MERMER" technique is one step in a process of many steps? Let's say we start with the technique of screening people by "flashing words or pictures relevant to a crime on a computer screen along with other, irrelevant, words or pictures. When a person recognizes information, specific electrical brain impulses that Farwell calls memory and encoding related multifaceted electroencephalographic responses (MERMERS) are involuntarily elicited. MERMERS are measured using a headband equipped with sensors. When details of a crime that only the perpetrator and investigators would know are presented, the perpetrator's brain emits a MERMER, but the brain of an innocent person does not..." So we sort out the ones who elicit MEMEMERS and also proceed with further testing of those who did and those who didn't using more devices, looking for confirmed positive and false positives as well as confirmed negatives and false negatives.

Then we proceed to further steps with the same subjects on the same subject. We use the modern CIA lie detector test, have the person talk to an empath, do a video analysis of their facial expression and have it viewed and scored by experts, monitor heartrate, blood pressure, blood supply around the eyes, facial and bodily tics, speech patterns, voice analysis, etc. We also do background investigations, re-examinations and so forth. Then we learn shortcuts, or indicators, that allow us to check with some other test using some other question to confirm or reject the likely truth or lie we suspect might be the case. What we need to do is essentially to simply organize and assimilate and correlate independent methods of lie detection, and then develop what we learn.

The Process of Establishing a Process

If we proceed in an organized fashion, we can outline here at least the preliminary steps of inventing and applying the Truth Machine to our judicial needs. Please feel free to pitch in and help, because we need this to pull off a real change in how society operates.

The first step is to get all the people who have been working on distinguishing honesty from bullshit together in one place so we can all meet and hear each other. We can have a nice long conversation, using dialogue and deliberation technology where everyone gets heard and everyone listens and we will write up our discoveries and conclusions and pass them around amongst ourselves and send them to others. (Read *The Tao of Democracy* by Tom Atlee and the next chapter in this book, because we will be using the new social technologies described therein for designing the true justice truth machine co-intelligently.)

We need to gather together several groups of people who are known for their skill and brilliance in determining truth from fiction. The first bunch is people who are known empaths, skilled in telling when someone else is lying. They are therapists, writers, trainers, corporate consultants, social workers, teachers, AA sponsors, counselors, group leaders, cab drivers, bartenders, and common people of all social classes who are accurately intuitive, mildly paranoid, and skillful in knowing when people are lying. (They are likely to be more honest than usual themselves because regular liars are generally less than intuitive.)

Some may have been successful liars and learned the benefits of honesty and adopted them, meaning they had the courage to start telling the truth in their personal lives.

For our diagnosticians to be useful at truth analysis in the way I am suggesting here, they must be able to apply their knowledge to accurately diagnose intentional lying.

These people exist and can be found. I know a bunch of them. And their ability can be scientifically validated using a whole series of lie detector tests and each other. They also must be willing to be videotaped and blood tested and brain scanned and God knows what else, and questioned and put to the test. They have to go through the Truth Machine themselves even if they are participants in being the Truth Machine. This is a mutual confirmation process and a way of building community among ourselves and developing empathy for the trials and tribulations of subjects being tested, as well as validation of the process.

Next, we collect together the people who have been working to establish a way to tell who is telling the truth and who isn't, using technology. The eventual goal is to use our empaths and the techies and technology in combination, to validate honesty in various kinds of human interactions—contracts, mergers, marriages, divorces, and so forth—not just lie detection but devious intention detection.

Help from the Evil Empire

Some new and effective ways of finding out if people are lying have been developed over the last thirty years by the evil agents of the military-industrial complex. This extensive technology could actually be used to benefit the world instead of destroy it. Instead of perennial adolescent old men using advanced technology to keep brainwashed adolescent boys wasting life on ridiculous posturing, ranting, warmaking, assassination, rigged elections, murder of innocents, setups, fraud, robbery, bribery, and other forms of chicanery and ignorant bullshit associated with the CIA and state terrorism, we could use the same technology for peace and integrity. What a concept!

Technicians skilled in voice analysis, brain area blood supply scans, improved traditional lie detector tests, video facial change analysis, sequential chemical analysis of blood, urine, and other secretions, and many other recent technical advances of all sorts, could to be used in sequence and the results combined with conclusions reached by empaths.

Already this year, due to advances in technology, magnetic resonance imaging (fMRI) brain scans have recently started being used as evidence in trials.[2]

Once we collect together everyone who has expertise to work together, they can design a sequence of tests that eventually becomes the Truth Machine, we are on our way. People who are skilled in ways to search out hidden thoughts working together with people who know how to use methods and devices to determine when people are lying could establish a way to catch enough liars and encourage enough truthtellers to establish a level of honesty that could dramatically change the world. Why try to lie if you know you can't get away with it?

We could actually establish the validity of the Truth Machine and determine the degree of accuracy with a series of scientific tests in a very short time. And then, when we add to all this the classical ways of vetting people for political office by using the Internet, hiring investigative specialists, following up on rumors, and then asking more questions we could double check ourselves a number of ways.

Going Public to Establish Legitimacy and Build Practice

We could quickly offer Truth Machine services to people in all walks of life and use their hiring of us to further validate our results. Our services could be used by courts, politicians, businesses, families, couples, and the government—*but once we agreed to determine what is true in any situation we would not allow our findings to be kept secret, since secrecy is merely another instance of lying in its most pernicious form—withholding—and our ability to find out the truth could be misused again by those who wish to keep it hidden.* So when people meet the challenge of facing the Truth Machine they also meet the challenge of everyone knowing that in our scientifically validated judgment they are liars or that they are honest.

That may give some people pause. If it does, it may give other people pause about them. Fine. We are here to challenge a totally fucked up system and the courage it takes to do this is required of both our subjects and us, and we have no reason to be in the least apologetic about it. If you don't want to go before the Truth Machine, fine. If you don't like the implication that if you don't you must be lying, God knows I'm sorry.

Like all contexts created for the sake of a bigger perspective, the cautions, resistances, and concerns for privacy and about the possible misuse of this technology help us distinguish what needs working on. All that being said, we can proceed now to create a degree of certainty and a collectively-intelligent design of using real lie detection skill. Here is a partial list of people who could be invited to participate in the initial design meetings:

Derrick Jensen, Andrew Sacks, George Monbiot, Charles Eisenstein, Jeremy Rifkin, and everyone else whose articles have been reprinted or reported on in this book so far.

Susan Campbell, author of *Getting Real* and many other books.

Gay and Kathlyn Hendricks, co-authors of *Conscious Living, Conscious Loving,* and twenty other books, who are skilled "body centered" psychotherapists and corporate trainers, and very savvy about lying and relationships.

Byron Katie, author of *Loving What Is,* and other books, and founder of *The Work,* who is a person skilled in distinguishing what is so from ideas about what is so.

Stephen Mitchell, co-writer of *Loving What Is,* and author of many other books.

Rita Mae Brown, author of *Venus Envy,* a brilliant story about honesty, and a great story teller and author of many other books of fiction.

Brad Blanton, author of *Radical Honesty, Practicing Radical Honesty,* and 5 other books about honesty. I am a skillful psychotherapist and personal growth seminar leader and can often tell when people are lying.

Neale Donald Walsch, author of the *Conversations with God* book series, and co-author of *Honest to God.*

James Halperin, author of *The Truth Machine* and *The First Immortal*, which are both brilliant and visionary science fiction novels in which the development of a Truth Machine that can tell, without fail, when people are lying brings about a whole new world.

Jett Psaris and Marlena Lyons, co-authors of *Undefended Love*, and skillful psychotherapists.

Thomas Lewis, Fari Amini, and Richard Lannon, three psychiatrists who are co-authors of *A General Theory of Love.* They would have much to contribute in terms of, among other things, a possible relationship between limbic brain scans and activity in the prefrontal lobe.

All the members and participants in *The Truth Summit* established by Susan Campbell and friends (mostly from California) could be called together in another meeting out there (forty or so people).

In addition to these folks we would invite other group leaders, consultants, authors, and experts from a variety of fields. As we learn more about people who are technically skilled in lie detection, we would get some funding and go to work on consciously evolving the Truth Machine process.

We may even have to include attorneys.

Lie Detection Brain Scan Could Be Used in Court for First Time
By Alexis Madrigal (*Wired Science*, May 4, 2010)[4]

A Brooklyn attorney hopes to break new ground this week when he offers a brain scan as evidence that a key witness in a civil trial is telling the truth, Wired.com has learned.

If the fMRI scan is admitted, it would be a legal first in the United States and could have major consequences for the future of neuroscience in court.

The lawyer, David Zevin, wants to use that evidence to break a he-said/she-said stalemate in an employer-retaliation case. He's representing Cynette Wilson, a woman who claims that after she complained to temp agency CoreStaff Services about sexual harassment at a job site, she no longer received good assignments. Another worker at CoreStaff claims he heard her supervisor say that she should not be placed on jobs because of her complaint. The supervisor denies that he said anything of the sort.

So, Zevin had the coworker undergo an fMRI brain scan by the company Cephos, which claims to provide "independent, scientific validation that someone is telling the truth."

Laboratory studies using fMRI, which measures blood-oxygen levels in the brain, have suggested that when someone lies, the brain sends more blood to the ventrolateral area of the prefrontal cortex. In a very small number of studies, researchers have identified lying in study subjects with accuracy ranging from 76 percent to over 90 percent. But some scientists and lawyers like New York University neuroscientist Elizabeth Phelps doubts those results can be applied outside the lab.

"The data in their studies don't appear to be reliable enough to use in a court of law," Phelps said. "There is just no reason to think that this is going to be a good measure of whether someone is telling the truth.

General fMRI data from research has been used in sentencing, but an individual's brain scan has yet to be entered as evidence in a civil or criminal trial to help the jury determine whether someone was telling the truth. Individual fMRI evidence was offered in at least one other case by a San Diego attorney defending a father accused of sexual abuse, but the evidence was eventually withdrawn and did not make it into the record.

The Interaction Between People and Technology Validated

The empathy and skill of the sensitive, good-at-calling-people-on-their-pretence, no-bullshit folks I am describing here will determine what questions to ask, while using the most advanced technology in lie detection. We then set up a structure for validation of the Truth Machine—to conduct research testing the ability of the group to determine the truth when the truth is known, but lying is attempted, by people who are good liars trying to fool the Truth Machine.

During the development phase, the original research group of questioners and technicians would give a simple pass/no pass report to people volunteering to be tested to determine the efficacy of the Truth Machine Process.

Applicants from the general public could come to the research group for assistance to resolve real conflicts and claims. These tests will be called Truth Machine Reviews. The members of the Truth Machine, will give a "Truth Machine validation" to people who are telling the truth, and a "Truth Machine no pass" to people they say are lying.

Once we develop a method of notification to the general public about the availability and possible use of services, and provide them with a way of actually requesting to book a Truth Machine Review (TMR), we can, with each application, further extend the validation of the Truth Machine's usefulness. Anyone can request the opportunity to be validated or invalidated using our process, with the one condition of the work from the beginning of its utilization is that *all results will be made public.* The validity and degree of reliability of the system at the time of each specific review would be a part of the report.

This system can initially operate along side of, or parallel to, our more primitive and antiquated systems of determining "the truth," such as Congressional hearings, civil courts, and the so-called (and well-named) criminal justice system.

Again, in order not to be captured by liars or corporate capitalist killers, it is critical to the success of this endeavor that *no findings of The Truth Machine will ever be kept secret!* That is one of the conditions of acceptance of any party that submits a request for validation that they are not lying.

Once the initial group of truth verifiers is established, there will be an expansion of the program to:

1. Build another living Truth Machine made up of another group of our best "empaths" and most skillful determiners of when people are telling the truth, in addition to, and in cooperation with the most reliable technical feedback currently available. Then we have two truth machines that can check up on each other.
2. Establish each Truth Machine group as an ongoing, evolving institution itself, perhaps with frequent meetings to share developmental information.
3. Check the findings of the two Truth Machines against each other, and possibly use them in sequence themselves (essentially do everything twice, but with different empaths).
4. Plan further replication of groups and systems of interactive validation (independent Truth Machines), and the establishment of the work of finding out who is lying.

Finally, when we come up with a document that summarizes our advances in truth determination we will see the beginning of a world where lying (along with all of its destructive consequences) has been rendered obsolete through accurate deceit-detection technology. In a world where we have developed a greater degree of certainty in our ability to tell when people are lying, people will know that if they lie they could be found out if challenged to face the Truth Machine, and they will have an incentive to go ahead and be honest in the first place. So people will stop lying because they know they can't get by with it! They can expect honesty from others for the same reason. The implications of this for everything that exists in the world as we know it are absolutely mind-boggling.

We Already have most of What We Need

As a rough estimate, I would guess that the technology already exists, right now, to determine with about 85 to 90 percent accuracy when people are lying. By using co-intelligent empaths cooperating to formulate questions, and contributing their observations and assessments of how the technology is being employed, and by conducting a little further research that takes advantage of the empaths input, we probably could quickly improve the percentage of accuracy of the whole "machine" to about 95 percent. It is obvious how much more effective this would be in comparison to the existing court system. With even further work, that level of accuracy could reach 98 percent, which is "good enough for government work."

"Truth certification" could initially supplement, and then quickly become a viable alternative to the judicial system. Since the current court system in the United States is one with which I am familiar, I know from many personal experiences that the ideal of justice there is a lie. I worked as a psychotherapist for dozens and dozens of attorneys, a few judges and law enforcement personnel, and a number of people tangentially related to the courts when I was in the full-time practice of clinical psychology in Washington, D.C. I also have some experience of being on trial myself for various charges from anti-war demonstrations, civil rights protests, and campaign finance reform demonstrations in and around the Capitol in Washington. All these gave me rare opportunities to have a different kind of relationship with the law than even some of my former clients. I have given expert testimony a few times, and with the help of the American Civil Liberty Union I have sued various governmental bodies and challenged a few edicts.

I mention all this history to assert that I have seldom, in all of these various circumstances, seen or heard about the court being the least bit interested in finding out the truth. *The system is not set up so that the truth emerges, but so that the persons who make the best case win.*

Justice, according to the court system, is about the best argument made about how this situation matches others previously ruled upon, not about the truth of what happened. The best case is the best justification according to previous law. They are tangentially interested in catching people lying now and then if it happens to help the case, but actually knowing what was going on was of little interest to them.

So when I say that the Truth Machine could be made central to a new system of justice based on honoring the being of human beings and of all living beings and that this is a clear alternative to the current system, it is a hell of an understatement. A system of justice based on finding out the truth is practically the opposite of the current system.

Truth Certification and Reconciliation

Once we have the capacity to establish at any given time in someone's life that they have told the truth we can certify at any given point in their lives they are even, honest, updated. They can confess previous crimes and details of cheating, stealing, hiding, and so on, and that confession can be verified as the truth. So someone who has stolen money, for example, could now be trusted still to work handling money, with agreements for occasional Truth Machine reviews, once they have fessed up about previous theft.

This also creates the possibility of people making things right by paying back or compensating in some way for their previous crimes and misdemeanors through working out agreements to do so. Once certified at a given point in time, a person would be freed up for a new beginning and have a chance of a new life without crime. With the security of the Truth Machine to assist individuals and society in keeping balance there is a greater possibility for forgiveness and new beginnings.

When people are violent and can't be rehabilitated we can have them for dinner. (They may not taste so good because they are kind of tough. They may need a lot of sauce or we may have to parboil them before we fry them.)

Established Forms of Permissible Crime and What We Can Do for Them

The biggest opponents of the Truth Machine will likely be all the people who are legally getting by with murder—namely, the corporate executives in charge of large banking and financial institutions, brokerage houses on Wall Street, defense industry contractors, and people and businesses with other vested interests. This legalized mafia will not leave without a fight. There are those among them intelligent enough to get that this ability to determine the truth would disrupt the very foundations of society as we know it, particularly corporate capitalist owned government, which is based on secrets and lies for the sake of "security". Our whole society is a bad joke based on deception and those of us interested in the truth are their mortal enemy.

I believe now that we will only be able to be set up this alternative system of justice if we are willing to kill those who are willing to kill us to prevent us from setting it up. It cannot be done non-violently prior to the total collapse of the system that is currently going down. It very likely will not be done non-violently even after the system collapses completely of its own accord—meaning, without our help. Our goons will have to outnumber and overpower their goons, or we will have to convert their goons to our side in order to do this. (At least there will be a lot of protein to eat for a while.)

Remember, there is a hell of a lot more of us than there are of them. Arm yourself and go into physical training, and then let's gather at the river.

If there is a way you can come up with to bring this about quickly without getting busy killing those in charge of established criminal law enforcement, I am open and eager to hear about it. For the sake of honesty though, I want to say that I currently do not think that when push comes to shove this can be done non-violently. If we want to build and use a Truth Machine, if they try to stop us we will probably have to kill a bunch of them and then end up being convicted of murder using our own device. Thus, the next chapter is about building a new method of governance that includes a new system of justice that lets us get by with this shit.

CHAPTER 10

Called by Each Other to Our Higher Selves:
Establishing Permanent Structures for Citizen Dialogue and Deliberation

"In knowing ourselves as an integral function of a multi-faceted Human Family Self, we evolve into beings whose actions, without struggle, are honest, intentional and grounded in Compassion. From this state we can no more go to war or allow destruction of our environment than we can stab our own hand. Intelligence, not intellect must dominate if our individual and collective lives are to be freed from the suffering caused by the illusions we live into."

—Joseph Chilton Pearce

"We are all longing to go home to some place we have never been—a place half-remembered and half-envisioned we can only catch glimpses of from time to time. Community. Somewhere a circle of hands will open to receive us, eyes will light up as we enter, voices will celebrate with us whenever we come into our own power. Community means strength that joins our strength to do the work that needs to be done. "

—Starhawk

"I need self-delusion. Otherwise I'd be so depressed about irrationality—and the general apocalyptic state of the world—that I couldn't function. I have learned this much about myself and my deeply flawed brain: I have to believe, irrationally, against all evidence, that humans can be rational."

—A. J. Jacobs, *The Guinea Pig Diaries*

"Would you rather have health and wellness, or wealth and hellness!?"
—John Margolis, (talking about the so-called health care debate)

It should be fairly clear by now that I have a political agenda as well as a scientific and social one. In order to salvage what we can from the already-too-late-to-fix upcoming tragedies in store for us, we have to take power in order to be in charge when bad things happen. We must take back the power of the nuts in charge of the nuthouse and feed their nuts to the other nuts that have been driven nuts by these nuts.

My friend John Speicher usually disagrees with me because he is a wealthy engineer who made his money in the defense industry and has an archaic traditional view of things. But he tries to keep an open mind nevertheless, as I do about his ideas. In response to an earlier draft of the first few chapters of this book, he wrote me. Here is part of what he said: "If you do not like business structures arranged as corporations, suggest an alternative form—basically, present some alternates to existing corporate procedures for forming, conducting and closing a business."

Sounds simple, doesn't it? So I will do that now. John's comment does remind me that two of the fundamental problems of governments and corporations are the top-down hierarchical structure of management and the fact that corporations never die and government bureaucracies last too damned long as well. If we had term limits for corporations and public officials—that might work! We could give them three or four years and then discorporate them and eat their management teams if they don't disband. That could work.

Obedience Training Is Not Education—and Vice Versa

The research by Stanley Milgram and the commentary reviewed in chapter 6 are background to understanding how we have set things up in our society so that people can become "sheeple" (people who act like sheep). Our whole system of education-as-obedience-training serves to prepare people for top-down control so they can be used by the system. It serves the cause of our government and phony justice for sheeple to act like slaves and be insatiable consumers, and arranges a way to punished them if they do not obey. Therefore a non-hierarchical, non-corporate-capitalist-cannibal-run government and system of justice would have to have a parallel non-hierarchical education system. To do this we have to overthrow or totally undermine the old educational system and take control from the people who keep it in place.

Reformation of education is a subject for another whole book. In the interest of brevity, I will proceed directly to the reformation of the justice system and save educational reform for later. There are other parts of government that need to be addressed as well, but the justice system is the most dangerously and egregiously unbalanced in our society.

Government by the People

In addition to having a new system of education that doesn't brainwash our children to be sheeple, and to have a new government we like we will require a new system of justice first. And we need a new way of judging in order to have a new system of justice. We need to take out people with power in the old system. We need to do that fairly, based on a real system of justice based on nurturance and sustainability for people and all living things. If we are going to be killing and eating justices in the name of justice, or at least removing them from power, we had better be clear and have structures for staying clear.

Along with the new system of justice we need to give collective intelligence a role of greater power in controlling people in power. For, as my friend Clinton Callahan says, "It is not that power corrupts, it is that corrupt people seek power." In his brilliant book, *The Power of Conscious Feelings* (Hohm Press, 2010), he shows how people who become economic and political leaders are basically sociopaths. The system is a sociopath maintenance program. I have little doubt that if we had killed and eaten some recent sociopaths early on, like, for example, the whole bunch that were the government of the United States during George W. Bush's regime, the whole world would have benefitted from it tremendously.

Until we take the money, property, and power away from those who keep control of the current sociopathic system, these individuals will prevent any social evolution beyond corporate fascism, therefore ending the possibility for survival of human beings on the planet. Nation-states controlled by the wealthy bring interminable war where 80 to 90 percent of those killed are innocent bystanders. The United States of America and its corporations are the main perpetrator of those wars in current times.

The inmates have taken over the asylum and we need a new way for the less sick to be put back in control. So the first step in taking back the power of the nuts in charge of the nut house and feeding their nuts to the other nuts that have been driven nuts by these nuts, is to build a parallel system of government.

First We Build a Parallel System

What I am proposing here is a new system of government based on term-limited honest co-intelligent dialogue and deliberation by people selected at random from voter registration lists. Citizens, drawn at random, and one group at a time, and then that series of groups is in charge of justice. They would have term limits, and they would interact with similar groups in charge of governance.

For the sake of conversation about a new form of government and system of justice utilizing what we are calling honest co-intelligent dialogue and deliberation, we must first answer these questions: What is honest co-intelligent dialogue and deliberation?

Why do its advocates call it "deep democracy"? *And is it a new kind of democracy*, different in some essential ways from what we have been calling democracy?

One of the best places to start this conversation about co-intelligence is to quote a definition of it from one of the best-known examples of how it operates, Wikipedia (a mutually-written online encyclopedia). The following excerpts are examples of co-creation where readers themselves can modify and expand upon existing text, improving and modifying as they go.

These following excerpts are both an apt introduction to co-intelligence and a limited example of how it actually works (limited because the best co-intelligence comes from face-to-face conversations.)

We will begin by distinguishing two concepts: collective wisdom and collective intelligence. The second phenomenon is more dynamic than the first, but understanding the first clarifies the distinction.

I have inserted notes in the middle in bracketed italics.

Collective Wisdom as Defined by Wikipedia, the Free Encyclopedia[1]

Collective wisdom, also called group wisdom and co-intelligence, is an emerging phenomenon researched in fields of inquiry such as psychology, social psychology, and philosophy. The solutions arrived at from such studies are applied to conflict resolution methods for individuals, groups and nations. There are far-reaching implications for long-term approaches to human relations. The results of shared research in subtopics of collective wisdom are being applied to new approaches to individual and group therapy, new understandings of expanded family and tribal units, conflict resolution work, collaborative projects in the arts, theatre and music, the business and corporate world, and politics.

Definition

Collective wisdom is shared knowledge arrived at by individuals and groups, used to solve problems and conflicts of all humanity. "Crowd wisdom" is used to describe the dark side of collective wisdom, incorporating the negative implications including the results incurred by the herd mentality or groupthink...

[We can distinguish co-intelligence from co-stupidity. The whole point of the social technologies we are introducing here is to actually counter what usually happens when groups of people get together to react unthinkingly, to be manipulated, or to fail to think at all. What we are going for is structures for interaction that guarantee that everyone gets to speak and everyone gets heard, not just symbolically, but thoroughly. And to guarantee that what is mined from our collective expression is the essence of the variety of perspectives and information that went into it, such that it becomes possible for a group genius to emerge that is superior to any possible individual genius

within the group. In essence, we do this so the cream rises to the top and the less valuable information or perspective sinks to the bottom, but only after thorough consideration and discussion and deep consideration of all perspectives. —Brad.]

Collective intelligence is basically consensus-driven decision making, whereas collective wisdom is not necessarily focused on the decision process...

History

...Drawing from the idea of universal truth, the point of collective wisdom is to make life easier/more enjoyable through understanding human behavior, whereas the point of collective intelligence is to make life easier/more enjoyable through the application of acquired knowledge... Dave Pollard's restatement of collective wisdom: "Many cognitive, coordination and cooperation problems are best solved by canvassing groups (the larger the better) of reasonably informed, unbiased, engaged people. The group's answer is almost invariably much better than any individual expert's answer, even better than the best answer of the experts in the group."[2] A well-known application of collective wisdom is the television show, "Who Wants to be a Millionaire?," where participants query the audience to help answer questions.

A Walk Through: The Story of a Process

The quotes from Wikipedia that precede and follow these comments are hard to digest all at once. So I will give you some story examples. You can get the general idea from both the stories and definitions of terms, that there may be a form of deliberation and dialogue that allows for a deep, collectively wise approach to problems of governance and could do so on an ongoing basis.

There are a growing number of books and practices that elaborate on the fundamental idea that maybe we can trust each other to be powerfully creative and brilliant together on a regular basis! For an example, let's talk about the *World Café* process created by Juanita Brown and David Isaacs, and explained in their book by that name, which they co-authored with the World Café Community (Berrett-Koehler Publishers, 2005).

What Is a World Café?

Generally what happens is that a group of people (let's say a group of forty) comes together to discuss a question they all have some interest in answering. The person conducting the meeting asks the group to divide into ten smaller groups of four people around café tables, which are covered by paper tablecloths and supplied with a bunch of pens and colored markers (so people can write on the tablecloth), some flowers, a little candy, and something nonalcoholic to drink.

The question being focused on is written large and posted in several locations around the room where every table can easily see it. This reminds people of the main thrust of the question if (or when) they get too far off the topic. The conductor of the café asks each table to elect a chairperson, whose job, in addition to discussing the question at hand like everyone else, is to keep notes on the conversation by writing on the paper tablecloth as the discussion goes on. Everyone else is also encouraged to make notes on the tablecloth whenever they like.

Once the preliminary instructions are over, the conversation begins. Each table has a "talking stick," which is held by the person who is talking, as he or she speaks, and can be passed to someone else or taken from them by any other participant when that other individual wants to speak. It also can be taken and handed to one of the four who has not said much when the others want to hear what the person thinks. People who are not holding the stick remain silent and listen until the stick is passed to them.

This conversation goes on for about twenty-five minutes. Then the person conducting the café rings a little bell and gives people a minute or so to wind up their conversations. The conductor asks the various table chairpersons to remain at their tables while the other three people at each table get up, split up, and wander around at random and find a seat at some other table where there is a different chairperson.

Once the tables have new groups of four folks, another twenty-five minute discussion ensues after the chairperson summarizes the previous conversation at that table by going over his or her notes written on the tablecloth. Of course, any of the participants is free to bring up ideas discussed at their previous meeting as well—and they do.

The new discussion, which is still being kept track of on the tablecloth by the chairperson, ends when a little bell rings. After a minute or two to wind up, everyone except the table chairperson is invited to wander around and join a new group again.

After the third iteration of this twenty-five-minute, four-person conversation, there is a short break so people can get a drink, go to the bathroom, and talk amongst themselves a little. Then there is a gathering of the whole group in one room in a big circle. In this circle, all former table chairpersons put their paper tablecloth with the notes, comments, pictures, and doodles from all of the conversations in front of themselves on the floor, so they can use the notes to speak about the ideas previously discussed. The larger group conversation begins with reports from all the table chairs on what was discussed in their three groups. As each of these reports is given, all participants are free to chime in if they think anything was left out or if they want to stress some particular idea.

The final meeting is usually loud and raucous, funny, inspiring, and stimulating, and generally everyone feels like a hell of a creator. Participants feel they have been listened to, that they have heard a lot of great ideas, and that they have wrought something new out of genuinely participating in a communication and co-creation with brilliant results.

The poem/song "I" wrote, "Human Photosynthesis," presented in chapter 5, came from me taking the tablecloths home from a world café that I conducted at the *No Mind Festival* in Sweden where, after watching Al Gore's movie, *An Inconvenient Truth*, participants focused on the question: *What can we do to be a part of the solution rather than a part of the problem with regard to global warming?* All the ideas for the verses to that song were on the tablecloths. I just made some of them rhyme and put a melody to it in order to try to get their brilliance out to the world and take credit for it myself.

What happens in these very exciting, fun, and creative co-intelligent experiences is a renewal of faith in each other and the possibilities for democracy, as well as a sense of satisfaction that is hard to top.

I have a few other stories that provide examples of how this and other similar social technologies work. This happened when I ran for Congress in 2006 against Eric Cantor, and incredibly stupid and corrupt Republican who outspent me two hundred to one using stolen money contributed by corrupt corporations. My campaign organized a World Café in a local community in my congressional district discussing the question: *"What should be the relationship between government and corporations?"*

I hoped that the structure of the World Café would allow people from my district of somewhat different persuasions to hear each other and to feel they had been heard, and for a collective perspective to evolve. I arranged for the event to be conducted by a person other than myself who was more practiced in running them, and so I could participate without having to run it.

Here are a few highlights: One unusual perspective came during one of the café table meetings came from a participant who was enrolled in a twelve-step program. He said, "I think both government and corporations need a twelve-step program." The conversation that ensued awakened us all to the possibility that personal addiction to power and money on the part of the folks in corporations and the government could possibly be dealt with in a compassionate way. We could cut them some slack and identify with their confusion in never knowing how much was enough and in being addicted to more, more, more. We came up with the idea that if there was some personal ownership of the problem on the part of people who are participants in this dysfunctional family, maybe some of the abuse of power due to addiction could be reduced. Maybe with some support from the rest of us, even corporate capitalists could be converted to compassionate sanity! It allowed for a compassionate, rather than a positional place to come from about corporations and government, even for me, in spite of my prejudices.

Though it took three hours from beginning to end of this meeting, at the end we had a hard time getting people to leave the building so it could be closed! Some people who had known each other for many years, even their whole lives, said they'd had the best conversations they had ever had with their neighbors.

A hilarious and inspiring discussion in the large group at the end came from us saying to the twelve-stepper, "Okay, we're convinced. What is the first step?"

He answered, "You have to admit that you have a problem."

We laughed and laughed. Ain't it the truth! I pretty much organized my whole campaign for Congress around that idea, and eventually one thing that idea led me to was this book.

I lost my race for Congress. Unlike my friend Ralph Nader, I withdrew a week and a half before the election when I knew I couldn't possibly win and asked my supporters in the Independent Green Party to support the Democrat who was running for Congress instead of me. I also asked them to support the Democratic Candidate for the Senate, Jim Webb. Our Independent Green Candidate for the Senate, because the race was so close, also said, with some encouragement from me, to all the Independent Greens, "If you can't vote for me in this very close race, at least vote for a change."

Along with a lot of work on the part of both Democrats and Independent Greens, we swung 30,000 Independent votes to Jim Webb, who won the race for Senate with a little over 9,300 votes! We know we accomplished this because in polls taken prior to the election our Independent Green candidate was polling a little over 2 percent, but when the election occurred she got only 1 percent—a little over 30,000 votes. A random check confirmed that we Independent Greens made the difference in unseating the incumbent Republican, George Allen, another dumb ass, and replacing him with Jim Webb, the fifty-first Senator who gave Democrats control of the Senate.

My losing campaign changed the balance of power in the United States Senate in 2006. That opened the way for further changes, which possibly included the advance of Barack Obama to the presidency. An important minor element of that shift of power, and perhaps a critical element, was holding authentic meetings of citizens where dialogue and deliberation techniques were used.

Of course, as Charles Eisenstein pointed out in his essay "*The Ubiquitous Matrix of Lies*," reprinted in chapter 3 of this book, the shift of power to the Democrats was only a change of brands, not a real change. We are still the empire and President Obama simply does not have the power to change things to the degree needed if we are to avoid the real catastrophe the U.S. is facing.

We are still in need of real—and incredibly quick—structural change. We need to hold a thousand World Cafés a week for a few years in order to save life on Earth, including our own.

Collective Intelligence as Defined by Wikipedia[3]

Collective intelligence is a shared or group intelligence that emerges from the collaboration and competition of many individuals. Collective intelligence appears in a wide variety of forms of consensus decision making in bacteria, animals, humans, and computer networks. The study of collective intelligence may properly be considered a subfield of sociology of business, of computer science, of mass communications, and of mass behavior—a field that studies collective behavior from the level of quarks to the level of bacterial, plant, animal, and human societies. The concept also frequently appears in science fiction, as telepathically linked species and cyborgs....[4]

Some figures like Tom Atlee prefer to focus on collective intelligence primarily in humans and actively work to upgrade what Howard Bloom calls "the group IQ." Atlee feels that collective intelligence can be encouraged "to overcome 'groupthink' and individual cognitive bias in order to allow a collective to cooperate on one process—while achieving enhanced intellectual performance."

...Collective Intelligence draws on this to enhance the social pool of existing knowledge. Henry Jenkins, a key theorist of new media and media convergence draws on the theory that collective intelligence can be attributed to media convergence and participatory culture.[5] Collective intelligence is not merely a quantitative contribution of information from all cultures, it is also qualitative.

One CI pioneer, George Por, defined the collective intelligence phenomenon as "the capacity of human communities to evolve towards higher order complexity and harmony, through such innovation mechanisms as differentiation and integration, competition and collaboration."[6] Tom Atlee and George Pór state that "collective intelligence also involves achieving a single focus of attention and standard of metrics which provide an appropriate threshold of action."...

With the development of the Internet and its widespread use, the opportunity to contribute to community-based knowledge forums, such as Wikipedia, is greater than ever before. These computer networks give participating users the opportunity to store and to retrieve knowledge through the collective access to these databases and allow them to "harness the hive" (Raymond 1998; Herz 2005 in Flew 2008). Researchers at the MIT Center for Collective Intelligence research and explore collective intelligence of groups of people and computers.[7]

General Concepts

Howard Bloom traces the evolution of collective intelligence from the days of our bacterial ancestors 3.5 billion years ago to the present and demonstrates how a multi-species intelligence has worked since the beginning of life.

Tom Atlee and George Pór, on the other hand, feel that while group theory and artificial intelligence have something to offer, the field of collective intelligence should be seen by some as primarily a human enterprise in which mind-sets, a willingness to share, and an openness to the value of distributed intelligence for the common good are paramount. Individuals who respect collective intelligence, say

Atlee and Pór, are confident of their own abilities and recognize that the whole is indeed greater than the sum of any individual parts.

From Pór and Atlee's point of view, maximizing collective intelligence relies on the ability of an organization to accept and develop "The Golden Suggestion," which is any potentially useful input from any member....

According to Don Tapscott and Anthony D. Williams, collective intelligence is mass collaboration. In order for this concept to happen, four principles need to exist. These are openness, peering, sharing, and acting globally.

Openness: In the early stage of communications technology, people and companies are reluctant to share ideas and intellectual property, or to encourage self-motivation because these resources provide the edge over competitors. However, in time people and companies began to loosen hold over these resources as they reap more benefits in doing so. Allowing others to share ideas and bid for franchising will enable products to gain significant improvement and scrutiny through collaboration.

Peering: This is a form of horizontal organization with the capacity to create information technology and physical products. One example is the 'opening up' of the Linux program where users are free to modify and develop it provided that they made it available for others. Participants in this form of collective intelligence have different motivations for contributing, but the results achieved are for the improvement of a product or service. As quoted, "Peering succeeds because it leverages self-organization—a style of production that works more effectively than hierarchical management for certain tasks."

Sharing: This principle has been controversial with the question being "Should there be a law against the distribution of intellectual property?" Research has shown that more and more companies have started to share some, while maintaining some degree of control over others, like potential and critical patent rights. This is because companies have realized that by limiting all their intellectual property, they are shutting out all possible opportunities. Sharing some has allowed them to expand their market and bring out products faster.

Acting Globally: The advancements in communication technology has prompted the rise of global companies, or e-Commerce that has allowed individuals to set up businesses at low to almost no overhead costs. The influence of the Internet is widespread, therefore a globally integrated company would have no geographical boundaries but have global connections, allowing them to gain access to new markets, ideas and technology.[8]

More Examples of Collective Intelligence

Ant societies exhibit more intelligence than any other animal except for humans, if we measure intelligence in terms of technology. Ant societies are able to do agriculture, in fact several different forms of agriculture. Some ant societies keep livestock of various forms, for example, some ants keep and care for aphids for "milking." Leaf cutters care for fungi and carry leaves to feed the fungi.

However, a majority will agree that the medium that displays collective intelligence in full is Wikipedia. It is an encyclopedia that can be altered by virtually anyone at any time. This concept is termed "wikinomics" by Don Tapscott and Anthony D. Williams in their book similarly named, they quote The Sunday Times, "Wikinomics" is the new force that is bringing people together on the net to create a giant brain."[9] Through this application, the lines between a consumer and producer have been blurred, inventing the term "prod-user" or "prosumer."

More examples on collective intelligence can be seen in games. Games such as The Sims, Halo, or Second Life are designed to be more non-linear and depend on collective intelligence for expansion. This way of sharing is gradually evolving and influencing the mindset of the current and future generations.[10] For them, collective intelligence has become a norm."

(Wikileaks and Julian Assange are a current fine example of the beginning of our mutual attack on corporate and military secrecy that lets governments and corporations get by with murder, by revealing secrets and lies classified as secret.—Brad)"

At a Scientific and Experimental Level, the Possibility of a New Kind of Community Brilliance has Already been Demonstrated

Though the processes and terminology are somewhat difficult and the structures to be put in place to allow for the continual re-invigoration of deep democracy, the potential for a whole new way of living together is tremendously exciting! Instead of having money do all the talking and top-down management and obedience training making it so the best we can hope for is benevolent dictatorships, we can have a truly democratic, egalitarian, co-intelligent community from which we establish rules of order and rules of law. This could be closer to heaven on earth than we have ever come before!

Deliberative Democracy as Defined by Wikipedia[11]

Deliberative democracy, also sometimes called discursive democracy, is a system of political decisions based on some trade-off between direct democracy and representative democracy that relies on citizen deliberation to make sound policy. In contrast to the traditional theory of democracy, in which voting is central, deliberative democracy theorists argue that legitimate lawmaking can arise only through public deliberation by the people....

Cohen's Outline

Joshua Cohen, a student of John Rawls, most clearly outlined some conditions that he thinks constitute the root principles of the theory of deliberative democracy in the article "Deliberation and Democratic Legitimacy" in the book *The Good Polity.* He outlines five main features of deliberative democracy, which include:

1. An ongoing independent association with expected continuation.

2. The citizens in the democracy structure their institutions such that deliberation is the deciding factor in their creation and that they allow deliberation to continue.

3. A commitment to the respect of a pluralism of values and aims within the polity.

4. The participants in the democracy regard deliberative procedure as the source of legitimacy and as such they also prefer those causal histories of legitimation for each law be transparent, and easily traceable back to the deliberative process.

5. Each member and all members recognize and respect the others having deliberative capacity.

This can be construed as the fact that in a deliberative democracy, we "owe" one another, in the legislative process, reasons.

Cohen presents deliberative democracy as more than a theory of legitimacy, and forms a body of substantive rights around it based on achieving "ideal deliberation":

It is free in two ways:

The participants regard themselves as bound solely by the results and preconditions of the deliberation. They are free from any authority of prior norms or requirements.

The participants suppose that they can act on the decision made, the decision through deliberation is a sufficient reason for compliance with it.

It is reasoned: parties to deliberation are required to state reasons for proposals, and proposals are accepted or rejected based on the reasons given, as the content of the very deliberation taking place.

Participants are equal in two ways:

Formal: Anyone can put forth proposals, criticize, and support measures. There is no substantive hierarchy.

Substantive: The participants are not limited or bound by certain distributions of power, resources, or pre-existing norms. "The participants…do not regard themselves as bound by the existing system of rights, except insofar as that system establishes the framework of free deliberation among equals."

Deliberation aims at a rationally motivated consensus: it aims to find reasons acceptable to all who are committed to such a system of decision-making. When consensus or something near enough is not possible, majoritarian decision making is utilized...

In Canada, there have been two prominent applications of deliberative democratic models. In 2004, the British Columbia Citizens' Assembly on Electoral Reform convened a policy jury to consider alternatives to the first-past-the-post electoral systems. In 2007, the Ontario Citizens' Assembly on Electoral Reform convened to consider alternative electoral systems in that province.

Similarly, three of Ontario's Local Health Integration Networks (LHIN) have referred their budget priorities to a policy jury for advice and refinement.

Strengths and Weaknesses

A claimed strength of deliberative democratic models is that they are more easily able to incorporate scientific opinion and base policy on outputs of ongoing research, because:

Time is given for all participants to understand and discuss the science

Scientific peer review, adversarial presentation of competing arguments, refereed journals, even betting markets, are also deliberative processes.

The technology used to record dissent and document opinions opposed to the majority is also useful to notarize bets, predictions and claims.

According to the proponents, another strength of deliberative democratic models is that they tend, more than any other model, to generate ideal conditions of impartiality, rationality and knowledge of the relevant facts. The more these conditions are fulfilled, the greater the likelihood that the decisions reached are morally correct. Deliberative democracy has thus an episemic value: it allows participants to deduce what is morally correct…

Liberation through Deliberation!

I know this is a lot to wade through and understand. But I just think this is so wonderful I want to jump up and down and holler every few days because of it. I have met and spent time with and talked to Tom Atlee and George Por and a number of other great people who have spent at least the last ten years of their lives on this. I belong to the National Coalition for Deliberation and Democracy (NCDD) and I occasionally keep up with their blogs. This whole endeavor is becoming a movement and not a second too soon! Let me talk about just one more brilliant leader and I will leave you alone about it and go on to speculate a little more about our future heaven on earth arising from the ashes of the corporatocracy.

Dynamic Facilitation

Jim Rough, whose Dynamic Facilitation process takes things even further beyond dialogue and deliberation, to *choosing and acting on ideas* when true consensus has been reached and everyone's interests are validated. This is about the application of deliberative democracy, with something called "The Creative Insight Council." What Jim calls Dynamic Facilitation is the process of supporting people to learn about and operate from, essentially, the principles and processes we have been talking about in this chapter up to this point. This is from Jim's upcoming book...

How Citizen Participation Can Solve Impossible Problems: Excerpts from The Future of Public Participation[12]
By Jim Rough

Lake Constance is at the heart of Europe bordering three countries: Germany, Austria, and Switzerland. On the Austrian border is the ancient city of Bregenz, capital of the wealthiest state in Austria, Vorarlberg. Dr. Manfred Hellrigl is Director of the Department of Future Related Issues for Vorarlberg and a pioneer in the art of democracy.

After a bitter public battle over the development of a key waterfront plot of land, Dr. Hellrigl proposed a new idea to the mayor of Bregenz for addressing the next high profile project. He suggested a new kind of public participation strategy, a way to involve mainstream citizens, not just the stakeholders, and where they really understand the issues, where everyone's points are valued, and where the process builds the spirit of community. Dr. Hellrigl proposed a Creative Insight Council (CIC) and the mayor agreed.

So twelve citizens were randomly selected from the voter registration roles. They met for two days and listened to the proposed plans and to a range of views about them. They were dynamically facilitated to reach a shared perspective. The CIC determined that this project offered a once-in-a-lifetime opportunity to link the city more tightly to the lake. That became their theme as they suggested major changes to the proposal. One main idea was to make the second floor of the project the center of gravity rather than the first. They suggested a wide bridge over the rail tracks, rather than the planned pedestrian underground path. Plus, they wanted a sweeping set of steps on the side toward the lake. With this new emphasis on the second level money could be saved because the parking garage no longer needed to go below ground level.

The CIC presented this unanimous perspective to the investors, architects, city planners and mayor. All were surprised by the depth of thinking and pleased. The principal investor who had been working on this project for two years said in approval, "We had been looking at the trees and didn't see the forest."

A few weeks later the CIC presented their perspective to a community gathering with a large media presence. One at a time each member of the CIC spoke about how enjoyable and how rewarding it was to be on the Council. Each of them was proud of the difference that their work may make in the community. At this meeting the investors, mayor, and architects also expressed their support.

There were about sixty citizens attending this community gathering, who then met in small group dialogues. Using the World Café model, they switched groups and so their dialogue would extend outward. The gathering was held in a spirit of celebration, community building and seeking what's best for all, rather than the usual grandstanding, posturing and arguing. This process is a way of generating a viewpoint that mainstream citizens can understand, consider and embrace. It's way that there can be a legitimate "public interest" perspective, rather than one portrayed by government or special interests....

What's Special?

The Creative Insight Council is a recent social invention that is unlike other forms of public participation. The group is random and speaks unanimously. So, it creates a legitimate voice of "the people." And the special thinking process used in the Council, builds a spirit of community and often generates breakthrough solutions better than what anyone had thought before....

The CIC seeks to facilitate this kind of talking in the community, by framing issues in a way that inspires people to think creatively. Consider how the Bregenz Wisdom Council framed the issue, for example, "How can we use this project to bring the city closer to the lake?"

Governments today face many difficult situations where the long-term needs of the environment must be balanced with the short-term need for jobs and economic growth. There are other issues too, like addressing the budget crisis, assuring fairness in taxes, designing a reliable election process, and balancing civil liberties and security. To address and effectively resolve controversial issues like these, government is increasingly seeking to involve the public through hearings, town meetings, citizen advisory groups, Citizens juries, stakeholder panels, and many different online approaches. These methods are more limited in scope.

When problems are really difficult, the CIC is called for because it involves mainstream people, generates better answers with more support, creates a legitimate voice of "the people" on the issue, and sparks more trust in government. Key in how it achieves this magic is the quality of conversation it elicits... choice creating instead of decision making.

Assuring Choice-creating

When people first hear about the CIC it's often difficult for them to appreciate how it's different from other forms of citizen participation, or how it might work at all. At first glance it seems similar to a citizens' advisory panel... or that more than twelve people would be needed... or that a random group of citizens could never address really difficult issues and achieve meaningful unanimous conclusions in a short time.

But these concerns are readily overcome in practice. It works because the CIC facilitates a quality of talking and thinking called "choice-creating," where people are open minded and open hearted, where they face the most important issues, and where they work creatively and collaboratively with their peers in trying to solve them. The group reaches a joint perspective via creative shifts and breakthroughs, rather than through the usual back and forth negotiation.

Consider these six different kinds of conversation a community might use to determine collective actions:

"Power struggle" where people seek to get their way by using argument, status or money. Our representative system is largely structured to use this form of decision-making. Public participation happens when people support candidates or political parties.

"Reasoned debate" where there is a thoughtful competition of ideas and a vote, where hopefully the best ideas win. To many this form of decision-making is how our system should work. Public hearings, debates between candidates or pundits on television, or stakeholder meetings are examples of this kind of public participation.

"Discussion" where government leaders present their intentions to the voters, answer questions, and listen. "Town meetings" and informal gatherings often follow this model of public participation.

"Deliberation" where experts, wise elders, informed citizens, or legislators investigate selected problems, carefully weighing the given options before recommending one to decision-makers. This process is used in citizen advisory panels, National Issues Forums, and Citizens Juries.

"Dialogue" where there is a large gathering of people or a network of small gatherings that explores topics open-mindedly. Conversation café's or salons are examples. In these dialogues people grow in their understandings of issues and one another, but group decisions are rare.

"Choice-creating" where diverse people address the most pressing issues collaboratively and creatively, evolving unanimous, win/win conclusions through "shifts" and breakthroughs. The Creative Insight Council and the Wisdom Council process, to be considered later, are examples of this kind of public participation.

Choice-creating is the ideal quality of thinking for a democracy, where everyone is involved equally and respectfully, seeking what's best for all. This form of thinking often occurs naturally in a crisis, when people recognize that the normal ways of thinking cannot work. Then they rise to the occasion to accomplish miracles. For example, maybe as a student you would wait until the last moment before starting an important assignment. This is an artificial crisis but it often evokes the best in a person.

Dynamic Facilitation (DF) is a way of helping a small group address its most pressing, seemingly impossible issues in the spirit of choice-creating. Rather than relying on agendas, guidelines, step-by-step thinking, or prepared questions, the dynamic facilitator uses four charts: Data, Solutions, Concerns and Problem-Statements. People just talk, but the dynamic facilitator structures the conversation so that all comments have a place and are valuable. No one feels judged and all feel included. He or she helps the group follow their energy in a way that a new, shared perspective emerges.

To achieve these results participants need not be trained ahead of time. They can just be themselves. As people feel fully heard they put aside their preconceived ideas and feelings and become open hearted and open minded. It's enjoyable. It builds the spirit of community and yields answers that all support...

A Vision of Change

Obviously, if there could somehow be a nationwide public conversation where all citizens are involved, facing the big issues creatively and collaboratively, and seeking answers that work for everyone, then many pressing, impossible-seeming issues would just go away. How, for instance, could racism or wars or terrorism exist, if all people were talking together in one respectful, listening conversation? How can we have a lopsided distribution of wealth or special interest dominance of politics if all are seeking what's best for everyone? And how could we continue to trash the planet if we have a way to work together in thoughtfully adjusting our system?...

By itself the Creative Insight Council offers a giant leap forward for government. In conjunction with the Wisdom Council process, it's possible to structure an ongoing, whole-system, creative public conversation, where wise and thoughtful perspectives result. This offers the prospect of a different kind of democracy, with all of us involved and with all-of-us-together ultimately in charge. We call it a "Wise Democracy."

Sum

Our society is encountering a rising number of crises. To address them all of us must become involved. But it's difficult to imagine being involved when the forms of citizen participation are so limited. However, three social inventions—Dynamic Facilitation, the Creative Insight Council, and the Wisdom Council—make it possible for government to achieve a whole new level of citizen involvement. They make it enjoyable and productive for ordinary citizens with different views to come together to work on the biggest issues we face collectively.

A simple, safe, first step promising immediate benefits might be for government to convene a Creative Insight Council on a difficult topic in the community. As elected officials and community leaders recognize the benefits of this approach, their trust in the capabilities of "the people" will rise. Then it becomes easier for a citizen group or government to make the choice-creating conversation ongoing using the Wisdom Council process.

In this approach there is no coercion of any kind and no identifiable risk. There is simply a new conversation in place about the big issues, where people are listening to one another and being creative together.

Five Key Messages

1. This article suggests a new way to enlist the intelligence and creative capability of citizens to solve difficult issues.
2. This process starts when government faces a difficult issue and convenes a Creative Insight Council to address it.
3. The next step is when this new public conversation is set up to be ongoing through the Wisdom Council process.
4. Both of these new social inventions work because of the heartfelt, creative quality of conversation, "choice-creating."
5. Dynamic Facilitation is used to assure choice-creating within both processes."

What Kind of World Could We Have if Co-intelligence Ruled?

Through the World Cafe and Creative Insight Councils and Wisdom Councils and many other carefully structured processes, we have developed ways to have regular people look at what is going on. And there are ways to have what they come up with used to intervene, control, and regulate the obsessive tendencies of people in power to conform to what has been and to make others conform as well. Obsessive trea-ditionalists sometimes hold on to traditional approaches whether or not they have ever been or are currently functional for everyone concerned. Wouldn't it be a relief to know that you or other citizens might be called upon and capable of actually influencing public policy so that it is really public policy? What if we had a form of world government that had the people of the world actually govern?

And what if we don't come up with an interruption of the lack of evolution of the corporate controlled government machine? Take a little break from hard study now, and read a wonderfully crafted story, from which you may learn even more, but effortlessly.

CHAPTER 11

The Machine Stops:
A Story by E. M. Forster (1909)

(Every so often, an individual formulates an amazing prediction about the future that turns out to be such an accurate foretelling of what actually occurs that there is a temptation to attribute supernatural powers to him or her. This story by E. M. Forster, written one hundred years ago, is one of those amazing predictions. It allows us the chance to interrupt a pathway to doom, because it so graphically imagines the steps along the way. It was first published in The Oxford and Cambridge Review.[1]

This fine work of fiction integrates our view of what needs fixing about the fix we are in—Brad)

I—The Air-ship

Imagine, if you can, a small room, hexagonal in shape, like the cell of a bee. It is lighted neither by window nor by lamp, yet it is filled with a soft radiance. There are no apertures for ventilation, yet the air is fresh. There are no musical instruments, and yet, at the moment that my meditation opens, this room is throbbing with melodious sounds. An armchair is in the centre, by its side a reading desk—that is all the furniture. And in the armchair there sits a swaddled lump of flesh—a woman, about five feet high, with a face as white as a fungus. It is to her that the little room belongs.

An electric bell rang.

The woman touched a switch and the music was silent.

"I suppose I must see who it is," she thought, and set her chair in motion. The chair, like the music, was worked by machinery and it rolled her to the other side of the room where the bell still rang importunately.

"Who is it?" she called. Her voice was irritable, for she had been interrupted often since the music began. She knew several thousand people, in certain directions human intercourse had advanced enormously.

But when she listened into the receiver, her white face wrinkled into smiles, and she said:

"Very well. Let us talk, I will isolate myself. I do not expect anything important will happen for the next five minutes—for I can give you fully five minutes, Kuno. Then I must deliver my lecture on 'Music during the Australian Period.'"

She touched the isolation knob, so that no one else could speak to her. Then she touched the lighting apparatus, and the little room was plunged into darkness.

"Be quick!" she called, her irritation returning. "Be quick, Kuno; here I am in the dark wasting my time."

But it was fully fifteen seconds before the round plate that she held in her hands began to glow. A faint blue light shot across it, darkening to purple, and presently she could see the image of her son, who lived on the other side of the earth, and he could see her.

"Kuno, how slow you are."

He smiled gravely.

"I really believe you enjoy dawdling."

"I have called you before, mother, but you were always busy or isolated. I have something particular to say."

"What is it, dearest boy? Be quick. Why could you not send it by pneumatic post?"

"Because I prefer saying such a thing. I want—"

"Well?"

"I want you to come and see me."

Vashti watched his face in the blue plate.

"But I can see you!" she exclaimed. "What more do you want?"

"I want to see you not through the Machine," said Kuno. "I want to speak to you not through the wearisome Machine."

"Oh, hush!" said his mother, vaguely shocked. "You mustn't say anything against the Machine."

"Why not?"

"One mustn't."

"You talk as if a god had made the Machine," cried the other.

"I believe that you pray to it when you are unhappy. Men made it, do not forget that. Great men, but men. The Machine is much, but it is not everything. I see something like you in this plate, but I do not see you. I hear something like you through this telephone, but I do not hear you. That is why I want you to come. Pay me a visit, so that we can meet face to face, and talk about the hopes that are in my mind."

She replied that she could scarcely spare the time for a visit.

"The air-ship barely takes two days to fly between me and you."

"I dislike air-ships."

"Why?"

"I dislike seeing the horrible brown earth, and the sea, and the stars when it is dark. I get no ideas in an air-ship."

"I do not get them anywhere else."

"What kind of ideas can the air give you?" He paused for an instant.

"Do you not know four big stars that form an oblong, and three stars close together in the middle of the oblong, and hanging from these stars, three other stars?"

"No, I do not. I dislike the stars. But did they give you an idea? How interesting; tell me."

"I had an idea that they were like a man."

"I do not understand."

"The four big stars are the man's shoulders and his knees. The three stars in the middle are like the belts that men wore once, and the three stars hanging are like a sword."

"A sword?"

"Men carried swords about with them, to kill animals and other men."

"It does not strike me as a very good idea, but it is certainly original. When did it come to you first?"

"In the air-ship—" He broke off, and she fancied that he looked sad. She could not be sure, for the Machine did not transmit nuances of expression. It only gave a general idea of people—an idea that was good enough for all practical purposes, Vashti thought. The imponderable bloom, declared by a discredited philosophy to be the actual essence of intercourse, was rightly ignored by the Machine, just as the imponderable bloom of the grape was ignored by the manufacturers of artificial fruit. Something "good enough" had long since been accepted by our race.

"The truth is," he continued, "that I want to see these stars again. They are curious stars. I want to see them not from the air-ship, but from the surface of the earth, as our ancestors did, thousands of years ago. I want to visit the surface of the earth."

She was shocked again.

"Mother, you must come, if only to explain to me what is the harm of visiting the surface of the earth."

"No harm," she replied, controlling herself. "But no advantage. The surface of the earth is only dust and mud, no advantage. The surface of the earth is only dust and mud, no life remains on it, and you would need a respirator, or the cold of the outer air would kill you. One dies immediately in the outer air."

"I know; of course I shall take all precautions."

"And besides—"

"Well?"

She considered, and chose her words with care. Her son had a queer temper, and she wished to dissuade him from the expedition.

"It is contrary to the spirit of the age," she asserted.

"Do you mean by that, contrary to the Machine?"

"In a sense, but—"

His image in the blue plate faded.

"Kuno!"

He had isolated himself.

For a moment Vashti felt lonely.

Then she generated the light, and the sight of her room, flooded with radiance and studded with electric buttons, revived her. There were buttons and switches everywhere—buttons to call for food for music, for clothing. There was the hot-bath button, by pressure of which a basin of (imitation) marble rose out of the floor, filled to the brim with a warm deodorized liquid. There was the cold-bath button. There was the button that produced literature. And there were of course the buttons by which she communicated with her friends. The room, though it contained nothing, was in touch with all that she cared for in the world.

Vashti's next move was to turn off the isolation switch, and all the accumulations of the last three minutes burst upon her. The room was filled with the noise of bells, and speaking-tubes. What was the new food like? Could she recommend it? Has she had any ideas lately? Might one tell her one's own ideas? Would she make an engagement to visit the public nurseries at an early date? —say this day month.

To most of these questions she replied with irritation—a growing quality in that accelerated age. She said that the new food was horrible. That she could not visit the public nurseries through press of engagements. That she had no ideas of her own but had just been told one-that four stars and three in the middle were like a man: she doubted there was much in it. Then she switched off her correspondents, for it was time to deliver her lecture on Australian music.

The clumsy system of public gatherings had been long since abandoned; neither Vashti nor her audience stirred from their rooms. Seated in her armchair she spoke, while they in their armchairs heard her, fairly well, and saw her, fairly well. She opened with a humorous account of music in the pre Mongolian epoch, and went on to describe the great outburst of song that followed the Chinese conquest. Remote and primeval as were the methods of I-San-So and the Brisbane school, she yet felt (she said) that study of them might repay the musicians of today: they had freshness; they had, above all, ideas. Her lecture, which lasted ten minutes, was well received, and at its conclusion she and many of her audience listened to a lecture on the sea; there were ideas to be got from the sea; the speaker had donned a respirator and visited it lately. Then she fed, talked to many friends, had a bath, talked again, and summoned her bed.

The bed was not to her liking. It was too large, and she had a feeling for a small bed. Complaint was useless, for beds were of the same dimension all over the world, and to have had an alternative size would have involved vast alterations in the Machine. Vashti isolated herself-it was necessary, for neither day nor night existed under the ground-and reviewed all that had happened since she had summoned the bed last. Ideas? Scarcely any. Events - was Kuno's invitation an event?

By her side, on the little reading-desk, was a survival from the ages of litter - one book. This was the Book of the Machine. In it were instructions against every possible contingency. If she was hot or cold or dyspeptic or at a loss for a word, she went to the book, and it told her which button to press. The Central Committee published it. In accordance with a growing habit, it was richly bound.

Sitting up in the bed, she took it reverently in her hands. She glanced round the glowing room as if someone might be watching her. Then, half ashamed, half joyful, she murmured "O Machine! O Machine!" and raised the volume to her lips. Thrice she kissed it, thrice inclined her head, thrice she felt the delirium of acquiescence. Her ritual performed, she turned to page 1367, which gave the times of the departure of the air-ships from the island in the southern hemisphere, under whose soil she lived, to the island in the northern hemisphere, whereunder lived her son.

She thought, "I have not the time."

She made the room dark and slept; she awoke and made the room light; she ate and exchanged ideas with her friends, and listened to music and attended lectures; she make the room dark and slept. Above her, beneath her, and around her, the Machine hummed eternally; she did not notice the noise, for she had been born with it in her ears. The earth, carrying her, hummed as it sped through silence, turning her now to the invisible sun, now to the invisible stars. She awoke and made the room light.

"Kuno!"

"I will not talk to you." he answered, "until you come."

"Have you been on the surface of the earth since we spoke last?"

His image faded.

Again she consulted the book. She became very nervous and lay back in her chair palpitating. Think of her as without teeth or hair. Presently she directed the chair to the wall, and pressed an unfamiliar button. The wall swung apart slowly. Through the opening she saw a tunnel that curved slightly, so that its goal was not visible. Should she go to see her son, here was the beginning of the journey.

Of course she knew all about the communication-system. There was nothing mysterious in it. She would summon a car and it would fly with her down the tunnel until it reached the lift that communicated with the air-ship station: the system had been in use for many, many years, long before the universal establishment of the Machine. And of course she had studied the civilization that had immediately preceded her own—the civilization that had mistaken the functions of the system, and had used it for bringing people to things, instead of for bringing things to people. Those funny old days, when men went for change of air instead of changing the air in their rooms! And yet—she was frightened of the tunnel: she had not seen it since her last child was born. It curved—but not quite as she remembered; it was brilliant—but not quite as brilliant as a lecturer had suggested. Vashti was seized with the terrors of direct experience. She shrank back into the room, and the wall closed up again.

"Kuno," she said, "I cannot come to see you. I am not well."

Immediately an enormous apparatus fell on to her out of the ceiling, a thermometer was automatically laid upon her heart. She lay powerless. Cool pads soothed her forehead. Kuno had telegraphed to her doctor.

So the human passions still blundered up and down in the Machine. Vashti drank the medicine that the doctor projected into her mouth, and the machinery retired into the ceiling. The voice of Kuno was heard asking how she felt.

"Better." Then with irritation: "But why do you not come to me instead?"

"Because I cannot leave this place."

"Why?"

"Because, any moment, something tremendous many happen."

"Have you been on the surface of the earth yet?"

"Not yet."

"Then what is it?"

"I will not tell you through the Machine."

She resumed her life.

But she thought of Kuno as a baby, his birth, his removal to the public nurseries, her own visit to him there, his visits to her—visits which stopped when the Machine had assigned him a room on the other side of the earth. "Parents, duties of," said the book of the Machine, "cease at the moment of birth. P.422327483." True, but there was something special about Kuno—indeed there had been something special about all her children—and, after all, she must brave the journey if he desired it. And "something tremendous might happen." What did that mean? The nonsense of a youthful man, no doubt, but she must go. Again she pressed the unfamiliar button, again the wall swung back, and she saw the tunnel that curves out of sight. Clasping the Book, she rose, tottered on to the platform, and summoned the car. Her room closed behind her: the journey to the northern hemisphere had begun.

Of course it was perfectly easy. The car approached and in it she found armchairs exactly like her own. When she signaled, it stopped, and she tottered into the lift. One other passenger was in the lift, the first fellow creature she had seen face to face for months. Few travelled in these days, for, thanks to the advance of science, the earth was exactly alike all over. Rapid intercourse, from which the previous civilization had hoped so much, had ended by defeating itself. What was the good of going to Peking when it was just like Shrewsbury? Why return to Shrewsbury when it would all be like Peking? Men seldom moved their bodies; all unrest was concentrated in the soul.

The air-ship service was a relic from the former age. It was kept up, because it was easier to keep it up than to stop it or to diminish it, but it now far exceeded the wants of the population. Vessel after vessel would rise from the vomitories of Rye or of Christchurch (I use the antique names), would sail into the crowded sky, and would draw up at the wharves of the south—empty. So nicely adjusted was the system, so independent of meteorology, that the sky, whether calm or cloudy, resembled a vast kaleidoscope whereon the same patterns periodically recurred. The ship on which Vashti sailed started now at sunset, now at dawn. But always, as it passed above Rheas, it would neighbor the ship that served between Helsingfors and the Brazils, and, every third time it surmounted the Alps, the fleet of Palermo would cross its track behind. Night and day, wind and storm, tide and earthquake, impeded man no longer. He had harnessed Leviathan. All the old literature, with its praise of Nature, and its fear of Nature, rang false as the prattle of a child.

Yet as Vashti saw the vast flank of the ship, stained with exposure to the outer air, her horror of direct experience returned. It was not quite like the air-ship in the cinematophote. For one thing it smelt—not strongly or unpleasantly, but it did smell, and with her eyes shut she should have known that a new thing was close to her. Then she had to walk to it from the lift, had to submit to glances from the other passengers. The man in front dropped his Book—no great matter, but it disquieted them all. In the rooms, if the Book was dropped, the floor raised it mechanically, but the gangway to the air-ship was not so prepared, and the sacred volume lay motionless. They stopped—the thing was unforeseen—and the man, instead of picking up his property, felt the muscles of his arm to see how they had failed him. Then some one actually said with direct utterance: "We shall be late" —and they trooped on board, Vashti treading on the pages as she did so.

Inside, her anxiety increased. The arrangements were old- fashioned and rough. There was even a female attendant, to whom she would have to announce her wants during the voyage. Of course a revolving platform ran the length of the boat, but she was expected to walk from it to her cabin. Some cabins were better than others, and she did not get the best. She thought the attendant had been unfair, and spasms of rage shook her. The glass valves had closed, she could not go back. She saw, at the end of the vestibule, the lift in which she had ascended going quietly up and down, empty. Beneath those corridors of shining tiles were rooms, tier below tier, reaching far into the earth, and in each room there sat a human being, eating, or sleeping, or producing ideas. And buried deep in the hive was her own room. Vashti was afraid.

"O Machine!" she murmured, and caressed her Book, and was comforted.

Then the sides of the vestibule seemed to melt together, as do the passages that we see in dreams, the lift vanished, the Book that had been dropped slid to the left and vanished, polished tiles rushed by like a stream of water, there was a slight jar, and the air-ship, issuing from its tunnel, soared above the waters of a tropical ocean.

It was night. For a moment she saw the coast of Sumatra edged by the phosphorescence of waves, and crowned by lighthouses, still sending forth their disregarded beams. These also vanished, and only the stars distracted her. They were not motionless, but swayed to and fro above her head, thronging out of one skylight into another, as if the universe and not the air-ship was careening. And, as often happens on clear nights, they seemed now to be in perspective, now on a plane; now piled tier beyond tier into the infinite heavens, now concealing infinity, a roof limiting for ever the visions of men. In either case they seemed intolerable. "Are we to travel in the dark?" called the passengers angrily, and the attendant, who had been careless, generated the light, and pulled down the blinds of pliable metal. When the air-ships had been built, the desire to look direct at things still lingered in the world. Hence the extraordinary number of skylights and windows, and the proportionate discomfort to those who were civilized and refined. Even in Vashti's cabin one star peeped through a flaw in the blind, and after a few hers' uneasy slumber, she was disturbed by an unfamiliar glow, which was the dawn.

Quick as the ship had sped westwards, the earth had rolled eastwards quicker still, and had dragged back Vashti and her companions towards the sun. Science could prolong the night, but only for a little, and those high hopes of neutralizing the earth's diurnal revolution had passed, together with hopes that were possibly higher. To 'keep pace with the sun,' or even to outstrip it, had been the aim of the civilization preceding this. Racing aeroplanes had been built for the purpose, capable of enormous speed, and steered by the greatest intellects of the epoch. Round the globe they went, round and round, westward, westward, round and round, amidst humanity's applause. In vain. The globe went eastward quicker still, horrible accidents occurred, and the Committee of the Machine, at the time rising into prominence, declared the pursuit illegal, unmechanical, and punishable by Homelessness.

Of Homelessness more will be said later.

Doubtless the Committee was right. Yet the attempt to "defeat the sun" aroused the last common interest that our race experienced about the heavenly bodies, or indeed about anything. It was the last time that men were compacted by thinking of a power outside the world. The sun had conquered, yet it was the end of his spiritual dominion. Dawn, midday, twilight, the zodiacal path, touched neither men's lives not their hearts, and science retreated into the ground, to concentrate herself upon problems that she was certain of solving.

So when Vashti found her cabin invaded by a rosy finger of light, she was annoyed, and tried to adjust the blind. But the blind flew up altogether, and she saw through the skylight small pink clouds, swaying against a background of blue, and as the sun crept higher, its radiance entered direct, brimming down the wall, like a golden sea. It rose and fell with the air-ship's motion, just as waves rise and fall, but it advanced steadily, as a tide advances. Unless she was careful, it would strike her face. A spasm of horror shook her and she rang for the attendant. The attendant too was horrified, but she could do nothing; it was not her place to mend the blind. She could only suggest that the lady should change her cabin, which she accordingly prepared to do.

People were almost exactly alike all over the world, but the attendant of the airship, perhaps owing to her exceptional duties, had grown a little out of the common. She had often to address passengers with direct speech, and this had given her a certain roughness and originality of manner. When Vashti swerved away from the sunbeams with a cry, she behaved barbarically—she put out her hand to steady her.

"How dare you!" exclaimed the passenger. "You forget yourself!"

The woman was confused, and apologized for not having let her fall. People never touched one another. The custom had become obsolete, owing to the Machine.

"Where are we now?" asked Vashti haughtily.

"We are over Asia," said the attendant, anxious to be polite.

"Asia?"

"You must excuse my common way of speaking. I have got into the habit of calling places over which I pass by their unmechanical names."

"Oh, I remember Asia. The Mongols came from it."

"Beneath us, in the open air, stood a city that was once called Simla."

"Have you ever heard of the Mongols and of the Brisbane school?"

"No."

"Brisbane also stood in the open air."

"Those mountains to the right—let me show you them." She pushed back a metal blind. The main chain of the Himalayas was revealed. "They were once called the Roof of the World, those mountains."

"You must remember that, before the dawn of civilization, they seemed to be an impenetrable wall that touched the stars. It was supposed that no one but the gods could exist above their summits. How we have advanced, thanks to the Machine!"

"How we have advanced, thanks to the Machine!" said Vashti.

"How we have advanced, thanks to the Machine!" echoed the passenger who had dropped his Book the night before, and who was standing in the passage.

"And that white stuff in the cracks? —what is it?"

"I have forgotten its name."

"Cover the window, please. These mountains give me no ideas."

The northern aspect of the Himalayas was in deep shadow: on the Indian slope the sun had just prevailed. The forests had been destroyed during the literature epoch for the purpose of making newspaper-pulp, but the snows were awakening to their morning glory, and clouds still hung on the breasts of Kinchinjunga. In the plain were seen the ruins of cities, with diminished rivers creeping by their walls, and by the sides of these were sometimes the signs of vomitories, marking the cities of to day. Over the whole prospect air-ships rushed, crossing the inter-crossing with incredible aplomb, and rising nonchalantly when they desired to escape the perturbations of the lower atmosphere and to traverse the Roof of the World.

"We have indeed advance, thanks to the Machine," repeated the attendant, and hid the Himalayas behind a metal blind.

The day dragged wearily forward. The passengers sat each in his cabin, avoiding one another with an almost physical repulsion and longing to be once more under the surface of the earth. There were eight or ten of them, mostly young males, sent out from the public nurseries to inhabit the rooms of those who had died in various parts of the earth. The man who had dropped his Book was on the homeward journey. He had been sent to Sumatra for the purpose of propagating the race. Vashti alone was travelling by her private will.

At midday she took a second glance at the earth. The air-ship was crossing another range of mountains, but she could see little, owing to clouds. Masses of black rock hovered below her, and merged indistinctly into grey. Their shapes were fantastic; one of them resembled a prostrate man.

"No ideas here," murmured Vashti, and hid the Caucasus behind a metal blind.

In the evening she looked again. They were crossing a golden sea, in which lay many small islands and one peninsula. She repeated, "No ideas here," and hid Greece behind a metal blind.

II—The Mending Apparatus

By a vestibule, by a lift, by a tubular railway, by a platform, by a sliding door—by reversing all the steps of her departure did Vashti arrive at her son's room, which exactly resembled her own. She might well declare that the visit was superfluous. The buttons, the knobs, the reading-desk with the Book, the temperature, the atmosphere, the illumination—all were exactly the same. And if Kuno himself, flesh of her flesh, stood close beside her at last, what profit was there in that? She was too well-bred to shake him by the hand.

Averting her eyes, she spoke as follows:

"Here I am. I have had the most terrible journey and greatly retarded the development of my soul. It is not worth it, Kuno, it is not worth it. My time is too precious. The sunlight almost touched me, and I have met with the rudest people. I can only stop a few minutes. Say what you want to say, and then I must return."

"I have been threatened with Homelessness," said Kuno.

She looked at him now.

"I have been threatened with Homelessness, and I could not tell you such a thing through the Machine."

Homelessness means death. The victim is exposed to the air, which kills him.

"I have been outside since I spoke to you last. The tremendous thing has happened, and they have discovered me."

"But why shouldn't you go outside?" she exclaimed, "It is perfectly legal, perfectly mechanical, to visit the surface of the earth. I have lately been to a lecture on the sea; there is no objection to that; one simply summons a respirator and gets an Egression-permit. It is not the kind of thing that spiritually minded people do, and I begged you not to do it, but there is no legal objection to it."

"I did not get an Egression-permit."

"Then how did you get out?"

"I found out a way of my own."

The phrase conveyed no meaning to her, and he had to repeat it.

"A way of your own?" she whispered. "But that would be wrong."

'Why?"

The question shocked her beyond measure.

"You are beginning to worship the Machine," he said coldly.

"You think it irreligious of me to have found out a way of my own. It was just what the Committee thought, when they threatened me with Homelessness."

At this she grew angry. "I worship nothing!" she cried. "I am most advanced. I don't think you irreligious, for there is no such thing as religion left. All the fear and the superstition that existed once have been destroyed by the Machine. I only meant that to find out a way of your own was——Besides, there is no new way out."

"So it is always supposed."

"Except through the vomitories, for which one must have an Egression-permit, it is impossible to get out. The Book says so."

"Well, the Book's wrong, for I have been out on my feet."

For Kuno was possessed of a certain physical strength.

By these days it was a demerit to be muscular. Each infant was examined at birth, and all who promised undue strength were destroyed. Humanitarians may protest, but it would have been no true kindness to let an athlete live; he would never have been happy in that state of life to which the Machine had called him; he would have yearned for trees to climb, rivers to bathe in, meadows and hills against which he might measure his body. Man must be adapted to his surroundings, must he not? In the dawn of the world our weakly must be exposed on Mount Taygetus, in its twilight our strong will suffer euthanasia, that the Machine may progress, that the Machine may progress, that the Machine may progress eternally.

"You know that we have lost the sense of space. We say 'space is annihilated', but we have annihilated not space, but the sense thereof. We have lost a part of ourselves. I determined to recover it, and I began by walking up and down the platform of the railway outside my room. Up and down, until I was tired, and so did recapture the meaning of 'Near' and 'Far.' 'Near' is a place to which I can get quickly on my feet, not a place to which the train or the air-ship will take me quickly. 'Far' is a place to which I cannot get quickly on my feet; the vomitory is 'far,' though I could be there in thirty-eight seconds by summoning the train. Man is the measure. That was my first lesson. Man's feet are the measure for distance, his hands are the measure for ownership, his body is the measure for all that is lovable and desirable and strong. Then I went further: it was then that I called to you for the first time, and you would not come.

"This city, as you know, is built deep beneath the surface of the earth, with only the vomitories protruding. Having paced the platform outside my own room, I took the lift to the next platform and paced that also, and so with each in turn, until I came to the topmost, above which begins the earth. All the platforms were exactly alike, and all that I gained by visiting them was to develop my sense of space and my muscles. I think I should have been content with this—it is not a little thing—but as I walked and brooded, it occurred to me that our cities had been built in the days when men still breathed the outer air, and that there had been ventilation shafts for the workmen. I could think of nothing but these ventilation shafts. Had they been destroyed by all the food-tubes and medicine-tubes and music-tubes that the Machine has evolved lately? Or did traces of them remain? One thing was certain. If I came upon them anywhere, it would be in the railway-tunnels of the topmost storey. Everywhere else, all space was accounted for.

"I am telling my story quickly, but don't think that I was not a coward or that your answers never depressed me. It is not the proper thing, it is not mechanical, it is not decent to walk along a railway-tunnel. I did not fear that I might tread upon a live rail and be killed. I feared something far more intangible—doing what was not contemplated by the Machine. Then I said to myself, 'Man is the measure,' and I went, and after many visits I found an opening.

"The tunnels, of course, were lighted. Everything is light, artificial light; darkness is the exception. So when I saw a black gap in the tiles, I knew that it was an exception, and rejoiced. I put in my arm—I could put in no more at first—and waved it round and round in ecstasy. I loosened another tile, and put in my head, and shouted into the darkness: 'I am coming, I shall do it yet,' and my voice reverberated down endless passages. I seemed to hear the spirits of those dead workmen who had returned each evening to the starlight and to their wives, and all the generations who had lived in the open air called back to me, 'You will do it yet, you are coming.'"

He paused, and, absurd as he was, his last words moved her.

For Kuno had lately asked to be a father, and his request had been refused by the Committee. His was not a type that the Machine desired to hand on.

"Then a train passed. It brushed by me, but I thrust my head and arms into the hole. I had done enough for one day, so I crawled back to the platform, went down in the lift, and summoned my bed. Ah what dreams! And again I called you, and again you refused."

She shook her head and said: "Don't. Don't talk of these terrible things. You make me miserable. You are throwing civilization away."

"But I had got back the sense of space and a man cannot rest then. I determined to get in at the hole and climb the shaft. And so I exercised my arms. Day after day I went through ridiculous movements, until my flesh ached, and I could hang by my hands and hold the pillow of my bed outstretched for many minutes. Then I summoned a respirator, and started.

"It was easy at first. The mortar had somehow rotted, and I soon pushed some more tiles in, and clambered after them into the darkness, and the spirits of the dead comforted me. I don't know what I mean by that. I just say what I felt. I felt, for the first time, that a protest had been lodged against corruption, and that even as the dead were comforting me, so I was comforting the unborn. I felt that humanity existed, and that it existed without clothes. How can I possibly explain this? It was naked, humanity seemed naked, and all these tubes and buttons and machineries neither came into the world with us, nor will they follow us out, nor do they matter supremely while we are here. Had I been strong, I would have torn off every garment I had, and gone out into the outer air unswaddled. But this is not for me, nor perhaps for my generation. I climbed with my respirator and my hygienic clothes and my dietetic tabloids! Better thus than not at all.

"There was a ladder, made of some primeval metal. The light from the railway fell upon its lowest rungs, and I saw that it led straight upwards out of the rubble at the bottom of the shaft. Perhaps our ancestors ran up and down it a dozen times daily, in their building. As I climbed, the rough edges cut through my gloves so that my hands bled. The light helped me for a little, and then came darkness and, worse still, silence which pierced my ears like a sword. The Machine hums! Did you know that? Its hum penetrates our blood, and may even guide our thoughts. Who knows! I was getting beyond its power. Then I thought: 'This silence means that I am doing wrong.' But I heard voices in the silence, and again they strengthened me.' He laughed. 'I had need of them. The next moment I cracked my head against something.'"

She sighed.

"I had reached one of those pneumatic stoppers that defend us from the outer air. You may have noticed them on the air-ship. Pitch dark, my feet on the rungs of an invisible ladder, my hands cut; I cannot explain how I lived through this part, but the voices still comforted me, and I felt for fastenings. The stopper, I suppose, was about eight feet across. I passed my hand over it as far as I could reach. It was perfectly smooth. I felt it almost to the centre. Not quite to the centre, for my arm was too short. Then the voice said: 'Jump. It is worth it. There may be a handle in the centre, and you may catch hold of it and so come to us your own way. And if there is no handle, so that you may fall and are dashed to pieces—it is till worth it: you will still come to us your own way.' So I jumped. There was a handle, and—"

He paused. Tears gathered in his mother's eyes. She knew that he was fated. If he did not die today he would die tomorrow. There was not room for such a person in the world. And with her pity disgust mingled. She was ashamed at having borne such a son, she who had always been so respectable and so full of ideas. Was he really the little boy to whom she had taught the use of his stops and buttons, and to whom she had given his first lessons in the Book? The very hair that disfigured his lip showed that he was reverting to some savage type. On atavism the Machine can have no mercy.

"There was a handle, and I did catch it. I hung tranced over the darkness and heard the hum of these workings as the last whisper in a dying dream. All the things I had cared about and all the people I had spoken to through tubes appeared infinitely little. Meanwhile the handle revolved. My weight had set something in motion and I span slowly, and then—

"I cannot describe it. I was lying with my face to the sunshine. Blood poured from my nose and ears and I heard a tremendous roaring. The stopper, with me clinging to it, had simply been blown out of the earth, and the air that we make down here was escaping through the vent into the air above. It burst up like a fountain. I crawled back to it—for the upper air hurts—and, as it were, I took great sips from the edge. My respirator had flown goodness knows here, my clothes were torn. I just lay with my lips close to the hole, and I sipped until the bleeding stopped. You can imagine nothing so curious. This hollow in the grass—I will speak of it in a minute—the sun shining into it, not brilliantly but through marbled clouds—the peace, the nonchalance, the sense of space, and, brushing my cheek, the roaring fountain of our artificial air! Soon I spied my respirator, bobbing up and down in the current high above my head, and higher still were many air-ships. But no one ever looks out of air-ships, and in any case they could not have picked me up. There I was, stranded. The sun shone a little way down the shaft, and revealed the topmost rung of the ladder, but it was hopeless trying to reach it. I should either have been tossed up again by the escape, or else have fallen in, and died. I could only lie on the grass, sipping and sipping, and from time to time glancing around me.

"I knew that I was in Wessex, for I had taken care to go to a lecture on the subject before starting. Wessex lies above the room in which we are talking now. It was once an important state. Its kings held all the southern coast from the Andredswald to Cornwall, while the Wansdyke protected them on the north, running over the high ground. The lecturer was only concerned with the rise of Wessex, so I do not know how long it remained an international power, nor would the knowledge have assisted me. To tell the truth I could do nothing but laugh, during this part. There was I, with a pneumatic stopper by my side and a respirator bobbing over my head, imprisoned, all three of us, in a grass-grown hollow that was edged with fern."

Then he grew grave again. "Lucky for me that it was a hollow. For the air began to fall back into it and to fill it as water fills a bowl. I could crawl about. Presently I stood. I breathed a mixture, in which the air that hurts predominated whenever I tried to climb the sides. This was not so bad. I had not lost my tabloids and remained ridiculously cheerful, and as for the Machine, I forgot about it altogether. My one aim now was to get to the top, where the ferns were, and to view whatever objects lay beyond.

"I rushed the slope. The new air was still too bitter for me and I came rolling back, after a momentary vision of something grey. The sun grew very feeble, and I remembered that he was in Scorpio—I had been to a lecture on that too. If the sun is in Scorpio, and you are in Wessex, it means that you must be as quick as you can, or it will get too dark. (This is the first bit of useful information I have ever got from a lecture, and I expect it will be the last.) It made me try frantically to breathe the new air, and to advance as far as I dared out of my pond. The hollow filled so slowly. At times I thought that the fountain played with less vigour. My respirator seemed to dance nearer the earth; the roar was decreasing."

He broke off. "I don't think this is interesting you. The rest will interest you even less. There are no ideas in it, and I wish that I had not troubled you to come. We are too different, mother.

She told him to continue.

"It was evening before I climbed the bank. The sun had very nearly slipped out of the sky by this time, and I could not get a good view. You, who have just crossed the Roof of the World, will not want to hear an account of the little hills that I saw—low colorless hills. But to me they were living and the turf that covered them was a skin, under which their muscles rippled, and I felt that those hills had called with incalculable force to men in the past, and that men had loved them. Now they sleep—perhaps forever. They commune with humanity in dreams. Happy the man, happy the woman, who awakes the hills of Wessex. For though they sleep, they will never die."

His voice rose passionately. "Cannot you see, cannot all you lecturers see, that it is we that are dying, and that down here the only thing that really lives is the Machine? We created the Machine, to do our will, but we cannot make it do our will now. It has robbed us of the sense of space and of the sense of touch, it has blurred every human relation and narrowed down love to a carnal act, it has paralyzed our bodies and our wills, and now it compels us to worship it. The Machine develops—but not on our lies. The Machine proceeds—but not to our goal. We only exist as the blood corpuscles that course through its arteries, and if it could work without us, it would let us die. Oh, I have no remedy—or, at least, only one—to tell men again and again that I have seen the hills of Wessex as Ælfrid saw them when he overthrew the Danes.

"So the sun set. I forgot to mention that a belt of mist lay between my hill and other hills, and that it was the colour of pearl."

He broke off for the second time.

"Go on," said his mother wearily.

He shook his head.

"Go on. Nothing that you say can distress me now. I am hardened."

"I had meant to tell you the rest, but I cannot: I know that I cannot: good-bye."

Vashti stood irresolute. All her nerves were tingling with his blasphemies. But she was also inquisitive.

"This is unfair," she complained. "You have called me across the world to hear your story, and hear it I will. Tell me—as briefly as possible, for this is a disastrous waste of time—tell me how you returned to civilization."

"Oh—that!" he said, starting. "You would like to hear about civilization. Certainly. Had I got to where my respirator fell down?"

"No—but I understand everything now. You put on your respirator, and managed to walk along the surface of the earth to a vomitory, and there your conduct was reported to the Central Committee."

"By no means."

He passed his hand over his forehead, as if dispelling some strong impression. Then, resuming his narrative, he warmed to it again.

"My respirator fell about sunset. I had mentioned that the fountain seemed feebler, had I not?"

"Yes."

"About sunset, it let the respirator fall. As I said, I had entirely forgotten about the Machine, and I paid no great attention at the time, being occupied with other things. I had my pool of air, into which I could dip when the outer keenness became intolerable, and which would possibly remain for days, provided that no wind sprang up to disperse it. Not until it was too late did I realize what the stoppage of the escape implied. You see—the gap in the tunnel had been mended; the Mending Apparatus; the Mending Apparatus, was after me.

"One other warning I had, but I neglected it. The sky at night was clearer than it had been in the day, and the moon, which was about half the sky behind the sun, shone into the dell at moments quite brightly. I was in my usual place—on the boundary between the two atmospheres—when I thought I saw something dark move across the bottom of the dell, and vanish into the shaft. In my folly, I ran down. I bent over and listened, and I thought I heard a faint scraping noise in the depths.

"At this—but it was too late—I took alarm. I determined to put on my respirator and to walk right out of the dell. But my respirator had gone. I knew exactly where it had fallen—between the stopper and the aperture—and I could even feel the mark that it had made in the turf. It had gone, and I realized that something evil was at work, and I had better escape to the other air, and, if I must die, die running towards the cloud that had been the colour of a pearl. I never started. Out of the shaft—it is too horrible. A worm, a long white worm, had crawled out of the shaft and was gliding over the moonlit grass.

"I screamed. I did everything that I should not have done, I stamped upon the creature instead of flying from it, and it at once curled round the ankle. Then we fought. The worm let me run all over the dell, but edged up my leg as I ran. 'Help!' I cried. (That part is too awful. It belongs to the part that you will never know.) 'Help!' I cried. (Why cannot we suffer in silence?) 'Help!' I cried. When my feet were wound together, I fell, I was dragged away from the dear ferns and the living hills, and past the great metal stopper (I can tell you this part), and I thought it might save me again if I caught hold of the handle. It also was enwrapped, it also. Oh, the whole dell was full of the things. They were searching it in all directions, they were denuding it, and the white snouts of others peeped out of the hole, ready if needed. Everything that could be moved they brought—brushwood, bundles of fern, everything, and down we all went intertwined into hell. The last things that I saw, ere the stopper closed after us, were certain stars, and I felt that a man of my sort lived in the sky. For I did fight, I fought till the very end, and it was only my head hitting against the ladder that quieted me. I woke up in this room. The worms had vanished. I was surrounded by artificial air, artificial light, artificial peace, and my friends were calling to me down speaking-tubes to know whether I had come across any new ideas lately."

Here his story ended. Discussion of it was impossible, and Vashti turned to go.

"It will end in Homelessness," she said quietly.

"I wish it would," retorted Kuno.

"The Machine has been most merciful."

"I prefer the mercy of God."

"By that superstitious phrase, do you mean that you could live in the outer air?"

"Yes."

"Have you ever seen, round the vomitories, the bones of those who were extruded after the Great Rebellion?"

"Yes."

"They were left where they perished for our edification. A few crawled away, but they perished, too—who can doubt it? And so with the Homeless of our own day. The surface of the earth supports life no longer."

"Indeed."

"Ferns and a little grass may survive, but all higher forms have perished. Has any air-ship detected them?"

"No."

"Has any lecturer dealt with them?"

"No."

"Then why this obstinacy?"

"Because I have seen them," he exploded.

"Seen what?"

"Because I have seen her in the twilight—because she came to my help when I called—because she, too, was entangled by the worms, and, luckier than I, was killed by one of them piercing her throat."

He was mad. Vashti departed, nor, in the troubles that followed, did she ever see his face again.

III—The Homeless

During the years that followed Kuno's escapade, two important developments took place in the Machine. On the surface they were revolutionary, but in either case men's minds had been prepared beforehand, and they did but express tendencies that were latent already.

The first of these was the abolition of respirators.

Advanced thinkers, like Vashti, had always held it foolish to visit the surface of the earth. Air-ships might be necessary, but what was the good of going out for mere curiosity and crawling along for a mile or two in a terrestrial motor? The habit was vulgar and perhaps faintly improper: it was unproductive of ideas, and had no connection with the habits that really mattered. So respirators were abolished, and with them, of course, the terrestrial motors, and except for a few lecturers, who complained that they were debarred access to their subject-matter, the development was accepted quietly. Those who still wanted to know what the earth was like had after all only to listen to some gramophone, or to look into some cinematophote. And even the lecturers acquiesced when they found that a lecture on the sea was nonetheless stimulating when compiled out of other lectures that had already been delivered on the same subject.

"Beware of first-hand ideas!" exclaimed one of the most advanced of them. "First-hand ideas do not really exist. They are but the physical impressions produced by life and fear, and on this gross foundation who could erect a philosophy? Let your ideas be second-hand, and if possible tenth-hand, for then they will be far removed from that disturbing element—direct observation. Do not learn anything about this subject of mine—the French Revolution. Learn instead what I think that Enicharmon thought Urizen thought Gutch thought Ho-Yung thought Chi-Bo-Sing thought Lafcadio Hearn thought Carlyle thought Mirabeau said about the French Revolution. Through the medium of these ten great minds, the blood that was shed at Paris and the windows that were broken at Versailles will be clarified to an idea which you may employ most profitably in your daily lives. But be sure that the intermediates are many and varied, for in history one authority exists to counteract another. Urizen must counteract the scepticism of Ho-Yung and Enicharmon, I must myself counteract the impetuosity of Gutch. You who listen to me are in a better position to judge about the French Revolution than I am. Your descendants will be even in a better position than you, for they will learn what you think I think, and yet another intermediate will be added to the chain. And in time" —his voice rose— "there will come a generation that had got beyond facts, beyond impressions, a generation absolutely colorless, a generation seraphically free from taint of personality, which will see the French Revolution not as it happened, nor as they would like it to have happened, but as it would have happened, had it taken place in the days of the Machine."

Tremendous applause greeted this lecture, which did but voice a feeling already latent in the minds of men—a feeling that terrestrial facts must be ignored, and that the abolition of respirators was a positive gain. It was even suggested that air-ships should be abolished too. This was not done, because air-ships had somehow worked themselves into the Machine's system. But year by year they were used less, and mentioned less by thoughtful men.

The second great development was the re-establishment of religion.

This, too, had been voiced in the celebrated lecture. No one could mistake the reverent tone in which the peroration had concluded, and it awakened a responsive echo in the heart of each. Those who had long worshipped silently, now began to talk. They described the strange feeling of peace that came over them when they handled the Book of the Machine, the pleasure that it was to repeat certain numerals out of it, however little meaning those numerals conveyed to the outward ear, the ecstasy of touching a button, however unimportant, or of ringing an electric bell, however superfluously.

"The Machine," they exclaimed, "feeds us and clothes us and houses us; through it we speak to one another, through it we see one another, in it we have our being. The Machine is the friend of ideas and the enemy of superstition: the Machine is omnipotent, eternal; blessed is the Machine." And before long this allocution was printed on the first page of the Book, and in subsequent editions the ritual swelled into a complicated system of praise and prayer. The word "religion" was sedulously avoided, and in theory the Machine was still the creation and the implement of man. But in practice all, save a few retrogrades, worshipped it as divine. Nor was it worshipped in unity. One believer would be chiefly impressed by the blue optic plates, through which he saw other believers; another by the mending apparatus, which sinful Kuno had compared to worms; another by the lifts, another by the Book. And each would pray to this or to that, and ask it to intercede for him with the Machine as a whole. Persecution—that also was present. It did not break out, for reasons that will be set forward shortly. But it was latent, and all who did not accept the minimum known as "undenominational Mechanism" lived in danger of Homelessness, which means death, as we know.

To attribute these two great developments to the Central Committee is to take a very narrow view of civilization. The Central Committee announced the developments, it is true, but they were no more the cause of them than were the kings of the imperialistic period the cause of war. Rather did they yield to some invincible pressure, which came no one knew whither, and which, when gratified, was succeeded by some new pressure equally invincible. To such a state of affairs it is convenient to give the name of progress. No one confessed the Machine was out of hand. Year by year it was served with increased efficiency and decreased intelligence. The better a man knew his own duties upon it, the less he understood the duties of his neighbor, and in all the world there was not one who understood the monster as a whole. Those master brains had perished. They had left full directions, it is true, and their successors had each of them mastered a portion of those directions. But Humanity, in its desire for comfort, had over-reached itself. It had exploited the riches of nature too far. Quietly and complacently, it was sinking into decadence, and progress had come to mean the progress of the Machine.

As for Vashti, her life went peacefully forward until the final disaster. She made her room dark and slept; she awoke and made the room light. She lectured and attended lectures. She exchanged ideas with her innumerable friends and believed she was growing more spiritual. At times a friend was granted euthanasia, and left his or her room for the homelessness that is beyond all human conception. Vashti did not much mind. After an unsuccessful lecture, she would sometimes ask for Euthanasia herself. But the death rate was not permitted to exceed the birth rate, and the Machine had hitherto refused it to her.

The troubles began quietly, long before she was conscious of them.

One day she was astonished at receiving a message from her son. They never communicated, having nothing in common, and she had only heard indirectly that he was still alive, and had been transferred from the northern hemisphere, where he had behaved so mischievously, to the southern—indeed, to a room not far from her own.

"Does he want me to visit him?" she thought. "Never again, never. And I have not the time."

No, it was madness of another kind.

He refused to visualize his face upon the blue plate, and speaking out of the darkness with solemnity said:

"The Machine stops."

"What do you say?"

"The Machine is stopping, I know it, I know the signs."

She burst into a peal of laughter. He heard her and was angry, and they spoke no more.

"Can you imagine anything more absurd?" she cried to a friend. "A man who was my son believes that the Machine is stopping. It would be impious if it was not mad."

"The Machine is stopping?" her friend replied. "What does that mean? The phrase conveys nothing to me."

"Nor to me."

"He does not refer, I suppose, to the trouble there has been lately with the music?"

"Oh no, of course not. Let us talk about music."

"Have you complained to the authorities?"

"Yes, and they say it wants mending, and referred me to the Committee of the Mending Apparatus. I complained of those curious gasping sighs that disfigure the symphonies of the Brisbane school. They sound like some one in pain. The Committee of the Mending Apparatus say that it shall be remedied shortly."

Obscurely worried, she resumed her life. For one thing, the defect in the music irritated her. For another thing, she could not forget Kuno's speech. If he had known that the music was out of repair—he could not know it, for he detested music—if he had known that it was wrong, "the Machine stops" was exactly the venomous sort of remark he would have made. Of course he had made it at a venture, but the coincidence annoyed her, and she spoke with some petulance to the Committee of the Mending Apparatus.

They replied, as before, that the defect would be set right shortly.

"Shortly! At once!" she retorted. "Why should I be worried by imperfect music? Things are always put right at once. If you do not mend it at once, I shall complain to the Central Committee."

"No personal complaints are received by the Central Committee," the Committee of the Mending Apparatus replied.

"Through whom am I to make my complaint, then?"

"Through us."

"I complain then."

"Your complaint shall be forwarded in its turn."

"Have others complained?"

This question was unmechanical, and the Committee of the Mending Apparatus refused to answer it.

"It is too bad!" she exclaimed to another of her friends.

"There never was such an unfortunate woman as myself. I can never be sure of my music now. It gets worse and worse each time I summon it."

"What is it?"

"I do not know whether it is inside my head, or inside the wall."

"Complain, in either case."

"I have complained, and my complaint will be forwarded in its turn to the Central Committee."

Time passed, and they resented the defects no longer. The defects had not been remedied, but the human tissues in that latter day had become so subservient, that they readily adapted themselves to every caprice of the Machine. The sigh at the crises of the Brisbane symphony no longer irritated Vashti; she accepted it as part of the melody. The jarring noise, whether in the head or in the wall, was no longer resented by her friend. And so with the moldy artificial fruit, so with the bath water that began to stink, so with the defective rhymes that the poetry machine had taken to emit. All were bitterly complained of at first, and then acquiesced in and forgotten. Things went from bad to worse unchallenged.

It was otherwise with the failure of the sleeping apparatus. That was a more serious stoppage. There came a day when over the whole world—in Sumatra, in Wessex, in the innumerable cities of Courland and Brazil—the beds, when summoned by their tired owners, failed to appear. It may seem a ludicrous matter, but from it we may date the collapse of humanity. The Committee responsible for the failure was assailed by complainants, whom it referred, as usual, to the Committee of the Mending Apparatus, who in its turn assured them that their complaints would be forwarded to the Central Committee. But the discontent grew, for mankind was not yet sufficiently adaptable to do without sleeping.

"Someone is meddling with the Machine—" they began.

"Someone is trying to make himself king, to reintroduce the personal element."

"Punish that man with Homelessness."

"To the rescue! Avenge the Machine! Avenge the Machine!"

"War! Kill the man!"

But the Committee of the Mending Apparatus now came forward, and allayed the panic with well-chosen words. It confessed that the Mending Apparatus was itself in need of repair.

The effect of this frank confession was admirable.

"Of course," said a famous lecturer—he of the French Revolution, who gilded each new decay with splendour— "of course we shall not press our complaints now. The Mending Apparatus has treated us so well in the past that we all sympathize with it, and will wait patiently for its recovery. In its own good time it will resume its duties. Meanwhile let us do without our beds, our tabloids, our other little wants. Such, I feel sure, would be the wish of the Machine."

Thousands of miles away his audience applauded. The Machine still linked them. Under the seas, beneath the roots of the mountains, ran the wires through which they saw and heard, the enormous eyes and ears that were their heritage, and the hum of many workings clothed their thoughts in one garment of subserviency. Only the old and the sick remained ungrateful, for it was rumored that Euthanasia, too, was out of order, and that pain had reappeared among men.

It became difficult to read. A blight entered the atmosphere and dulled its luminosity. At times Vashti could scarcely see across her room. The air, too, was foul. Loud were the complaints, impotent the remedies, heroic the tone of the lecturer as he cried: "Courage! Courage! What matter so long as the Machine goes on? To it the darkness and the light are one." And though things improved again after a time, the old brilliancy was never recaptured, and humanity never recovered from its entrance into twilight. There was an hysterical talk of "measures," of "provisional dictatorship," and the inhabitants of Sumatra were asked to familiarize themselves with the workings of the central power station, the said power station being situated in France. But for the most part panic reigned, and men spent their strength praying to their Books, tangible proofs of the Machine's omnipotence. There were gradations of terror—at times came rumors of hope-the Mending Apparatus was almost mended—the enemies of the Machine had been got under—new "nerve-centers" were evolving which would do the work even more magnificently than before. But there came a day when, without the slightest warning, without any previous hint of feebleness, the entire communication-system broke down, all over the world, and the world, as they understood it, ended.

Vashti was lecturing at the time and her earlier remarks had been punctuated with applause. As she proceeded the audience became silent, and at the conclusion there was no sound. Somewhat displeased, she called to a friend who was a specialist in sympathy. No sound: doubtless the friend was sleeping. And so with the next friend whom she tried to summon, and so with the next, until she remembered Kuno's cryptic remark, "The Machine stops."

The phrase still conveyed nothing. If Eternity was stopping it would of course be set going shortly.

For example, there was still a little light and air—the atmosphere had improved a few hours previously. There was still the Book, and while there was the Book there was security.

Then she broke down, for with the cessation of activity came an unexpected terror—silence.

She had never known silence, and the coming of it nearly killed her —it did kill many thousands of people outright. Ever since her birth she had been surrounded by the steady hum. It was to the ear what artificial air was to the lungs, and agonizing pains shot across her head. And scarcely knowing what she did, she stumbled forward and pressed the unfamiliar button, the one that opened the door of her cell.

Now the door of the cell worked on a simple hinge of its own. It was not connected with the central power station, dying far away in France. It opened, rousing immoderate hopes in Vashti, for she thought that the Machine had been mended. It opened, and she saw the dim tunnel that curved far away towards freedom. One look, and then she shrank back. For the tunnel was full of people—she was almost the last in that city to have taken alarm.

People at any time repelled her, and these were nightmares from her worst dreams. People were crawling about, people were screaming, whimpering, gasping for breath, touching each other, vanishing in the dark, and ever and anon being pushed off the platform on to the live rail. Some were fighting round the electric bells, trying to summon trains that could not be summoned. Others were yelling for euthanasia or for respirators, or blaspheming the Machine. Others stood at the doors of their cells fearing, like herself, either to stop in them or to leave them. And behind all the uproar was silence—the silence which is the voice of the earth and of the generations who have gone.

No—it was worse than solitude. She closed the door again and sat down to wait for the end. The disintegration went on, accompanied by horrible cracks and rumbling. The valves that restrained the Medical Apparatus must have weakened, for it ruptured and hung hideously from the ceiling. The floor heaved and fell and flung her from the chair. A tube oozed towards her serpent fashion. And at last the final horror approached—light began to ebb, and she knew that civilization's long day was closing.

She whirled around, praying to be saved from this, at any rate, kissing the Book, pressing button after button. The uproar outside was increasing, and even penetrated the wall. Slowly the brilliancy of her cell was dimmed, the reflections faded from the metal switches. Now she could not see the reading-stand, now not the Book, though she held it in her hand. Light followed the flight of sound, air was following light, and the original void returned to the cavern from which it has so long been excluded. Vashti continued to whirl, like the devotees of an earlier religion, screaming, praying, striking at the buttons with bleeding hands. It was thus that she opened her prison and escaped—escaped in the spirit: at least so it seems to me, ere my meditation closes. That she escapes in the body—I cannot perceive that. She struck, by chance, the switch that released the door, and the rush of foul air on her skin, the loud throbbing whispers in her ears, told her that she was facing the tunnel again, and that tremendous platform on which she had seen men fighting. They were not fighting now. Only the whispers remained, and the little whimpering groans. They were dying by hundreds out in the dark.

She burst into tears.

Tears answered her.

They wept for humanity, those two, not for themselves. They could not bear that this should be the end. Ere silence was completed their hearts were opened, and they knew what had been important on the earth. Man, the flower of all flesh, the noblest of all creatures visible, man who had once made god in his image, and had mirrored his strength on the constellations, beautiful naked man was dying, strangled in the garments that he had woven. Century after century had he toiled, and here was his reward. Truly the garment had seemed heavenly at first, shot with colours of culture, sewn with the threads of self-denial. And heavenly it had been so long as man could shed it at will and live by the essence that is his soul, and the essence, equally divine, that is his body. The sin against the body—it was for that they wept in chief; the centuries of wrong against the muscles and the nerves, and those five portals by which we can alone apprehend—glazing it over with talk of evolution, until the body was white pap, the home of ideas as colorless, last sloshy stirrings of a spirit that had grasped the stars.

"Where are you?" she sobbed.

His voice in the darkness said, "Here."

"Is there any hope, Kuno?"

"None for us."

"Where are you?"

She crawled over the bodies of the dead. His blood spurted over her hands.

"Quicker," he gasped, "I am dying—but we touch, we talk, not through the Machine."

He kissed her.

"We have come back to our own. We die, but we have recaptured life, as it was in Wessex, when Ælfrid overthrew the Danes. We know what they know outside, they who dwelt in the cloud that is the color of a pearl."

"But Kuno, is it true? Are there still men on the surface of the earth? Is this—tunnel, this poisoned darkness—really not the end?"

He replied: "I have seen them, spoken to them, loved them. They are hiding in the midst and the ferns until our civilization stops. Today they are the Homeless—tomorrow—"

"Oh, tomorrow—some fool will start the Machine again, tomorrow."

"Never," said Kuno, "never. Humanity has learnt its lesson."

As he spoke, the whole city was broken like a honeycomb. An air-ship had sailed in through the vomitory into a ruined wharf. It crashed downwards, exploding as it went, rending gallery after gallery with its wings of steel. For a moment they saw the nations of the dead, and, before they joined them, scraps of the untainted sky.

Now and Then, Someone Seems to Hit the Nail on the Head

This story was written one hundred years ago. This was written one hundred years ago. This man wrote this insightful vision of the future, a full one hundred years ago...and I think this quote, in particular, speaks out to us from both the past and the future:

"Cannot you see, cannot all you lecturers see, that it is we that are dying, and that down here the only thing that really lives is the Machine? We created the Machine, to do our will, but we cannot make it do our will now. It has robbed us of the sense of space and of the sense of touch, it has blurred every human relation and narrowed down love to a carnal act, it has paralyzed our bodies and our wills, and now it compels us to worship it. The Machine develops—but not on our lies. The Machine proceeds—but not to our goal. We only exist as the blood corpuscles that course through its arteries, and if it could work without us, it would let us die. Oh, I have no remedy—or, at least, only one—to tell men again and again that I have seen the hills of Wessex..."

Can We Be as Brilliant Together as E. M. Forester was Alone?

Let's continue this story and write at it's end, a new beginning, about which someone will say, a hundred years from now, two or three times, "My God! This was written a hundred years ago!"

PART THREE

What's the Big Idea?

Earth Song
By Michael Jackson[1]

What about sunrise?
What about rain?
What about all the things
That you said we were to gain?
What about killing fields?
Is there a time?
What about all the things
That you said was yours and mine?
Did you ever stop to notice
All the blood we've shed before?
Did you ever stop to notice
The crying Earth, the weeping shores?

Aaaaaaaaaah Aaaaaaaaaah

What have we done to the world
Look what we've done

What about all the peace
That you pledge your only son?
What about flowering fields?
Is there a time?
What about all the dreams
That you said were yours and mine?
Did you ever stop to notice
All the children dead from war?
Did you ever stop to notice
The crying Earth, the weeping shores?

Aaaaaaaaaah Aaaaaaaaaah

I used to dream
I used to glance beyond the stars
Now I don't know where we are
Although I know we've drifted far
Aaaaaaaaaah Aaaaaaaaaaah Aaaaaaaaaah
Aaaaaaaaaah
Hey, what about yesterday?
(What about us)
What about the seas?
(What about us)
The heavens are falling down
(What about us)
I can't even breathe
(What about us)
What about the bleeding Earth?
(What about us)
Can't we feel its wounds?
(What about us)
What about nature's worth?
(ooo,ooo)
It's our planet's womb
(What about us)
What about animals?
(What about it)
We've turned kingdoms to dust
(What about us)
What about elephants?
(What about us)

Have we lost their trust?
(What about us)
What about crying whales?
(What about us)
We're ravaging the seas
(What about us)
What about forest trails?
(ooo, ooo)
Burnt despite our pleas
(What about us)
What about the holy land
(What about it)
Torn apart by creed?
(What about us)
What about the common man
(What about us)
Can't we set him free?
(What about us)
What about children dying
(What about us)
Can't you hear them cry?
(What about us)
Where did we go wrong?
(ooo, ooo)
Someone tell me why
(What about us)
What about babies?
(What about it)
What about the days?
(What about us)
What about all their joy?
(What about us)
What about the man?
(What about us)
What about the crying man?
(What about us)
What about Abraham?
(What was us)
What about death again?
(ooo, ooo) Do we give a damn?

If—
By Rudyard Kipling[2]

If you can keep your head when all about you
Are losing theirs and blaming it on you,
If you can trust yourself when all men doubt you,
But make allowance for their doubting too;
If you can wait and not be tired by waiting,
Or being lied about, don't deal in lies,
Or being hated, don't give way to hating,
And yet don't look too good, nor talk too wise:

If you can dream—and not make dreams your master;
If you can think—and not make thoughts your aim;
If you can meet with Triumph and Disaster
And treat those two impostors just the same;
If you can bear to hear the truth you've spoken
Twisted by knaves to make a trap for fools,
Or watch the things you gave your life to broken,
And stoop and build 'em up with worn out tools:

If you can make one heap of all your winnings
And risk it on one turn of pitch-and-toss,
And lose, and start again at your beginnings
And never breathe a word about your loss;
If you can force your heart and nerve and sinew
To serve your turn long after they are gone,
And so hold on when there is nothing in you
Except the Will which says to them: 'Hold on!'

If you can talk with crowds and keep your virtue,
Or walk with kings—nor lose the common touch,
If neither foes nor loving friends can hurt you,
If all men count with you, but none too much;
If you can fill the unforgiving minute
With sixty seconds' worth of distance run—
Yours is the Earth and everything that's in it,
And—which is more—you'll be a Man my son!

CHAPTER 12

A Simple Question:
How Can We Heal or Replace the Collective Mental Illness Called Corporate Capitalist Civilization?

"Symptoms may shift and particular forms of dis-ease may be exchanged for others. The basic condition remains. Transformation of society is the only real cure."

—George Leonard

What follows here is George Leonard's description of the work of Fritz Perls, who trained me in Gestalt therapy, and whose work is central to the work I do with individuals, couples, families, and groups, and from which Radical Honesty is an extension.

To begin to answer the mega question—what's the big idea? —that makes up the primary focus of this third section of the book, I want to focus on some smaller questions that lead us to information usable in creating the big answer. The questions for the beginning of this chapter and for the beginning of some dialogue and deliberation sessions among us, as we continue to think this thing through together, are:

How can we integrate into ongoing life in society the same kind of opportunity for family or institutional growth as we are capable of offering for personal growth for individuals? (How do we have an ongoing growing therapeutic community?)

Can ongoing opportunities for the re-enlightenment for citizens be designed into society itself (ongoing education and renewal)?

Can personal growth and spiritual renewal, having to do with the primacy of observing, noticing, describing, and sharing—over thinking—be converted into a collective therapeutic transformation of society itself? Is there a therapeutic social renewal that repeats itself, one which renews the perspective on life for participants in the society?

To answer these more general questions about a new therapeutic social order we need to start by taking a good look at how psychotherapy works at an individual level. So as background, to shed light on all these questions, here is George Leonard talking about Fritz Perls.

George Leonard on Fritz Perls[1]

Frederick S. Perls, the founder of Gestalt therapy, was a master showman. He was also a master craftsman. Even his critics have had to grant that he could get to the heart of a neurosis with stunning speed and accuracy. We are not privileged to view Freud at work with his patients. Even if electronic recording devices had been widely available in his time, Freud's mode of treatment probably would have precluded their use. Perls, on the other hand, believed that the presence of a group or even a large audience is necessary, for one thing, to keep the therapist honest.

Thousands of people watched him work, and his sessions were recorded on hundreds of hours of tape, videotape, and film before his death in 1970. His dreamwork demonstrations were particularly spectacular, since he would work with his "victim" before a sizable audience, making explanatory asides at key points in the procedure much in the manner of a surgeon describing a tricky operation to a group of medical men in a surgical theater. Those in the audience could see, in a few minutes, just how much a person loves his neurosis, how desperately he clings to it, how cunningly he manipulates the environment to keep it propped up, how he will resort to charm, humor, intelligence, deafness, blindness, dumbness, confusion, pity, outrage, amnesia, anything to avoid the loss of this, his most precious possession, his adored disease.

[I will insert commentary occasionally in parentheses referring to the analogy between social structures and personality structures. What George Leonard refers to here is at the heart of Fritz Perls brand of gestalt therapy. Entropy, or resistance to change of something one is attached to whether it is functional or not, is as true of the institutions of society as of suffering, self-torturing individuals. We have our collective conspiracies to keep things the same whether they work or not—take Congress, for example—please! People en masse are as attached to resisting social structural change as they are to changing their individual neuroses. —Brad]

A pleasant sense of anticipation pervaded the dining room at Esalen Institute on the California Coast on those nights when Perls was scheduled to give one of his demonstrations. Tables were quickly cleared away. A partition was moved to expand the gallery where he would perform. Chairs were set up and a fire was built in the large brick fireplace at the end of the room. As soon as the doors were opened the room would fill to overflowing. Perls, an Old Testament prophet in a white jump suit, would take his place on a low platform near the fireplace. In addition to his easy chair, the platform was provided with two empty straight chairs—one the "hot seat" for the victim, the other a place where the victim would sit while enacting one of the phantom cast of characters with which he keeps his neurosis alive and active.

After a brief talk, Perls would ask for volunteers. About a third of the hundred or so people present generally would raise their hands, eager to be diagnosed, dissected, and stripped of their most intimate pretenses before curious onlookers. A victim would mount the platform, take the hot seat, and start to describe a dream. Perls would miss nothing. He would find clues, not just in the cognitive content of the words, but in the voice, the gestures, the breathing, and the posture. Sometimes he would make the victim aware of what his hands were doing, and then ask for a dialogue between the right and the left.

Sometimes, hearing different tones of voice in different situations, he would create a dialogue between, for instance, the victim's whining voice and his domineering voice. The victim would move from one chair to the other as he played the two parts. The dream itself would come alive in a reconstituted present tense. Instead of talking about the people and things in the dream, the victim would be asked to become each person and thing; the dream, after all, is entirely his and every element in it some aspect of his being.

Perls often commented that a neurotic is someone who does not see the obvious. He would make the obvious explicit, then cut off the escape routes the victim may have painstakingly and cleverly maintained over the years. Relentlessly, Perls would follow the trail that leads directly to the neurosis. If the victim began trembling, Perls would have him "go into" the trembling, exaggerate it, personify it. He would never shy away from the victim's anxiety or terror; he took this to be a very good sign that he was nearing a neurotic center.

Finally the moment would come when the victim's escape routes were entirely cut off, when all the props that had supported the neurosis had been knocked out. Perls called this moment "the impasse." Here the victim is offered the opportunity for an existential leap past the neurosis, a sort of death of the ego structure and a rebirth, however temporary, into a state of pure being in the here and now. The impasse is a moment of high drama. Getting past it demands a headlong dive into unfamiliar waters.

Once Perls brought a heavy stammerer to the impasse by having him increase his stammer. As he stammered, Perls asked him what he felt in his throat. "I feel like choking myself," he answered. Perls gave him his arm and said, "Now, choke me." "God damn," the man said, "I could kill you." As his anger became explicit, his stammer disappeared. He spoke loudly, without difficulty. Perls pointed out that he now had an existential choice, to be an angry man or a stammerer.

These short demonstrations were by no means cures. But they were often remarkably powerful. They cast doubt on the efficacy, and the real function, of the five-year long, five-day-a-week therapies.

I once saw Perls bring a handsome and ingratiating young man to his impasse in a period of about fifteen minutes. Within ten minutes it was perfectly obvious to everyone in the room except the victim that he was keeping himself in a constant condition of dis-ease with a fear—clearly a false fear—of homosexuality. He was unwilling to confront this simple fact. His chief escape modes, his ways of squirming around the truth, were charm and humor. Fritz cut these out from under him. There was a tiger in the young man's dream, snarling and clawing up at him from a deep ditch. But when he became the tiger, the snarls and threats were less than frightening. The tiger was paper. The fear was false.

We may balk at accepting the fact that a person wouldn't be quite happy to realize that his worst fear is false. But that is almost always the case when it is part of a neurosis. As the charming young man was brought closer and closer to the truth, he was overcome with dismay. His once mobile, ingratiating countenance became blank. His memory failed. He couldn't hear what Perls was saying to him. At this point Perls turned to the audience and, in a classic aside, murmured, "Ah, the impasse!" The victim broke through in a flood of tears.

The next morning, I met the young man walking on the edge of the cliff by the sea. His face was transformed, no longer ingratiating or "charming." His smile was fresh and real. He had the soft, tremulous, vulnerable look of one reborn. And all this from one fifteen-minute demonstration. How often I have seen that look on the faces of friends and family who have had the good fortune to experience the little transformations that are offered at Esalen. I have seen how beautiful people can be. And I have seen that beauty fade within a period of weeks after reentry into the world we so thoughtlessly call "real."

One Friday evening in the autumn of 1967, I came home to find a stranger sitting in the middle of my living room rug. I recognized him soon enough as one of my closest friends, Leo Litwak, who had driven straight from Big Sur after a five-day encounter experience with William Schutz. Litwak's early years as child of a labor leader in Detroit had been far from tranquil. His World War II service as a medic with General George Patton's forces in Europe was by all odds the most harrowing I had ever heard. These formative experiences, along with his long study of Western philosophy, had contributed to a habitual expression that lay between sadness and skepticism. But now he simply shimmered. His eyes—there is no other way to say it—were like stars. When he rose to embrace me, I had an impression of a butterfly just emerging from a cocoon—moist, trembling, and unquestionably newborn. Later, Litwak described his experience for *The New York Times Magazine*. The article has since appeared in over a dozen anthologies and remains one of the very best written on a subject that generally defies graceful description. Its final paragraph speaks directly to the subject of this chapter: The condition of vulnerability is precious and very fragile. Events and people and old routines and old habits conspire to bring you down. But not all the way down.

There is still the recollection of that tingling sense of being wide-awake, located in the here and now, feeling freely and entirely, all constraints discarded. It remains a condition to be realized. It could change the way we live. I, too, have experienced that tingling sense of being wide-awake. And I have felt it fade under the relentless, often unrealized pressures of daily existence. Much criticism of some of the early Esalen-type experiences [Gestalt, encounter, sensory awakening —Brad] has centered on the proposition that they "don't last."

Of course they don't last. *It becomes painfully obvious that no one can live safely and successfully in civilized society without some kind of going numb defense. [The words are George Leonard's, the italics mine. —Brad]* This is the heart of the matter for both individual personality change from dysfunctional to functional. It is the place where social change and personal change are intimately related.

It is also obvious that some sort of long-term psychotherapy is needed to effect what is generally termed a "cure" for a neurotic condition. The Esalen experiences, despite some popular misunderstanding, were never meant to "cure" people who consider themselves "sick." But let us ask what the usual long-term therapy really accomplishes. It certainly does not take very long to isolate a neurosis and cast it out. Perls, among others, has demonstrated this point again and again. Diagnosing and casting out neuroses, however, is by no means the basic function of most psychotherapy. According to Perls, "Anybody who goes to a therapist has something up his sleeve. I would say roughly 90 percent don't go to a therapist to be cured, but to be more adequate in their neurosis."

Let us at least consider this possibility: that the main function of the conventional therapies is not curing the patient of neurosis, but helping him build, polish, tune up, and test a new neurosis to replace the old. The new neurosis will continue to keep the patient discontented with his own being *[so that he will be successful in civilization—Brad])*, but it will do so in a manner that is more acceptable to himself and those around him.

[So becoming acceptable enough to fit into a sick society is a primary goal of the conspiracy between therapist and client. Clearly, in the realm of politics and social change the same principle applies. —Brad]

What Can We Do to Heal Ourselves of the Social Disease Called Corporate Capitalist Civilization?

This ending insight by George Leonard that the main purpose of conventional therapies are to make people stay sick enough to maintain civility (and thus civilization), do their jobs, and keep their mouths shut. Why can't we just up and decide to remake civilization so people are not so ill and unhappy trying to force themselves to fit? Could we possibly reform civilization through healing people of the effects of civilization and have them pass it on, and renew it on an ongoing basis? How could we have this work on personal growth provided for citizens and have it result in the evolution of culture?

One possible design for deepening organized community living and making our whole social life more gratifying, growing and self healing in every way is to develop community and personal health models that support each other. How do we do this? How do we heal people both individually and collectively at almost the same time?"

Gene Marshall and I have been talking about this...

Gene: The face-to-face work that you do and I do is so important in enabling real changes in personal lives.

However, I want to dialogue further with you about social-change vision, strategy, and action.

Brad: Thanks Gene!

The vision of a possible and viable future seems first to require an acknowledgement of what didn't work or no longer works. Then we need proposals and experiments to invent/discover some new ways for humans to live together—and for consciousness to enhance, rather than wipe out the living conditions of people and other living beings.

Gene: On this we entirely agree.

Brad: Given that all diagnoses are reductionist, we have to use the best combinations of simplistic thinking to undermine faith in what used to work, or the way things used to work, and demythologize the past. In individual and couple's therapy participants have to come to the impasse where they acknowledge that continual persistence in trying to make the unworkable work has to be given up on. I think when you talk about how to throw a monkey wrench into the "machine" of social habit so we all have a "wrenching experience" is good for our mutual disenchantment and the opportunity for mutual new beginnings. And I agree that having diagnosed what is now dysfunctional, whether or not it once was, we need to spread the word of the possibility for renewal. And now that we can predict the likely downfall or destruction of our form of life if we persist in our old ways, we need to come up with a vision for a functional, less destructive model that is not just reactionary (to tribal times) or excluding of the advances of deadly civilization. We want to hold on to certain scraps from the demise of what once worked, but works no more, to cannibalize, if we can, certain still useable parts, like electricity, for example. And that is what I would like to have more dialogue about

Gene: Me too.

Brad: As you know, I am fascinated with the healing potential of deep democracy based on honest sharing. And I am convinced that co-hearted co-intelligence in a context of honesty is a cut or two deeper than being civilized in the usual obedient neurotic survivalist mode. And I think the egalitarianism of being to being sharing that creates the possibility of co-hearted co-intelligence and everyone participating in inventing and modifying new social forms on an ongoing basis, is the best game in town. That's why we are discussing co-consciousness, or the love that nurtures and kills and renews, as the fundamental path to psychological as well as social healing.

Co-consciousness that comes from co-operation and co-facilitation, mutual honesty, forgiveness, and support for change like that provided in AA and similar groups is a fine model for social reform. This means, I think, people getting used to being in charge one day and a servant of others in charge the next, while life flows on. We had this for a while in Haight-Ashbury in San Francisco in the Sixties, and for a while in the Seventies all over the country. We were renewed, awake, happy, and making new social reforms on an hourly basis then. In hopes that recalling what it was like to be in a climate of social reform based on liberation from pre-existing frames of mind, here is an excerpt from my autobiography, *Some New Kind of Trailer Trash* (Sparrowhawk Press, 2011):

I was in San Francisco at the Peace Rally at Kezar Stadium, and in the march to the stadium and away from the stadium. This was at beginning of the massive protests against the war in Vietnam and the spark that was the start to what became the summer of love in Haight-Ashbury that year.

I don't know how we did it except by sheer numbers. We were many tens of thousands strong and we were fed up with all the bullshit about the war and anti-communism and a dozen other things about conventional society and we had experienced altered states of consciousness and we knew that we knew things people older than us just didn't know. We were people who could not be dominated by conventional forces, and the police and the government didn't really know what to do with us. So they made agreements with us to keep the peace. We made a deal with the cops that they would remain entirely outside the stadium while we had our rally and concert inside. We didn't want to be interfered with for smoking pot, being too loud, getting out of hand, cursing the fucking establishment, or any goddamned, jack leg fucking excuse the cops might come up with to interfere with us.

Everyone was there from The Fillmore—Janice, The Dead, The Airplane… and many more. There was a big bandstand in the middle of the stadium with sound that reverberated throughout. There were 70,000 hippies packed in there. As we walked among the bleachers to find a seat, people handed us a joint and we'd take a toke and hand it to the next person down the row. Then we would take a toke from the next person and pass it on to the the next person. The whole damned stadium had a cloud of marijuana smoke inside and above it. It was a peace rally as well as an anti-war rally. Everyone was high and everyone was happy. Everyone was dancing and the stadium was rocking, and I do mean rocking—shaking, bouncing, moving, and maybe near to collapsing. We were in there four or five hours—all afternoon.

When the concert, speeches, dancing, and singing were over, we streamed out of there and headed for the park and Haight-Ashbury. As we streamed toward the Haight there were a few people walking toward us though the flow of people—the Provos (They were a group that started in Amsterdam, just creating social services for people in general for free—like putting out bicycles and maintaining them so people could just ride all over town and leave the bikes wherever they got to and someone else who needed to go somewhere else could take it and go). The Provos were wearing big black hats like Abraham Lincoln used to wear, and they took them off and turned them up to collect money. They held out their hats and said, "If you need money take some. If you have money put some in."

People were doing that. And it worked! People who had money put it in and people who needed some took it out. Every hippy in San Francisco had food and a place to stay that night! We made sure of it! And for a while there, at least through that summer (I went back later in "the summer of love" for a about a month), there was an economy of love and sharing that really worked. I can't tell you how wonderful it was.

My brother Jimmy was living there then, too, and many friends of mine from Texas. Everyone rode free bycicles to wherever they were going and dropped them off there, and others took them and went where they wanted. The Provos re-distributed bikes and repaired them and kept things going. People hitchhiked all over the city and all over California. If you had a car, you gave people rides. If you wanted to go somewhere, you went out on the road and stuck your thumb out.

Sometimes, traveling during those days, people would give everything they owned to each other. I had a hitchhiker in a car I was driving say to me, "I think I'll leave you this back pack. I've had it for a while." I said, "Great, take mine," and he did.

Once me and my friend Jim were driving up to Mendocino from San Francisco and we picked up a hitchhiker who was headed for Las Vegas. He told us he was going to see his mom who was very sick. When we got to the turn off toward Nevada, Jim pulled over, reached into the glove box, took out the title to the car, signed it, and handed it to the hitchhiker. He said, "I think your need to see your mom is more pressing than any we have. You take the car. We'll hitch the rest of the way." And we did.

Once, at another time (I can't remember all the times completely clearly because I was stoned a lot. That's why we say, "If you remember the 60's you must not have been there."), I was down somewhere south of Big Sur, off Highway One, a few miles up a creek called Bear Creek. There were a bunch of people there (from a dozen to about twenty as the group ebbed and flowed) without any clothes on all day and all night. We would sleep in sleeping bags under the open air or sometimes in tents. Every day at about noon we would gather at the fire site and draw straws. Two people who got short straws would have to go put on some clothes and get the sack and the sign (the sign said, "FOOD"), and walk the couple of miles out to the highway and hold the sign up at one of the pulloffs. People would stop, we would drink a beer and smoke a joint with them, and they would leave something for us to put in the sack—something to eat or get high on.

At around five or six o'clock, the two people would bring the sack back, we would all open the cans, cut up the veggies, add a little water and salt and throw in the dope into the big cook pot over the fire. When it got hot, or it seemed the right time, we would eat the food and wait to see what happened to us. I remember one day when we woke up we had all the sleeping bags unzipped and either under us or over us covering everyone in the group. We thought we might have had an orgy the night before, but nobody could remember.

I remember meeting an ex-Episcopal priest there, who had just quit preaching and become a hippie. He was kind of making his way down Highway One in no particular hurry to get anywhere.

One night, there at Bear Creek, sitting around the fire talking and playing the guitar, at one of the lulls in the music I noticed the earring the fellow across from me had in his ear. "I like that earring," I said. "It looks good on you." He stood up, came over to me, and took another earring out of his pocket like the one he was wearing. He also had a needle. He stuck the needle through my ear, and inserted the earring. I thanked him, and laughed and bled a little. I kept that earring right there for several years.

You might say we were all very interested in the possibility of what could be a new way of living together for human beings. We didn't know what it would be, but we figured it was more a matter of discovery than thinking, so we went about investigating and researching alternative ways of living.

So this is a kind of hippy-dippy vision from me, a former stoner in Haight-Ashbury who lives alone in a tent on a hill from which he can see the downfall of man and the birth of "some new beast, it's time come round at last... stumbling toward Bethlehem to be born."

Gene: I love that poem. It has always been the monastics, contemplatives, and other outcasts of the current social consensus who live in a locus of consciousness that enables them to be relatively objective about both past and future and therefore create new possibilities that have long-range promise.

Brad: One mind in charge is usually a terrible thing, but a bunch of minds of people who love and are in love can correct the tendency of that one-minded way of being, and guard against the extremes of injustice of our learned, civilized, mentally ill ways of being.

So here is the simple question: What is the best governmental, economic, and educational structure for the ongoing re-creation of agreements, laws, standards, and modes of operation that maximizes the possibility of happiness, security, freedom, and love between and among human beings and their sentient contemporaries so that joy happens a lot throughout life for most sentient beings—and co-hearted, co-intelligent, co-consciousness rules?

Gene: Yes, you are describing a group of people that I call "the invisible league (or church)." It is invisible because no human being knows the boundaries of this league. But we discover one another from time to time and our co-hearted, co-intelligent, co-conscious conversations build the consensus that can be taught to the awakening masses and thereby empower cultural, political, and economic institutions, and change the course of history.

Brad: My vision is not clear, but it looks like government by a whole bunch of World Cafés in comedy clubs all over the world, televised and analyzed on the nightly news.

Gene: Here I want to insert a bit of caution. We must not confuse government with the invisible league. The governmental establishment is always "next to last," never the first part of society to embrace new innovations. Lincoln, for example, was not the first wave of slavery abolition, but the next to last. The last stage was cleaning up through law and order the stubborn minority who still resisted this massive change. The first stage is represented by people like Frederick Douglas and other abolitionists who slaved away during many earlier decades. This principle also applies to our current political situation. The Obama administration is the next to last stage of a set of change directions that are now a couple of decades old. The current invisible league is a decade or more ahead of what the Obama administration will be clear about or politically able to do.

Brad: Well, your analysis is eloquent and undoubtedly accurate as an understanding of how things have worked in the past. The problem is that there is an escalation of entropy here that we can't afford to let follow its natural course. Jeremy Rifkin, in *The Empathic Civilization* says that though we humans have become increasingly empathic, as we have evolved, because of many things that had us being with and learning more about each other. One thing, over the last hundred years or so, was electricity, which let us know so much more about each other and our commonality. But the very advances that made this possible have built up an entropic debt of such proportions that by the time we get to complete empathy or "atmospheric consciousness," we will have killed ourselves with the pollution from corporatocracy-controlled nation-states which created a deadly mess while creating the possibility of empathy. This is ironic to such a degree that we may only be able to exit laughing and crying at the same time. Real comedians are real tragedians anyway, and when the joke is so much on us we may just die laughing.

Mutually admired, appalled, laughed at, and taken with a grain of salt, we stumble on together, drunk on God, and occasional other substances. Cheerful Easy Laughter Church Court Legislature is in session, and they are discussing fart jokes on the way to modifying the interest rates and taxes for the next quarter, in preparation for building mass graves. My point is, either the invisible league catches up with the government (or the government speeds up in recognizing the wisdom of the invisible league) or we all die laughing and vice versa.

My view of the way around this hilarious tragic end to life as we know it is to structure into government an early warning system for creative, disruptive, but life-sustaining ideas.

As different World Cafés are conducted to focus on major questions, and ideas are brought forth, they are formulated into referenda for the public to vote up or down every six weeks. Those passed would be carried out by elected representatives who actually would get paid to serve the public for limited terms (no professional politicians). Sometimes the collective of people who come up with brilliant ideas get hired for a while longer and are assigned to manage bringing into being what they dreamed up. Then there could be referenda on what people think about the job they do and/or did once it is over. Talk shows and comedy routines would get the word out about what is in process and what's coming up in the way of referenda.

Gene: Here you are talking about the tactics of various organizations of the invisible league, not the government.

Brad: No, that would have been true in the past, but will no longer be true in the future. There would be two weeks of open voting on the Internet using fingerprint and voiceprint identification. In my vision, commentary is also requested and made public—blogged about and summarized on the news—over the course of the two weeks of open voting before the count is taken. Once everyone who wants to, votes something in, the comedy cafés and the short-term elected representatives hire, assign, and accept volunteers to do the job.

Gene: Now you are talking about governmental structures. But I do not trust Internet voting. I think we need to continue going to polling places, and every part of the voting process needs to be supervised carefully by people not just machines. Also, I have a preference for conventions as a replacement for ballot boxes wherever that is practical. Certainly this works well for electing delegates to state and national party conventions.

I have a wider point that is not clearly articulated so far in this dialogue. Government is a power structure using specific rules of law and order, punishments, and coercive force (where needed) to enforce the consensus that has already been arrived at through the democratic discussion we want to vastly increase and empower. We need democratically-founded government institutions to enforce the last stage of any progressive change as well as preserve previous progressive changes from being revoked. This governmental role is needed in spite of the fact any empowered government that does this job will be behind the times and, thus, act as a block to be overcome in making the next sequence of progressive changes. This, dynamic, I believe, is just a tragic given within human history.

Brad: I think this is brilliant and probably accurate, and still it seems very sad and fated to fail in this time of escalating crisis. And I don't want to accept it... I do think a better design could lessen the problem. I still want the invisible league to become visible much more quickly and it's benefits put into place more efficiently, and I want the maintainers of social order replaced more rapidly. Just because you have accurately described the way this has functioned in past history doesn't mean it must persist into the future. What if the invisible league governed?

Gene: These governmental-to-invisible-league relationships are not being clearly understood by the more libertarian and hippy-happy elements of the invisible league. If we want actually to win, we have to learn how to work this relationship realistically.

Brad: Well a lot of new thought has to be funny and brilliant and applicable quickly. Comedians rule! Everyone's a comedian! That can be our call to each other's arms!

Gene: Yes, comedians are crucial in the life of the invisible league. And governmental officials also need a broad sense of humor. But we have to describe the role of statesperson as something more than a comedian sort of role. It includes competent, courageous, careful, step-by-step decision-making within the always ambiguous, but deadly serious options of history.

Brad: Okay, I agree. We can keep a few serious noses to the grindstone. We can have committed, hard working people around as long as we can crack a lot of jokes about them, and replace them periodically when we thank them, retire them, and provide for them in gratitude. Thanks for this whole dialogue.

CHAPTER 13

Radical Honesty as a Prelude to Deep Democracy: The Antidote for Compliant Cowardice

So far there is still no real honesty in politics. No politician is honest with another in public. People in political roles shun honesty. And honesty is what is needed in order to transform politics into effective action in the real world, and to iron things out with a sense of irony. That is a dilemma for the ages, and also for the end of the human experiment.

People who lie to protect their images are not very funny. And they are boring. Hitler and Bush and Cheney, for example, were simply not very amusing. In fact, except for their unbelievable destructiveness, they were very, very boring. Not the kind of folks you would want to hang out with. Image-protecting people, like these men, know how to be hateful and dominate, but they have no idea of how actually to handle conflict so that resolution occurs. Hateful thoughts and hateful actions remain. They are all perfomance and no connection, no substance.

In my work with people in conflict in Radical Honesty groups I encourage people to go ahead and have conflict out loud, to cuss and holler and raise hell, but not to fight physically. Then I coach them to get very specific about what they resent about each other by naming exactly the behavior that pissed them off and expressing it by saying, at whatever volume seems appropriate to the level of energy they are experiencing, "I resent you for... (and fill in the blank with a specific named behavior that both people can remember). We find that in conversations between individuals who are angry at each other, when the honest expression of resentment and open disagreement and all attending emotion are expressed contactfully—meaning, they are attended to and experienced as sensation in the body—the information and the experience can be shared and gotten over at the same time. The process of experiencing the experience in the presence of the other person, with nothing repressed, and having the expression of it vociferous and intense, allows it to increase, then decrease, then go away *as a sensate experience.*

This is how forgiveness occurs. Forgiveness occurs through losing your mind and coming to your senses—where you attend to experienced sensation first, and thought second. When people on both "sides" experience the bodily sensate experience in their own bodies and see the intensity of experience on the other side, the issues that used to divide can then serve as a beginning point of mutual recognition and a new dialogue, and the mutual co-creation of a solution.

Dialogue after forgiveness almost always ends up being truly brilliant, creative, and accepted by people not as compromise, but as transformation and co-creation. It is the benefit of the process of intense, honest, contactful self expression, mutual recognition and forgiveness.

That is why I say non-violent communication (NVC) is bullshit system of rationalization that never resolves anything and seldom leads to any authentic forgiveness. Obama's phony attempt to be open to, and "communicate with" the stupid, brainwashed, sold-out, asshole, cowardly Blue Dog Democrats and shit-for-brains Republicans—is another fine example of how well compromise without full self-expression works. It sucks! People who start out with the intent to compromise are not virtuous; they are stupid. Watching any of Obama's "summits" can show you that in a minute or two. They would better be called "valleys."

Our next excerpt is an essay, which is a fine example of something in writing that, if expressed face to face with a Republican, would be a good start. First, the global accusations about behavior and intent could be expressed just as they are in what follows. Then, as the Republicans come back with their own accusations, the fight would get more specific. If both "sides" stood in for the entire comeback until it was fully vented, they could be coached to be more and more specific. This kind of open conflict and sticking to it until it is done could lead to actual creative results and authentic solutions, rather than total bullshit legislation like the fucking train wreck called the "health care bill" where in 2010 bribery won and the people lost again and a lot of poor people are dying from it as we speak.

Until Obama and the dumb-assed Blue Dog Democrats start out this way, no real creativity will occur and compromise, even if reached, will still be dissatisfying to everyone except the rich bastards who make a profit from it, and keep us sick literally and figuratively as individuals and as a society. We need something much more creative and therapeutic than compromise. We need confrontation, personal transformation, and mutual social transformation.

Here is a fine article that would make for a good beginning of a dialogue between actual Democrats and actual Republicans (including the Republicans still in the Democratic Party).

Subject: Dear Republicans[1]

Fuck you. No, I'm not joking. I'm sick of this bullshit.

I'm sick of the way you've corrupted the public discourse. The way you've made it acceptable to hurl any insult you like at public officials. The way you blame us for the current atmosphere of hatred by accusing us of starting it with hating Bush. Like Bush didn't come on the heels of eight years of your tireless efforts to destroy Clinton by any means necessary, like Bush didn't give us good reason to complain. A couple of posters on a website compared Bush to Hitler and you've used it as free license to compare Obama to Hitler 24/7 and I'm sick of your hypocrisy, where it's acceptable to say shit about Obama that you would have had an apoplectic fit (and did) if anything remotely similar had been said about your guys. Keith Olbermann calls Cheney a fascist when he was actually using fascist tactics and you think that gives you the freedom to call Obama a fascist, socialist, Marxist constantly for no reason at all. Fuck you and your bullshit false equivalency.

I'm sick of the way you've made the populace stupid. Around a fifth of your populace thinks the sun orbits the earth, over half think evolution never happened. Your populace actually believes the media has a liberal bias. Not because it has, we have the most conservative media in the free world, but because you've shouted it so loud and so often that you've brainwashed the public into believing it, like the battered wife who parrots her husband's insults. You've got a whole segment of the populace shouting about socialism and fascism and none of them know what the fucking words mean. You've convinced them that fascism is a left-wing thing. You've got them so turned around that some of them actually believe global warming isn't happening. Fuck you.

I'm sick of the way you try to destroy the whole concept of government. You've tricked the people into believing that government can't do anything right, always being careful to exclude the army because you love your bullets and bombs, but you've so destroyed the public's ability to reason that they don't even think of interstate highways, the space program, the national parks program, and so on. Government is always great when it's doing what you tell it, and inevitably corrupt when it isn't. Fuck you.

I'm sick of your rewriting of history. You've bleated so loud and long that Reagan was a great president, that the New Deal didn't work, that cutting taxes increases revenues, that you actually have the people believing this bullshit. And these are the same people who will go on to become teachers and fill their student's heads with this self-same bullshit. Reagan was a mediocre president at best, who had the good fortune to be in power when the USSR collapsed under it's own weight, and you bastards have turned him into the Second Coming. You've rewritten history so that everything foul and hateful and wrong can be attributed to a Democrat while everything worthwhile is a Republican's glory. Fuck you.

I'm sick of your dragging the center ever further to the right. How many whack job fringe ideas have you dragged into the mainstream, such as the aforementioned idea that tax cuts increase revenues, the Laffer Curve, the idea that welfare harms the poor, the idea that there's rampant fraud in welfare, and the idea that whatever is good for corporations is good for the country? You push these ideas through your corporate media and you do it so long and so loudly that they become part of the accepted political landscape. And then, because it is easier to tell a lie than to debunk one, we never get away from this rancid shit. Fuck you.

I'm sick of your casual criminality. Teddy Kennedy, a man who's boots you were not worthy to lick, was just buried and all I've heard from my rightist friends for days is Chappaquiddick, Chappaquiddick, Chappaquiddick. Your fucking golden boy, George Bush, raped the Constitution, mainly because he wanted to; tortured random people (and water boarding is torture, fuck you, too) essentially because he wanted to; spent like a drunken sailor, essentially because he wanted to; invaded a sovereign nation, essentially for the loot (and in the process destroyed people's lives), and you bastards are obsessed with a fucking accident a Democrat had decades ago? You don't go on about Laura Bush killing some guy decades ago. Fuck you.

I'm sick of you praising pure evil. You're letting Dick Cheney be the standard-bearer for Republicanism. Dick Cheney, a man so nakedly evil that even his friends call him "Darth," a man so callous that Lex Luthor would recoil in terror; a man who probably has dismembered hitchhikers in those man-sized safes, and kills plants by his mere proximity. Fuck you.

I'm sick of your attempts to tilt the playing field permanently in your favor. Democrats filibustered a few of Bush's most hateful judicial picks and you pricks started screaming about doing away with the filibuster, but now while you're in the minority, you're filibustering absolutely everything you can and whining when you don't get the chance. You ignored everything the Democrats had to say when you had power and now that you don't, you scream that everyone must be bipartisan. You don't budge a fucking inch on anything, but you insist that everyone else must compromise to meet you. That's your idea of politics: Don't move an inch, force the other guy to come to the right to meet you, and call the result a "compromise." Fuck you.

I'm sick of your corporatism. You dress it up in false populism but anyone with half a brain can see that you're the bought and paid for subsidiary of big business. You keep pushing tax cuts as the answer for absolutely everything. You keep sabotaging every attempt to control the excesses of big business. You genuinely think the world would be a better place if it was a combination of Bill Gibson's dystopian vision of a corporate dominated world and Ayn Rand's bullshit objectivism, yet another entry in mankind's endless attempts to find a moral justification for naked greed.

You've taken the clinically insane spewing of a woman literally to the right of Hitler (pardon my Godwins) and the 1984-like vision of a dystopian author and convinced yourselves that would be a good place to live.

Big business is the enemy of the people, always has been. The ideal for the corporate class is to have a small pool of people rich enough to buy their fucking crap and a much larger pool of people so poor and with so few options that they can be used and abused at the corporation's whim. A corporation's objective is not to look after you; it is to make ever-larger profits by any means necessary.

You bastards want to reinstate fucking slavery to the corporate class and you've made the public so fucking stupid that they actually swallow the bullshit you're serving up, they actually want to enslave themselves to the corporations that abuse them at every turn. They actually care more about the corporations right to make obscene profits than they care about their children's right to live on a habitable planet. Fuck you.

Fuck you, you scum-ridden shite hawks. You make me sick. Just fuck off and die."

Curses that Precede Forgiveness

Now that is what I call a good start! There is a potential beginning of a real dialogue! Though at a mostly name-calling stage, all that happens in this kind of communication is the first volley of loosening up and heading for the truth. It is inpiring to me and would be to all parties concerned! When everybody wakes up and comes alive and sticks with it good things happen! This is a necessary first beginning. What follows this in a committed environment for resolution would be—eventually—forgiveness and co-creation.

Compromise is bullshit. If we decided to eat the biggest liar each day, along with the world's uber-rich, we might modify the tendency to bullshit our way around things rather than deal with them. ("Eating a liar a day keeps the doctor away.") Until people have honest vociferous disagreements and yell, holler, cuss, and name-call for quite a while (but stay on task nevertheless), no real change can occur. If we did this intensely and on purpose, it could take us only days, instead of years, to reach powerful, creative solutions. There is no way around doing it because without feeling our way through to forgiveness our creativity is so hampered as to be almost nonexistent.

Authentic dialogue and deliberation must first be authentic. Without authenticity—communicating with exact, descriptive language and to the degree of intensity that is accurate for all involved—there can be no dialogue and deliberation that leads to anything that will work or last.

I hate most corporate executive billionaires. Well, at least all but the 40 or so who recently agreed to give most of their fortunes away to charities of their choosing. I can't get close enough to any of them to forgive them. Of course I think if you've got any goddamned sense, you hate them too. But think of the fine conversation we might have with the folks at these corporations found to be the worst of 2008, coming up in the next chapter—just in case we don't get to kill and eat them but actually have to re-create the social structures of the world with them.

CHAPTER 14

Examples of Corporate Hardheartedness and Irresponsibility: The Opposite of Empathy

"When plunder becomes a way of life for a group of men living together in society, they create for themselves in the course of time a legal system that authorizes it and a moral code that justifies it."

—Frederic Bastiat

"America now has far more people in its prisons than on its farms. One percent of Americans farm for a living. Two and one half percent of Americans are in prisons, and several times that number are on parole or being monitored by the U.S. prison systems (Pew Research Center). As to the farms that remain, about 8 percent of America's farms, the megafarms of agribiz, produce 75.5 percent of agricultural products (measured by dollars). The rest, the little guys attempting to farm, are people holding fulltime jobs and essentially farming on the side, though they hate to describe it that way."

—Joe Bageant

Stanley Milgram's research says that the nature of human beings is irredeemable because they act, and always will act, in obedience to external authority whether or not that authority contradicts their own personal values—that obedience and fear trumps, and will always trump, personal integrity.

George Monbiot says we are living in the Age of Coercion and that our only hope for survival is to bring about the Age of Consent that is worldwide, not mediated by nation-states, and has the selfish interests of sub-segments of humankind under the control of some form of democracy. He thinks a worldwide democratic revolution, though imperfect, is the only alternative to being doomed by corporate-state capitalism. He says that without a global transformation, national transformations are impossible. His attempted solution is to put corporate and state in opposition to each other, and to keep the balance of power, somehow, slightly in favor of government.

Here is one brief, summary assertion from Monbiot's book *The Age of Consent* (HarperPerennial, 2004): "Democracy is unattainable unless it is brokered by institutions, mandated by the people and made accountable to them, whose primary purpose is to prevent the strong from oppressing the weak and to prevent people of all stations from resolving their differences by means of violence. The collective noun for such institutions is government. So democratic government, of one kind or another, appears to be the least bad system we can envisage. It is the unhappy lot of humankind that an attempt to develop a least-worst system emerges as the highest ideal for which we can strive. But if democracy is the only system that could deliver the Age of Consent we seek, we immediately meet a paradox. The reason why democratic governance is more likely to deliver justice than anarchism is that it possesses the capacity for coercion: the rich and powerful can be restrained, by the coercive measures of the state, from oppressing the rest of us."[1]

The problem is, as Monbiot says, "The global citizen, whose class interests extend beyond the state (and are seldom represented by the state), is left without influence over the way the global economy develops.... Our task is surely not to overthrow globalization, but to capture it, and to use it as a vehicle for humanity's first global democratic revolution."[2]

Sheeple Pleasers

The problem here is that most people are sheep. We submit to control. People willing and primarily interested in dominating, will—because they can. Sociopaths rise to the top. People who we tend to call "leaders" are essentially people psychopathically obsessed with dominance and control. Sheep dogs. We have to figure out how to have the sheep do something very un-sheepish. They have to limit the power of the sheep dogs. We have to figure out how we can control the sheep dogs.

Sheep are suckers. The question is, can the sheep actually change their nature or must they simply be suckered forever? Monbiot again: "Partly as a result of the dictatorship of vested interests, partly through corruption and misrule, and the inequality and destructiveness of an economic system which depends for its survival on the issue of endless debt, the prosperity perpetually promised by the rich world to the poor perpetually fails to materialize."[3]

No shit, George.

He continues: "Almost half the world's population live on less than two dollars a day: one fifth on less than one. Despite a global surplus of food, 840 million people are officially classified as malnourished, as they lack the money required to buy it. *[That stat has change now, at the end of the first quarter of 2010 these people now number over one billion—Brad]*

"... One hundred million children are denied primary education. One-third of the people of the poor world die of preventable conditions, such as infectious disease, complications of giving birth, and malnutrition. The same proportion has insufficient access to fresh water.

"... Much of the farming in the poor world has been diverted from producing food for local people to feeding the livestock required to supply rich people with meat."[4]

Monbiot's list of cheerful conditions just goes on and on. I highly recommend reading more detail in his brilliant book. I have oversimplified his point with this phrase: Governments! You can't live with them and you can't live without them! What are we to do, I ask, sheepishly?

And now I answer, not so sheepishly. I say what we need to do is to institute a new form of democracy, deep democracy. Here is what it looks like. The real focus of our work could be to figure out how to create an institution that perpetuates deep democracy.

Because there is so much available to be known now about the secrets and lies of Wall Street and banking institutions leading up to the almost collapse of the economy in 2009, I want to include the wider range of criminals less often mentioned, who show how built into the economic system lying, cheating, and being heartless actually is.

Multinational Monitor List of the Ten Worst Corporations of 2008[5]

What a year for corporate criminality and malfeasance!

As we compiled the "Multinational Monitor list of the Ten Worst Corporations of 2008," it would have been easy to restrict the awardees to Wall Street firms. (And *just think of the 2009 Wall Street Firms and Banks that joined this list in 2009!!—Brad)*

But the rest of the corporate sector was not on good behavior during 2008 either, and we didn't want them to escape justified scrutiny.

So, in keeping with our tradition of highlighting diverse forms of corporate wrongdoing, we included only one financial company on the Ten Worst list.

Here, presented in alphabetical order, are the Ten Worst Corporations of 2008.

AIG: Money for Nothing

There's surely no one party responsible for the ongoing global financial crisis. But if you had to pick a single responsible corporation, there's a very strong case to make for American International Group (AIG), which has already sucked up more than $150 billion in taxpayer supports. Through "credit default swaps," AIG basically collected insurance premiums while making the ridiculous assumption that it would never pay out on a failure—let alone a collapse of the entire market it was insuring. When reality set in, the roof caved in.

Cargill: Food Profiteers

When food prices spiked in late 2007 and through the beginning of 2008, countries and poor consumers found themselves at the mercy of the global market and the giant trading companies that dominate it. As hunger rose and food riots broke out around the world, Cargill saw profits soar, tallying more than $1 billion in the second quarter of 2008 alone.

In a competitive market, would a grain-trading middleman make super-profits? Or would rising prices crimp the middleman's profit margin? Well, the global grain trade is not competitive, and the legal rules of the global economy—devised at the behest of Cargill and friends—ensure that poor countries will be dependent on, and at the mercy of, the global grain traders.

Chevron: "We Can't Let Little Countries Screw Around with Big Companies"

In 2001, Chevron swallowed up Texaco. It was happy to absorb the revenue streams. It has been less willing to take responsibility for Texaco's ecological and human rights abuses.

In 1993, 30,000 indigenous Ecuadorians filed a class action suit in U.S. courts, alleging that Texaco over a twenty-year period had poisoned the land where they live and the waterways on which they rely, allowing billions of gallons of oil to spill and leaving hundreds of waste pits unlined and uncovered. Chevron had the case thrown out of U.S. courts, on the grounds that it should be litigated in Ecuador, closer to where the alleged harms occurred. But now the case is going badly for Chevron in Ecuador—Chevron may be liable for more than $7 billion. So, the company is lobbying the Office of the U.S. Trade Representative to impose trade sanctions on Ecuador if the Ecuadorian government does not make the case go away.

"We can't let little countries screw around with big companies like this—companies that have made big investments around the world," a Chevron lobbyist said to Newsweek in August. (Chevron subsequently stated that the comments were not approved.)

Constellation Energy: Nuclear Operators

Although it is too dangerous, too expensive, and too centralized to make sense as an energy source, nuclear power won't go away, thanks to equipment makers and utilities that find ways to make the public pay and pay.

Constellation Energy Group, the operator of the Calvert Cliffs nuclear plant in Maryland—a company recently involved in a startling, partially derailed scheme to price gouge Maryland consumers—plans to build a new reactor at Calvert Cliffs, potentially the first new reactor built in the United States since the near-meltdown at Three Mile Island in 1979.

It has lined up to take advantage of U.S. government-guaranteed loans for new nuclear construction, available under the terms of the 2005 Energy Act. The company acknowledges it could not proceed with construction without the government guarantee.

CNPC: Fueling Violence in Darfur

Sudan has been able to laugh off existing and threatened sanctions for the slaughter it has perpetrated in Darfur because of the huge support it receives from China, channeled above all through the Sudanese relationship with the Chinese National Petroleum Corporation (CNPC).

"The relationship between CNPC and Sudan is symbiotic," notes the Washington, D.C.-based Human Rights First, in a March 2008 report, "Investing in Tragedy." "Not only is CNPC the largest investor in the Sudanese oil sector, but Sudan is CNPC's largest market for overseas investment."

Oil money has fueled violence in Darfur. "The profitability of Sudan's oil sector has developed in close chronological step with the violence in Darfur," notes Human Rights First.

Dole: The Sour Taste of Pineapple

A 1988 Filipino land reform effort has proven a fraud. Plantation owners helped draft the law and invented ways to circumvent its purported purpose. Dole pineapple workers are among those paying the price.

Under the land reform, Dole's land was divided among its workers and others who had claims on the land prior to the pineapple giant. However, wealthy landlords maneuvered to gain control of the labor cooperatives the workers were required to form, Washington, D.C.-based International Labor Rights Forum (ILRF) explains in an October report. Dole has slashed it regular workforce and replaced them with contract workers.

Contract workers are paid under a quota system, and earn about $1.85 a day, according to ILRF.

GE: Creative Accounting

In June, former New York Times reporter David Cay Johnston reported on internal General Electric documents that appeared to show the company had engaged in a long-running effort to evade taxes in Brazil. In a lengthy report in Tax Notes International, Johnston reported on a GE subsidiary's scheme to invoice suspiciously high sales volume for lighting equipment in lightly populated Amazon regions of the country. These sales would avoid higher value added taxes (VAT) in urban states, where sales would be expected to be greater.

Johnston wrote that the state-level VAT at issue, based on the internal documents he reviewed, appeared to be less than $100 million. But, he speculated, the overall scheme could have involved much more.

Johnston did not identify the source that gave him the internal GE documents, but GE has alleged it was a former company attorney, Adriana Koeck. GE fired Koeck in January 2007 for what it says were "performance reasons."

Imperial Sugar: Fourteen Dead

On February 7, an explosion rocked the Imperial Sugar refinery in Port Wentworth, Georgia, near Savannah. Days later, when the fire was finally extinguished and search-and-rescue operations completed, the horrible human toll was finally known: fourteen dead, dozens badly burned and injured.

As with almost every industrial disaster, it turns out the tragedy was preventable. The cause was accumulated sugar dust, which like other forms of dust, is highly combustible.

A month after the Port Wentworth explosion, Occupational Safety and Health Administration (OSHA) inspectors investigated another Imperial Sugar plant, in Gramercy, Louisiana. They found one-quarter- to two-inch accumulations of dust on electrical wiring and machinery. They found as much as forty-eight-inch accumulations on workroom floors.

Imperial Sugar obviously knew of the conditions in its plants. It had in fact taken some measures to clean up operations prior to the explosion. The company brought in a new vice president to clean up operations in November 2007, and he took some important measures to improve conditions. But it wasn't enough. The vice president told a Congressional committee that top-level management had told him to tone down his demands for immediate action.

Philip Morris International: Unshackled

The old Philip Morris no longer exists. In March, the company formally divided itself into two separate entities: Philip Morris USA, which remains a part of the parent company Altria, and Philip Morris International. Philip Morris USA sells Marlboro and other cigarettes in the United States. Philip Morris International tramples the rest of the world.

Philip Morris International has already signaled its initial plans to subvert the most important policies to reduce smoking and the toll from tobacco-related disease (now at five million lives a year). The company has announced plans to inflict on the world an array of new products, packages and marketing efforts. These are designed to undermine smoke-free workplace rules, defeat tobacco taxes, segment markets with specially flavored products, offer flavored cigarettes sure to appeal to youth and overcome marketing restrictions.

Roche: "Saving Lives Is Not Our Business"

The Swiss company Roche makes a range of HIV-related drugs. One of them is enfuvirtid, sold under the brand name Fuzeon. Fuzeon brought in $266 million to Roche in 2007, though sales are declining.

Roche charges $25,000 a year for Fuzeon. It does not offer a discount price for developing countries.

Like most industrialized countries, Korea maintains a form of price controls—the national health insurance program sets prices for medicines. The Ministry of Health, Welfare and Family Affairs listed Fuzeon at $18,000 a year. Korea's per capita income is roughly half that of the United States. Instead of providing Fuzeon, for a profit, at Korea's listed level, Roche refuses to make the drug available in Korea.

Korean activists report that the head of Roche Korea told them, "We are not in business to save lives, but to make money. Saving lives is not our business."

I Know Reading this Shit Probably Makes You Feel Sick and Angry, but...

What I like about this list is that it is so "business as usual" and it goes on and on. There are ten more for 2009, and ten more for 2010, and a thousand more getting by with far worse shit secretly, paid for by the sheep. Finally, just one recent report from this year (2010). Just think of all the nice profit this brings!

The U.S. Is Shipping Tons of Deadly Weaponry to Pakistan
By Jeremy Scahill (*The Nation*, May 12, 2010)[6]

U.S. drones bomb Pakistan regularly. Now, Washington set up to deliver twenty F-16s and surveillance planes to Islamabad along with a thousand five hundred-pound bombs.

Last week, the Los Angeles Times reported on a 2008 authorization by the Bush administration, continued by the Obama administration, that expanded the U.S.

drone attacks in Pakistan. Citing current and former counterterrorism officials, the paper reported that the CIA had received "secret permission to attack a wider range of targets" allowing the Agency to rely on "pattern of life" analysis.

"The information then is used to target suspected militants, even when their full identities are not known," according to the report. "Previously, the CIA was restricted in most cases to killing only individuals whose names were on an approved list. The new rules have transformed the program from a narrow effort aimed at killing top Al Qaeda and Taliban leaders into a large-scale campaign of airstrikes in which few militants are off-limits, as long as they are deemed to pose a threat to the U.S., the officials said."

There is no doubt that the Obama administration has dramatically expanded the use of drones in Pakistan and that the drone attacks are unpopular. It is far from a radical position to assert that the bombings are creating fresh enemies, inspiring militants and empowering the Taliban. On Monday, I reported on the comments of Lt. Col. Tony Schaffer and Georgetown Professor Christine Fair on the issue. Shaffer said he was against the drone attacks because they create a reality where the "Taliban are more motivated than ever to come at us... the Predator program is having the same effect [it had] in Afghanistan two years ago in killing innocents" that it is now having in Pakistan. Shaffer is no anti-war activist—on the same show he advocated deploying U.S. "boots on the ground" in Pakistan. Fair, a respected former UN advisor in Afghanistan, made the ridiculous claim that "the drones are not killing innocent civilians," adding that the "residents of FATA [the Federally Administered Tribal Areas] generally welcome the drone strikes because they know actually who's being killed."

It is indisputable that, across Pakistan, the drone strikes are passionately opposed. According to a poll conducted by Gallup last year, only 9 percent of Pakistanis support the strikes.

What a Mess

There are endless examples of corporate greed in charge of government policy, but none more telling than the profitable ongoing conduct of war. The military-industrial-congressional-media complex isn't called that for nothing.

We have got to create something better.

Here is another fine set of candidates for the broiler, and I will shut up for now. I quote from the website of Project Polluter Watch: "Big corporations know that the public doesn't trust them. So they funnel millions of dollars to front groups to do their dirty work. No one has perfected this over the years quite like Exxon-Mobil and their CEO Rex Tillerson. That's why we started Project PolluterWatch—to hold people like Mr. Tillerson accountable by educating the public about polluter influence peddling and propaganda."[7]

A Vision of Planetary Democracy and a System of Justice for the Prevention of Corporate Control

Wouldn't it be great to have a system of justice that selected these folks either for psychological processing or for food processing in a fair way? If we ate only fifty of the corporate executives from this list, maybe five hundred million people would be positively given new life! If we raised hell with them and forgave them, and had them forgive us, I wonder what kind of creative solutions we could come up with? If we didn't kill or eat them, and told them what we actually thought of them and had a radically honest exchange about it what might we accomplish?

The War on Wealth!

I invite you to join me and my friends in the next step in the war on poverty—namely: the war on wealth. I sent my friends the following excerpt from recent writing by Derrick Jensen, which I have taken to heart.

Resistance Resisters: It's Time to Lead, Follow, or Get Out of the Way
By Derrick Jensen (*Orion*, March/April 2010)[8]

Another 120 species went extinct today; they were my kin. I am not going to sit back and wait for every last piece of this living world to be dismembered. I'm going to fight like hell for those kin who remain—and I want everyone who cares to join me. Many are. But many are not. Some of those who are not are those who, for whatever reason, really don't care. I worry about them. But I worry more about those who do care but have chosen not to fight. A fairly large subset of those who care but have chosen not to fight assert that lifestyle choice is the only possible response to the murder of the planet. They all carry the same essential message—and often use precisely the same words: Resistance isn't possible. Resistance never works.

Meanwhile, another 120 species went extinct today. They were my kin.

There are understandable personal reasons for wanting to believe in the invincibility of an oppressive system. If you can convince yourself the system is invincible, there's no reason to undertake the often arduous, sometimes dangerous, always necessary work of organizing, preparing to dismantle, and then actually dismantling this (or any) oppressive system. If you can convince yourself the system is invincible, you can, with fully salved conscience, make yourself and your own as comfortable as you can within the confines of the oppressive system while allowing this oppressive system to continue. There are certainly reasons that those in power want us to see them as invincible. Abusive systems, from the simplest to the most sophisticated, from the familial to the social and political and religious, work best when victims and bystanders police themselves. And one of the best ways to get victims and bystanders to police themselves is for them to internalize the notion that the abusers are invincible and then, even better, to get them to attempt to police anyone who threatens to break up the stable abuser/victim/bystander triad.

And meanwhile, another 120 species went extinct today.

But those who believe in the invincibility of perpetrators and their systems are wrong. Systems of power are created by humans and can be stopped by humans. Those in power are never supernatural or immortal, and they can be brought down. People with a lot fewer resources collectively than any single reader of Orion have fought back against systems of domination, and won. There's no reason the rest of us can't do the same. But resistance starts by believing in it, not by talking yourself out if it. And certainly not by trying to talk others out of it... Some people may be willing to give up on life on this planet without resisting. I'm not one of them."

A New Kind of Culture War:
Underthrow the Government and It's Owners

I consider myself an ally of Derrick Jensen. I have stopped resisting and joined the resistance. I have been a resistance resister myself, but I have been working at giving up on giving up. I invite you to join. You can help us underthrow the government! You can have your caring count! I have the beginning of a plan!

My friends and I are already doing some things to undercut, undermine, undermind, and underthrow the government. These are small, conscious-living resistances. Here are a few things we are doing for some examples:

1. We are screening everything we do to keep from giving any more money to any big corporations. (I canceled my Anthem Blue Cross health insurance when the fuckers defeated the public option on health care and I will refuse to buy health insurance from the kill-for-profit corporations created by the government they bought, and I encourage everyone I know to do the same.)

2. I sold my house and some of my land and I live in a Yurt. I no longer have a mortgage, and no goddamned home owners insurance. If my yurt burns down I can replace it for less than $20,000 with a little help from my friends.

3. I quit buying at Wal-Mart unless I can steal something from them at the same time.

4. I only buy what gasoline I need from small oil companies.

5. I don't ever pay retail anywhere when I travel.

6. I don't pay taxes (When book sales surge or a big seminar comes up, I pay somebody to lie to the government for me instead of paying them, just like rich people do).

7. I maintain a bad credit rating as a matter of integrity. If my credit score gets good enough that a bank would approve a credit card for me I do something to fuck some big company out of something I owe them for in order to get my credit score

down to where it ought to be.

8. I use only debit cards, not credit cards, and I screw as many big corporations out of as much money as I can. (I originally attained this status when I screwed a lot of credit card companies out of a lot of money by taking their fucking rip off cards and running them to the limit and then not paying them back and telling them and all their collectors to go fuck themselves. It was very gratifying and I recommend it.)

9. I bought a used Prius and traded in my pickup on it.

10. I work in a collective garden with friends here in our group called Sustainable Shenandoah and we meet and watch subversive videos and pick, can, freeze, and eat food that we grow.

11. I eat deer meat and other game and a lot of raw vegetables grown locally, or right next to my yurt, or in our community garden.

12. I have become a "loan guppy" to undermine loan sharks by using the rest of the money I made on selling my house to provide loans to people I know. They can pay off debt, and my interest rate is a third to a half the interest they have been paying, yet still more than the fucking banks will give me for using my money. And I lie to the government about what little I make from that.

13. I help people "negotiate" with debt to big corporations by telling said corporations to go fuck themselves as an opening gambit.

14. I am sponsoring a contest among my friends where we compete to see who can make debt collector callers hang up on us the fastest! (We start telling the poor person calling to collect for their corporate masters to quit that job and take up something that contributes to other people's happiness, and give up that miserable and misery making fruitless and damaging job working for killers).

15. All my Christmas gifts this year and from now on will be donations to non-profit charities for food, health care, and housing for children in poverty. I donate to them in the name of the kith and kin I am giving the present to.

16. I am writing this book. The War on Wealth is central to the War on Poverty!

17. I am quitting eating tuna and will no longer eat at sushi restaurants, and I am quitting ocean fish and non-organic red meat, and eating chicken only when I know it is free range.

18. I will be sending a newsletter out and keeping a blog active on a regular basis, with new articles every month on ways to resist, and offers of tools for resistance, and information about the takedown of the system of rich people running everything carelessly for profit. Our motto is "All the news printed in a fit!"

This barely scratches the surface of what thousands of our friends are doing in our evolution of revolution projects and enterprises. This also barely scratches the surface of taking down the corporate criminal conspiracy in complete control of the government.

Just because it is not enough doesn't mean we shouldn't do it. Anything worth doing is worth doing poorly. (And anything worth poo-ing is worth poo-ing dourly.) There are dozens of fun, entertaining, exciting, adventurous, and good-to-do-when-stoned-or-imbibing-in-other-joyfully-illegal activities. There are many things that are fun and destructive to right wingers and fundamentalists of every ilk! It is invigorating and it is good exercise for staying awake. It is like a walking meditation for liberation to save our nation and change the station of those suffering occupation by corporate constipation. We have things to offer that are destructive and dangerous to the status quo and the freaks of the past currently in control of starving people for profit in the present.

The more our resistance accumulates, the weaker the kill-for-profit economy becomes. As we prepare for, and cheer on the upcoming collapse, we can rejoice in how well things are going our way. I am sure there were many people in Rome who rejoiced at what history called the downfall. Our resistance could merge into underwhelming entropy that finally brings this gigantic kill-for-profit machine to a halt. These are the pathetic beginnings of an (eventually) underwhelming entropy.

PART FOUR

Some Good News and Positive Results from Big Experiments

"Enough for everyone's need but not for everyone's greed."

—Mahatma Gandhi

We have the limbic brain equipment to love our children—to compassionately, lovingly, and joyfully get more pleasure from watching them eat than we do from eating something ourselves! From this impulse, we have the capacity to nurture each other. What if we built on that rather than on our capacity to control and defend? What if we came up with a five-year, a fifty-year, and a five-hundred-year plan actually to build an empathic civilization?

This is one question addressed quite well in *The Empathic Civilization* by Jeremy Rifkin (J.P. Tarcher, 2009). This book is an inspiration. Excellent! Wonderful! It is an amazing reinterpretation of history that gives us heart by allowing us to see that we collectively have one—and it is growing! The big question is whether or not we will overcome the entropic debt we have built up in the course of becoming more capable of identifying with each other and learning to relate to life itself before we wipe ourselves out? We are just on the verge of learning to love and care for each other and for life.

What if we built an entirely new way of living together while the current empire collapses around us? What if we built instead a worldwide, locally-supported, world commonwealth-protected heaven on earth? What if kindness was the heart of the matter and we still had a chance for it to win?

My heart is full of joy and grief, both emotions turned up full volume like being on an acid trip, laughing and crying at the same time. We could do this. We could come close, and fail to do this, too.

Kindness
By Naomi Shihab Nye[1]

Before you know what kindness really is
you must lose things,
feel the future dissolve in a moment
like salt in a weakened broth.
What you held in your hand,
what you counted and carefully saved,
all this must go so you know
how desolate the landscape can be
between the regions of kindness.
How you ride and ride
thinking the bus will never stop,
the passengers eating maize and chicken
will stare out the window forever.

Before you learn the tender gravity of kindness,
you must travel where the Indian in a white poncho
lies dead by the side of the road,
You must see how this could be you,
how he too was someone
who journeyed through the night with plans
and the simple breath that kept him alive.

Before you know kindness as the deepest thing inside,
you must know sorrow as the other deepest thing.
You must wake up with sorrow.
You must speak to it till your voice
catches the thread of all sorrows
and you see the size of the cloth.

Then it is only kindness that makes sense anymore
only kindness that ties your shoes
and sends you out into the day to mail letters and
purchase bread,

only kindness that raises its head
from the crowd in the world to say
It is I you have been looking for
and then goes with you everywhere
like a shadow or a friend.

I love this poem. How more clearly can one state the key to our survival? It is only kindness that makes sense anymore, indeed.

This last section of The Korporate Kannibal Kookbook lists some amazing accomplishments that have resulted from people coming together and solving problems with love drawn from their limbic brains and technological skill drawn from their frontal lobes.

These projects are at different stages of development—but they are all things that are taking humanity in the right direction due to the miracle of love and logic.

I have saved what good news there is until last in this book. Whether or not what we are doing is futile, we may as well do it in case we are wrong in the assessment of the futility. It would be hell to realize at a later date that the terminal hell we are living in could have been avoided had we not so accurately predicted it.

Chapter 15

Conscious Participation in Evolution:
How Can We Help?

The idea of consciously participating in our own evolution, as we proceed forward, makes all the questions and ways of asking the questions about conscious caring relevant. The best view of all history and current events is the widest view. The list of the horrors and ecstasies, and everything in between, gives us a perspective and allows for more information before we reduce the view again to determine future action. There is an oscillating pattern of divergence and convergence that allows for transcendent love and courage to emerge and win the day, if the day is to be won.

If we hold creating heaven on earth as a constant objective, while acknowledging a wide and terrifying look at what currently is, and what appears to be on the horizon, and we keep sharing honestly as we go, we can begin to actually help determine the direction of evolution toward an agreed upon objective.

From almost any view of history, it is safe to say that we have actually been greatly impacting evolution for some time with very little consciousness on our part. So many things have been put in motion without any awareness. Being able to be okay with our lack of control is a bitch though, given how we all have been raised and acculturated. We humans tend to want to fight amongst ourselves about control when we get frustrated about not having enough of it. It is this family feud that is killing us and destroying the network of life within which we live.

Regression in the name of Progress

It may be that we need to regress in order to progress. If we go back to the most violent, but also most impotent age we all live through, the age when we are about three years old, we may be able to access some of the things we learned then and later forgot. This wisdom may serve us to develop a new kind of co-intelligence.

Two- to three-year-olds are my favorite people most of the time, and there may be a clue there about reducing our capacity to do violence down to sticks and stones again. My friend Taber Shadburne speaks in a recent email to me about regression progression in talking about some of the wisdom in Buddhism: "In Buddhism there's the concept of the 'single enlightenment' possessed by animals and small children—a beautiful simplicity and one-pointededness, an honest form of self-centeredness. But this is distinguished from 'full enlightenment,' which in some ways looks like a return to childhood (if you would enter heaven 'become as little children'), with the addition of a whole new capacity for self-awareness, deeper compassion, and an honest form of selflessness."[1]

Maybe evolution is on the way to helping us get less able to magnify our destructive powers by having the military-industrial complex (or dilatory-combustible complex) blow itself up along with a few billion extras. A vision of humanity's likely future keeps coming back to me. We reach the epicenter of enlightenment and the epicenter of destructiveness at almost exactly the same time, and, luckily, the enlightenment precedes the destruction by a few minutes. Everyone on earth finally says, "Ohhh! I seeeee! Amazing!!! My God!! Reality is God!! Reality is love and I love reality!" Suddenly we are Jesus and the Buddha and Charlie Chaplin all wrapped up into one, washing each other's feet and not kissing each other's asses. And then someone from our parallel evolutionary brothers and sisters pushes a button and ... BOOM! Suddenly, we're all gone.

I am obviously not the only one who has come up with this idea, because having had it for years, I now see it showing up all over the place:

Sudden Mass American Enlightenment Puzzles Congress and Causes National Security Alert
By Ignatius O'Reilly (Scott.net, April 1, 2010)[2]

A sudden and unexplained mass enlightenment of the US population leads to jubilant celebrations. Washington. President Obama, U.S. congressmen, and their aides held an emergency four hour-long meeting Wednesday to decide what action to take to stem a sudden and unprecedented mass enlightenment of the U.S. population that threatens to destabilize the Government and create a fiscal crisis.

Millions of citizens jubilantly celebrated their new awareness as they suddenly realized they have been lied to all their lives on just about everything by their psychopathic, conscienceless leaders of major corporations and government and security agencies.

Residents in all major cities across the United States awoke Wednesday morning complaining that they were experiencing an inexplicable mental clarity that was causing them to realize the way they were about to spend their day was utterly pointless, a potential health threat, and would only add energy and finances to a powerful wealthy elite that had been ruling their lives since as long as they could remember.

Congress was thrown into chaos when a majority of staff decided to simply stop showing up for work until their bosses resign; in a move of solidarity, energy companies turned off the power to government buildings and military bases, while water companies shut down their water supply; repair people refused to carry out repairs for the politically well-connected; and television network staff refused to report the lies they are routinely ordered to tell by their editors.

One Chicago resident's report was consistent with many similar accounts coming in from across the country. Joe, 42, told us how he had become aware of the diversionary divide and conquer machinations of the psychopathic oligarchs, especially in relation to abortion, health care, immigration, global warming, peak oil, 9/11, fake terrorism, both current wars and past wars, "necessary police actions," empire building and resource plundering, left vs. right, evolution vs. creationism, and fundamentalists vs. everybody else!

"Wow! I sort of felt things weren't right, but to suddenly be able to see the true nature of all the lies we've been bombarded with by media and Big Government is just mind-boggling," Joe exclaimed.

"The public seems to have finally understood that they're so sick and going bankrupt because of the FDA/AMA medical mafia and Big Pharma's Gestapo death grip over absolutely everything! I've noticed how food companies, Monsanto, and Big Pharma's share prices have exploded over the past few years," said Joe. "I can see it's because they have bought Congress and have a complete monopoly over our food supply, health, and non-existent consideration for others' well-being."

Reports are flooding in of people deciding to buy or trade for goods with hand crafters in their own region instead of shopping at Wal-Mart. Rather than buying GMO foods at the supermarket chain stores, they've formed co-ops with their neighbors, bought fresh food in bulk, and are getting together to can foods, smoke meats and pickle vegetables—followed by a barbecue. Feeling so connected and enthused by that, ordinary people across the nation are organizing all kinds of meetings to learn all the old skills that their grandparents knew that made them independent.

People are leaving the cities in droves and, en masse, have established themselves on previously restricted government land. This resulted in a veritable frenzy of house building and barn raising parties followed, once again, by barbecues where homemade pickles were enjoyed by all.

The reasons for the mass awakening are as yet unclear. One possible explanation has been given by the U.S. Environmental Protection Agency where officials have discovered that the normally high levels of fluoride added to the nation's drinking water were "accidentally omitted." It's suspected that workers at water plants are responsible. Government health officials have advised all citizens to carry on working as normal, eat lots of fast-food, and stay glued to their TV sets in the hope that any thoughts generated in people by seeing the reality of the situation will be pacified by toxins, apathy, and a return to the steady atrophy of their brains.

Citizens have been urged by the Obama administration to report anyone they witness behaving in a non-consumer-capitalist manner to Homeland Security who, with the help of FEMA, will permanently detain anyone found more than five meters from a television screen.

Funny Things Happened on the Way to the Slaughterhouse...Compassionate, Wise, Poetic, Celebratory, and Hilarious Responses by Friends and Allies with Regard to the Cure for Corporate Cannibalism

What if we, somehow (knowing that we need to revise ourselves to achieve a healthier state of being, just as the potted plant knows it needs to bend to the light) were to laugh at what used to scare us, laugh at who used to intimidate us, and consciously shrug off that part of ourselves reinforcing fear and insecurity? What if we cleaned up our mess by cleaning up the most mess-chievius amongst us?

From Jack Stork[3]

Hey Brad,

The cannibalism concept is, without question, out of the box. Then why do I like it so much? Corporate Kookbook, made me laugh. You can come up with some wildly funny shit my friend.

A lot of the people that I admire, for example Nearing, Gandhi, Tolstoy, Thoreau, Fuller, admitted that they refused to think about money. I think that a part of that is that these integrated souls do not need money.

In my own experience, every time in my life that my focus became money, it put me in a real funk and I wound up shooting myself in the foot.

The moneygrubbers that I know personally seem to be working their ass off in an attempt to overcome inadequacy. Once someone gets on that train, there is never enough money because it will not work. They cannot abandon the idea however, and just need more and more money and will bend some rules to get it.

Like any good sociopath, they develop an ability to justify anything to themselves at shallow levels of the mind, but the depths of the mind hold terror.

The stories of the wealthy bailing out of upper-story windows at the news of the crash in 1929 are real enough, and even today there are unusual numbers of big money people committing suicide at the idea of being poor or being found out.

There are people at all levels who are without money for one reason or another, that would never commit suicide over it.

I see the desperate homeless, many of whom are mentally ill, figuring out how to live and even manage to get a laugh or two out of life. Life does not seem to scare them. It does piss them off at times. Me too.

Both Camus and Sartre claimed that they were never so alive as when they were in the French underground, living hand to mouth, living in the sewers, printing anti-Nazi materials, and with the Nazis hunting for them continually.

In the end, I cannot see myself getting angry with the greedy rich. I can get away from them, they cannot. Hang in there, be like a ping-pong ball in the river, kick back and watch the scenery go by, and see where it takes you.

Jack.

From Taber Shadburne... Again[4]

Actually I think there are some problems with the question, "Where did we go wrong?" I think it springs from the retro-romantic notion of the noble savage, which was just an updated version of the original sin doctrine, the idea of some previous time in Eden with a subsequent fall from grace (caused by some terrible moral failing on our parts, some awful mistake we made in the past—the results of which we now reap).

We want to believe that there was some idyllic time when everything wasn't all fucked up (and that now everything is). We want to believe that animals and babies and hunter-gatherers exist in a natural state of grace, that we lost access to through some mistake.

I say this is a mistaken notion, which springs from a desire to prop up the illusion of control: "If only had just done X, then I wouldn't be suffering like this now."

We have way more powerful ways of shooting ourselves in the foot, now than we ever had before, but we always suffered from the tendencies that are now being magnified to such horrific extremes: chimps will hunt down and kill the members of neighboring bands to keep them out of their turf. Baboons suffer from stress, depression, and social anxiety disorders.

Hunter-gatherers were often homicidally xenophobic, and they caused mass extinctions (see the works of Jared Diamond). Modern humans are actually most violent at age two or three (though they lack the means to do serious damage).

There was no previous state of perfection and grace, nor is everything fucked up now. It has been a mixed bag all along—evolution mixed with amplification of error, transcendence mixed with repression, empowerment mixed with oppression. Like Sufism's levels of consciousness, growth doesn't always mean a decrease in suffering. The developments that have led us to the brink of self-annihilation have also led us to the brink of self-liberation.

The cultural evolution that has created such extreme forms of suffering has also created the possibility of us consciously creating our culture, a possibility which has never existed to the same degree before. So you could say, everything's totally fucked up an' goin' to hell in a hand basket. True... and not. Or you could say things have never been better. True... and not. Or you could say things are fucked up and have never been better. True... and not... And that it's always been this way. True... and not.

Ultimately, since all these stories about history, our culture, ourselves, and so on, are nothing more than mental fictions with an emotional axe to grind, the question becomes not which stories are true, but which are the most useful? What are the implications of holding a given story? Is it just an attempt at emotional solace and egoic compensation? Or is it a means of guiding and orienting constructive action, a way of empowering creativity?

So, I guess I don't think the question "Where did we go wrong?" and it's answer are all that useful, at least not if it's framed as some singular turning point, some original sin and fall from grace. Perhaps it would be more useful if it were coupled with, "Where did we go right?" Or, better yet, "How have we been wrong (and right) all along?" and, "How have things been getting worse and how have they been getting better?"

We've had a paranoid fearful/greedy reptile brain from the start, which has often hijacked evolution, and yet pretty pockets of transcendence, compassion, and awareness have been breaking out more and more often. I find models like Ken Wilber's or Don Beck's version of *Spiral Dynamics* useful ones that emphasize evolutionary development—but one rife with repression and wrong turns along the way; one, like all natural evolutionary developments, with no guarantee of "success," a fickle, flawed, yet somehow glorious "slouch toward Bethlehem" with ever and ever greater potential present in the system, more and more potential for disaster and catastrophe, and more and more potential for the creation of something at least approaching Eden... the first one ever.

Love, Taber

Babbling on in Babylon

It looks like going sane and going insane are very hard to distinguish...

—What If We Go Sane?
By James Howard Kunstler (Kunstler.com, March 29, 2010)[5]

Nations go crazy. It's terrifying when it happens, especially to a major nation with the ability to project its craziness outward. We look back on the psychotic break of Germany in 1933 and still wonder how the then-best-educated population in Europe could fall under the sway of a sociopathic political program. We behold the carnage and devastation left in the wake of that episode, and decades later you still can do little more than shake your head in bewilderment.

China had a psychotic break in the 1960s in its "cultural revolution," provoked by the mad neo-emperor Mao. He sent cadres of Chinese baby boomer youths rampaging across the land, turned every institution upside down, and let millions starve. Mao's China lacked the ability then to export this mischief, but enough of his own people suffered.

Cambodia was the next humdinger of a national nervous breakdown when the Paris-educated classic Marxist Pol Pot decided to make the world's biggest omelet by cracking a million eggs. He took everybody wearing eyeglasses, everybody who appeared to have a thought in his or her head, and sent them out to the bush to be worked to death, or shot in ditches, or disposed of otherwise. The mounds of skulls remain to tell the tale.

Lately we've had the Hutu-Tutsi genocides in Rwanda, the craziness in former Yugoslavia, the cruelty of Darfur, the international suicide-bomber craze (including today's blasts in Moscow). Surely, I've left a few out... but these are minor episodes compared to what be coming next.

Am I the only one who senses it might be America's turn to go nuts? I don't mean a family squabble, like the Boomer-Hippie-Vietnam uproar that was essentially an adolescent rebellion against bad parenting in the national household. I mean a genuine descent into madness, with the very high probability of persecution, violence, murder, and mayhem—all more or less sponsored by various authorities and institutions.

The Republican Party is doing a great job in provoking such a dangerous episode by making consensual governance impossible in a time of awful practical problems and challenges. They're in the process, right now, of transforming themselves from the party of "no" to the party of no decency, no common sense, no ideas, no conception of the public interest, and no respect for the traditions that they pretend to stand for, like due process of law. In the days since the passage of health care reform, they've gone as far as inciting mobs to violence against their fellow congressmen and senators—bricks thrown through windows, death threats made, coffins placed in the yards of their adversaries. One day soon, somebody with a gun or an explosive device, someone with a very sketchy sense-of-self, and perhaps a recent record of personal failure and humiliation, is going to sacrifice himself to become the Tea Party's first martyr by shooting up a shopping mall in some blue district.

Republican leaders' avidity to ally themselves with the followers of hate-monger entertainers like Glenn Beck, Rush Limbaugh, Ann Coulter, and the Fox News gang is only the beginning of the process that will lead to a political convulsion possibly worse than the one that started at Fort Sumter, South Carolina, 1861. If it comes, it will certainly be a far more incoherent conflict. The guerilla forces of the radical right will not know whether they are fighting for Wal-Mart, or the Financial Services arm of General Electric, or against abortions, or for bigger and better freeways, or the rights of thoracic surgeons to drive families into bankruptcy, or against the idea of climate change or evolution, or Jews-in-the-media, or their neighbors having something they feel envious about.

In the background, of course, is an economy just barely holding together with political baling wire and duct tape. It has very poor prospects for continuing in the way it was designed to run, on cheap oil and revolving debt. The upshot is an economy now destined for permanent contraction, and nobody has a plan for managing that contraction—which will include awful failures in food production, in disintegrating water systems, electric grids, roadway systems, schools... really anything that requires ongoing public investment. It includes a financial system that cannot come up with capital deployable for productive purpose, or currencies that can be relied on to hold value, or markets that function without interference.

For its part, the Democratic Party has done a poor job of clearly articulating the realities of these things, and in actions like bailouts they've given the false impression that the nation can somehow engineer a return to the reckless hedonism of the late 20th century. My guess is that the situation is so desperate now that President Obama and his supporters can't risk telling the truth about the comprehensive contraction we face.

The health care reform act was a tortured way of dealing with some of this indirectly. It will absolutely lead to a kind of health care "rationing," but rationing is unavoidable in an economy where there is less of everything that people need, and fewer resources to spread around. The difference between the Democrats and the Republicans is that the Republicans would prefer to see the rationing accomplished by money-grubbing health insurance companies denying coverage to policy-holders who get sick, or by the bankrupting of households (i.e. losers who deserve to die anyway), while the Democrats want to at least try to distribute what we can a little more fairly. The larger failure of both factions to emulate better systems running in sister societies like Canada and France is something that history will judge.

I was in favor of the health care reform act for the reason of that basic difference between the Right and the Left. For all its flaws—and perhaps even the prospect that we are too far gone in national bankruptcy to ever get all its provisions running—I believe it was necessary for our national morale to pass the bill, to prove that we could do something besides remain stuck in paralysis and bickering indefinitely. And it was necessary to smack down the Party of Cruelty, to inform ourselves that we are not quite ready to go completely crazy.

Whatever his flaws, omissions, and failures, I'm impressed with President Obama's ability to conduct himself like an adult, like a good father, in the face of the most unseemly provocations by his red-faced adversaries John Boehner, Mitch McConnell, Michelle Bachman, Sarah Palin, Jim DeMint, and all the other apoplectic opportunists trying so desperately to turn the United States into a high-definition

Jesus tele-theocracy of Perpetual NASCAR. As economic conditions worsen—I believe they will—I hope Mr. Obama can discipline these maniacs. I would like to see him start by instructing his attorney general to look into the connection between Republican officials (including staff members) and the threats of violence and murder that were made last week around the country.

James Howard Kunstler is the author of The Long Emergency, *and the novel* World Made By Hand, *and its sequel,* The Witch of Hebron.

From My Friends at Public Education and Empowerment Resource Service (PEERS)[6] and Excerpts from Creating a New Paradigm By PEERS[7]

Our world appears to be making a profound shift from one paradigm to another. The old paradigm served humanity for many, many years, and in some ways serves us still. Yet an exciting new paradigm is paving the way for a more loving, harmonious way of living and interacting with all around us. The comparison below is an attempt to capture the spirit of the old and new paradigm without the intention of making one better than the other, yet also inviting us to join in welcoming inspiring new ways which can support us all in being the best we can be and making a difference in our lives and world.

Old: Man is born into sin, essentially corrupt at the core.

New: All people in their core essence are beautiful and worthy of love.

Old: Hatred and vengeance are justified for wrongs suffered. An eye for an eye.

New: Love is the most transformative force. Forgiveness is an act of courage and compassion.

Old: Don't show real feelings, or you will get hurt. Create a convincing persona to present to the world.

New: Welcome authenticity and vulnerability. It's all about being honest and real with each other.

Old: Emphasis on hierarchies. Focus on competition so that the best rise to the top of the hierarchy.

New: Emphasis on equality. Focus on cooperation in order to support the greatest good for all.

Old: Tend to avoid personal responsibility by blaming those above or below them in the hierarchy.

New: Take personal responsibility for actions and learn from our mistakes.

Old: People need to be led or controlled by those believed to be better or more capable.

New: Each individual is a powerful creator capable of meeting their needs with the help of others.

Old: The mind and science is supreme. The scientific paradigm supersedes God and religion.

New: The heart and personal relationships are of paramount importance. The deepest essence of life is a divine mystery to be welcomed and explored.

Old: Don't question the accepted scientific paradigm. Focus on three-dimensional, five-sensory world.

New: Foster fluid intelligence. Explore the edges of consciousness, especially other dimensions and capabilities not believed to be possible under the old paradigm.

Old: Categorizing and dissecting nature allows us to better control it and to profit from it.

New: Recognizing the interconnectedness of all life leads to greater growth and harmony.

Old: Focus on order, discipline.

New: Welcome flexibility and even occasional chaos and disorder as means to see new possibilities.

Old: Value boundaries, borders, and divisions. These give security, safety, and comfort.

New: While respecting and honoring differences, look for shared vision and ways to work together. Take risks in order to grow. Short-term pain can bring long-term gain.

Old: You can't trust anyone.

New: Surrender to and trust in a divine force greater than our egoic selves.

Old: Focus on defeating and conquering the enemy, us versus them. War against evil.

New: Committed to transforming and integrating life's challenges. The external reflect the internal.

Old: Focus on details, complexity.

New: Remember the bigger picture. Identify simple principles behind the complexities of life.

Old: Look outwards for guidance. Don't trust self. Have rigid rules and beliefs.

New: Look inwards for guidance. Develop intuition. Have flexible guidelines and beliefs.

We all have our feet in both paradigms. How much we live in each paradigm is only a matter of degree. The old paradigm is not necessarily something to be shunned or avoided. There are times when principles of both paradigms can be useful and beneficial. Yet overall, the new paradigm invites more love, support, and deeper connection into our lives and world. In every moment we can consciously choose the paradigm to which we give our focus, time, and energy.

Remember that all of us to some degree are afraid of our shadows. At times we avoid looking at the disturbing parts of ourselves and our world. Yet consider that a willingness to explore and even dance with these shadows can be a potent catalyst to a new paradigm. And when we set a clear life intention to choose and support what's best for all, our lives can't help but become richer and more fulfilling.

"All the darkness of the world cannot put out the light of a single candle."

The Old Paradigm: Together, we can and will create a new paradigm on Earth. Yet in order to give meaningful suggestions for this, we first need to speak candidly about what's happening in the world at present. It appears that there are factions within the world's power elite who desire to exert as much control as possible over the world. *Their primary means for establishing control are through promoting fear, secrecy, and polarization, and through distracting people from their deeper purpose in life.* When these factions gain greater power and control, our freedoms and liberties are increasingly taken away, sometimes without our even realizing it.

Fear is used as a powerful tool of control by these factions of the global elite. "The terrorists want to kill us all. Your job, savings, and retirement are no longer secure. You are either for us or against us. We might be attacked at any time." All of these messages push us towards fear. And by encouraging us to focus blame on others such as terrorists and "evil" leaders, the global power brokers push us away from feeling in control of our lives and towards the role of powerless victims. The more we slip into fear and being victims, the easier it is for us to be manipulated.

Secrecy leads to control through preventing the exposure of hidden agendas, and through breeding distrust, suspicion, and paranoia in the world. In the name of "national security," we have been told ever more frequently that we should not know what is happening behind closed doors in government. Yet we are encouraged to keep vigilant watch over our neighbors, over those who question the government, and over those who look or act different from us, as they could secretly be terrorists in sheep's clothing. Rampant suspicion and secrecy cause us to lose touch with the common humanity we share with all around us."

Laugh and Cry and Think You're Gonna Die

Once you get so high and you laugh and cry and think you're gonna die, you see clearly, not denying anything, and you see how you can laugh at the tremendous joke of very serious business, like the following article from Onion News Network.

U.S. Flag Recalled After Causing 143 Million Deaths
By Onion News Network (April 13, 2010)[8]

Washington. Citing a series of fatal malfunctions dating back to 1777, flag manufacturer Annin & Company announced Monday that it would be recalling all makes and models of its popular American flag from both foreign and domestic markets.

Representatives from the nation's leading flag producer claimed that as many as 143 million deaths in the past two centuries can be attributed directly to the faulty

U.S. models, which have been utilized extensively since the 18th century in sectors as diverse as government, the military, and public education.

"It has come to our attention that, due to the inherent risks and hazards it poses, the American flag is simply unfit for general use," said Annin & Company president Ronald Burman, who confirmed that the number of flag-related deaths had noticeably spiked since 2003. "I would like to strongly urge all U.S. citizens: If you have an American flag hanging in your home or place of business, please discontinue using it immediately."

Added Burman, "The last thing we would want is for more innocent men and women around the world to die because of our product."

Millions of U.S. flag-related injuries and fatalities have been reported over a 230-year period in locations as far flung as Europe, Cuba, Korea, Gettysburg, PA, the Philippines, and Iraq. In addition, the company found that U.S. flag exports to Vietnam during the late 1960s and early 1970s resulted in hundreds of thousands of deaths, a clear sign that there was something seriously wrong with its product.

Despite fears about the flag's safety—especially when improperly used or manipulated in ways not originally intended—sales continued unabated over the years, potentially putting billions of unsuspecting people in danger.

"At first, we wanted one of our flags in every home in America," Burman said. "Unfortunately, the practical applications of this product are far outnumbered by the risks it presents. Millions have died needlessly, and when you ask people why, they point to the flag." Unfortunate casualties of Old Glory's near-continuous 230-year use.

Added Burman, "Frankly, we should have pulled it off the market decades ago."

Studies conducted by the Annin & Company research and development department revealed that faulty U.S. flags have caused more than just injuries and deaths. During the mid-1950s, the flags were found to have the bizarre side effect of causing fear, paranoia, and hysterical behavior among millions of Americans. This was dismissed as an isolated event until September 2001, when similar symptoms re-emerged on a massive scale.

As hazardous as the flags may be on their own, Annin & Company officials claimed the products become even more dangerous when used in conjunction with other common household items.

"When combined with alcohol, excessive patriotism, grief, or well-intentioned but ultimately misguided ideals, U.S. flags transform into ticking time bombs, just waiting to go off," Burman said.

Manufacturers are addressing the flag's unsafe and potentially lethal alignment of stars and stripes by designing a revised model that they hope will cut down on deaths in the United States and overseas, where experts say the flag is nearly 1,000 times as deadly.

In the meantime, Annin & Company is advising all Americans to either ship their flags back to the manufacturer or, if no time permits, dispose of them in an efficient manner.

"I understand that people might be reluctant to stop using a product they have found to be reliable over the years," Burman told reporters. "But I can't in good conscience allow them to use something I know to be dangerous. We'll try to make adjustments soon and come up with something that benefits everybody rather than hurting them."

Added Burman, "In the interim, I would recommend that all Americans switch to the Canadian flag, which seems to be working just fine."

Chapter 16

The Pathway to Salvation, If There Is One:
Rooting Out a Route

This next fine example of co-intelligence emerged from my friend Rabbi Michael Lerner and his friends in the Tikkun magazine community. Though this is more moderate than almost anything I have proposed, it takes all kinds of people and all kinds of effort to bring about social change. I want to align myself with people as committed, as easy to love, and as articulate in diagnosing the problem of human self-destruction through corporate capitalism as Michael is.

Taking On a Personal Commitment for Social Change

Rabbi Michael Lerner for The Tikkun Community and the Network of Spiritual Progressives invites us to take on this commitment and rewrite it in ways that would make it real for us and sign and date it, and then re-read what we've written once a week. He suggests: "Circulate this invitation to a personal commitment on the environment to everyone you know, including all the groups to which you have access both on email, on the web, and in person. You can also place this on your website or share it on Facebook or Twitter references to it at www.spiritualprogressives.org where it will be on the home page." Here is what he suggests we pass around.

Personal Environmental Commitment
By Rabbi Michael Lerner (*Tikkun,* 2010)[1]

The following emerged from our work in supporting environmental sanity, and is shared in a spirit of humility, knowing how much we all have a long distance to go to be doing all that we could and should to save the planet from the destruction to which our current economic and political system contributes, and knowing that you can probably devise an even better statement of a personal environmental commitment that more fully fits your own situation, capacities, and limitations.

1. I will learn more of the details of the multiple levels in which we are undermining the life support systems of the planet, from overpopulation to over consumption to dumping our garbage, to destroying the air and the water, to excessive use of the resources of the planet to… endless other ways. I will work within some community of which I am a part in order to raise the issues of environmental degradation and what we can do not only as individuals but as a community to challenge our government to take all steps necessary to reduce the carbon in the air to below 350 parts per million.

2. I will carefully follow the activities of my elected representatives in Congress to ensure that they do not adopt compromise measures which they justify as "politically realistic" but which do not adequately reflect the actual needs of the planet for immediate and drastic action to reverse all the ways in which we are destroying the life support systems upon which we, the animals, fish and birds depend. I will then let neighbors, friends and members of any group or community to which I have access know about the behavior of these elected officials.

3. I will myself take significant steps to reduce my own misuse of the environment, starting with:
A.
B.
C.

4. Recognizing that one reason I do not act politically on these issues is my own sense of powerlessness, I will take the following steps in the next few months to reverse that sense of powerlessness:
A.
B.
C.

5. Recognizing that a central problem is that people in this society believe that there is no limits to what is possible to take from the earth and no limits to the capacity of the oceans and the land and the air to absorb the polluting garbage that we create, and that "progress" means endlessly extracting from the earth its minerals and endlessly producing new chemical combinations whose long-term impact on the planet we have no way of knowing in order to produce new items for consumption, and recognizing that all this is supported by notions of "success" for an economy that do not take into account the health, welfare, happiness, spiritual fulfillment, intellectual development or psychological health of the world's inhabitants but instead focuses on production of material goods, I will take the following steps to challenge that notion of progress or success whenever I hear people alluding to it:

A.

B.

6. Recognizing that I myself and many others sometimes feel I need to consume something, buy the newest something, overeat, immerse in a computer (or fill in what you do) in order to fill up my own sense of loneliness, despair, depression, inadequate recognition by others, inadequate love from others, or fear that I won't have enough or that there will not be enough later on, or as a way of diverting my attention from other unmet needs, I will do the following:

A. The next time I feel that need, I will refuse to do what I normally do to avoid it or fill it up.

B. If I find that I'm too addicted to that behavior to stop, I will take some specific steps to limit it in the next few weeks, and see how that feels. I will buy less, eat less, give less time to drinking or drugs or sexual excess or to whatever other addictive behavior I use to fill up or divert my attention from my unhappiness or yearning, and instead will focus on the source of those feelings and how to overcome them.

C. Failing that, I will seek help from others to find another way besides my current attachments to fill up those needs-including some spiritual path like Shabbat, prayer, meditation, walks in nature or listening to music, building community with others, and working for Tikkun-the healing and transformation of our world to rebuild it in ways that are ecologically sustainable, socially just, non-violent, and filled with love and generosity, and awe and wonder at the grandeur of all that is."

Accumulating Successful Models of Change

Making commitments for change and affiliating with people who make similar commitments seems to be taking on a life of its own The accumulation of millions of voices for change, that could eventually overthrow the masters of war is now happening. Here is another example...

Charlie Bloom Telling the Story of Dr. Ariyaratne of Sri Lanka
(Bloomwork.com. May 2010)[2]

We wrote in an earlier newsletter about our friend in Sri Lanka who has often been compared to Gandhi. There were years and years of war in Sri Lanka between religious groups. After a peace settlement was brokered by the Norwegians, Dr. Ariyaratne invited the followers of his movement to gather to hear his vision of the future of Sri Lanka. Over 650,000 people showed up at the gathering, in which he proposed a 500 year peace plan saying that "It's taken us 500 years to create the suffering that we're in now", making reference to the effects of 400 years of colonialism and 500 years of religious strife between Hindus, Buddhists, and Muslims, "and it will take us 500 years to change these conditions.

Dr. Ariyaratne then laid out a plan in which after the cease-fire, all parties would learn each other's languages and cultures and economic injustices would be corrected. Included in the plan was a commitment to meet in council every hundred years and assess how the plan is going. This plan would necessitate the involvement of an informed, educated and engaged citizenry that not only understands the causes of suffering, but is committed to taking whatever actions are necessary in order to attend to the social wounds that need to be healed.

...I met and briefly spoke with Dr. Ariyaratne before the opening session. Although he is slightly built and soft-spoken, Dr. Ariyaratne embodies his commitment to peace and justice through a powerful and compelling presence that radiates both compassion and fierce intentionality. Shortly after our meeting, Dr. Ariyaratne addressed the conference in his opening keynote presentation, which followed the welcoming talk by Congresswoman Lynn Woolsey.

His address was both inspiring and challenging. In it he reminded all of us that the creation of an economic system that is based upon sustainable rather than exploitative (of people as well as natural resources) practices, is primarily a spiritual matter, and secondarily, a technological one. This process requires the transformation of consciousness, from which alternative economic and political systems will inevitably follow, rather than the reverse order. As an organization that is dedicated to personal and social transformation, the Saravodaya Shramadana movement supports the cultivation of mindfulness and the practice of awareness as a means of promoting clarity and deeper understanding of ourselves and our world. All organizational gatherings, from the smallest local groups to those in which there are thousands in attendance, begin with meditation.

Dr. Ariyaratne spoke of how when the mind is clear and open, it becomes possible to cultivate right understanding of a situation, which leads to right thoughts, which promotes right speech, which generates right actions, which creates right livelihood for all. This is not an abstract theory, but a reality that applies to us all and one that the Saravodaya movement has put into practice and has altered the lives and destinies of millions. It offers a means of awakening to the truth of who we are and our relationship with all beings while we honor and fulfill the needs and requirements of both the material and spiritual planes of existence.

In its forty-seven-year history, the Saravodaya movement has grown to include over 15,000 Sri Lankan villages and has built over 5,000 schools, community health centers, libraries, and banks, and dug many thousands of wells. "True community, states Dr. Ariaratne, "requires nourishing the body as well as the spirit; the melding of a sense of mutual responsibility and self-help that comes from living the truth of compassion, loving kindness, joy in the happiness of others, and equanimity."

When we integrate these principles into our lives, whether we are inhabitants of a small rural village or residents of a major urban metropolis, our quality of life will transform to one in which we experience an "abundance of sufficiency." As Gandhi reminded us, "there is enough for everyone's need, but not for everyone's greed." Knowing the distinction between these two and living accordingly may be the essence of true spiritual wisdom."

Participating in the Great Spiritual Alliance

All of us are allies. Those of us who teach psychological maturation, spiritual growth, economic revolution, and scientific progress to relieve stress on ourselves and our fellow species, revolutionaries both violent and non-violent, creators of alternative lifestyles and communities, and so on. It takes all kinds of people working together in a gigantic whirlpool of psychological, emotional, spiritual, and physical change—to become aware of each other, just as Dr. A.T. Ariyaratne advocated that all the religious groups of Sri Lanka get to know each other and engage in a common task of evolving the society to a new place of thriving instead of conflict and ignorance. These immense acts of inclusion are actually escalating. We all are, in fact, becoming more aware of each other through the Internet and through our many affiliations.

Ed Greville Telling about Willie Smits[3]

"Absolutely amazing! This is a miracle that the world needs to know about!" That is how my friend Ed introduced me to the TED 2009 talk by Willie Smits on how he restored the rainforest and saved orangutans and human beings. *[See end notes for the specific link so you can watch that Ted talk too. —Brad]*

Willie Smits: Conservationist
TED Speaker Profile[4]

Willie Smits works at the complicated intersection of humankind, the animal world, and our green planet. In his early work as a forester in Indonesia, he came to a deep understanding of that triple relationship, as he watched the growing population of Sulawesi move into (or burn for fuel) forests that are home to the orangutan. These intelligent animals were being killed for food, traded as pets or simply failing to thrive as their forest home degraded.

Smits believes that to rebuild orangutan populations, we must first rebuild their forest habitat—*which means helping local people find options other than the short-term fix of harvesting forests to survive.* His Masarang Foundation raises money and awareness to restore habitat forests around the world—and to empower local people. In 2007, Masarang opened a palm-sugar factory that uses thermal energy to turn sugar palms (fast-growing trees that thrive in degraded soils) into sugar and even ethanol, returning cash and power to the community and, with luck, starting the cycle toward a better future for people, trees and orangs.

The talk by Smits on TED is a must-see. He actually, with the help of many local people who were given the opportunity to thrive on helping each other improve their living environment, *recreated a rain forest and changed the weather, which started expanding the forest!* And the local people became the defenders of the forest! If you can watch this talk and the standing ovation at the end of it without crying your heart out with joy, you have done something I have been unable to do through many viewings!

Realizing that in order to rebuild the Orangutan population he had to rebuild the human population and have them restore the almost already destroyed environment. And they did it! I am leaving this one reference in the text of this book rather than listing it in the bibliography because it is critical to my presentation of successful solutions to big problems here. This man, Willie Smits, and his friends have created and proven a working model of how we might actually work together to restore the earth.

"This man has dedicated his life to saving the world, and for this he earns our deepest respect." —Jean Kern, Ode

The People's Agreement
From the World People's Conference on Climate Change and the Rights of Mother Earth in Cochabamba, Bolivia, 2010[5]

Today, our Mother Earth is wounded and the future of humanity is in danger.

If global warming increases by more than 2 degrees Celsius, a situation that the "Copenhagen Accord" could lead to, there is a 50 percent probability that the damages caused to our Mother Earth will be completely irreversible. Between 20 percent and 30 percent of species would be in danger of disappearing. Large extensions of forest would be affected, droughts and floods would affect different regions of the planet, deserts would expand, and the melting of the polar ice caps and the glaciers in the Andes and Himalayas would worsen. Many island states would disappear, and Africa would suffer an increase in temperature of more than 3 degrees Celsius. Likewise, the production of food would diminish in the world, causing catastrophic impact on the survival of inhabitants from vast regions in the planet, and the number of people in the world suffering from hunger would increase dramatically, a figure that already exceeds 1.02 billion people. The corporations and governments of the so-called "developed" countries, in complicity with a segment of the scientific community, have led us to discuss climate change as a problem limited to the rise in temperature without questioning the cause, which is the capitalist system.

We confront the terminal crisis of a civilizing model that is patriarchal and based on the submission and destruction of human beings and nature that accelerated since the industrial revolution.

The capitalist system has imposed on us a logic of competition, progress and limitless growth. This regime of production and consumption seeks profit without limits, separating human beings from nature and imposing a logic of domination upon nature, transforming everything into commodities: water, earth, the human genome, ancestral cultures, biodiversity, justice, ethics, the rights of peoples, and life itself.

Under capitalism, Mother Earth is converted into a source of raw materials, and human beings into consumers and a means of production, into people that are seen as valuable only for what they own, and not for what they are.

Capitalism requires a powerful military industry for its processes of accumulation and imposition of control over territories and natural resources, suppressing the resistance of the peoples. It is an imperialist system of colonization of the planet.

Humanity confronts a great dilemma: to continue on the path of capitalism, depredation, and death, or to choose the path of harmony with nature and respect for life.

Books about Current Social Change that Elaborate this Theme

A book I have mentioned before here, *Blessed Unrest* by Paul Hawken (Viking, 2007), is absolutely full of encouraging news about the awakening of humanity. I won't presume to summarize it here except to say that it is a quick and encouraging read. Like Rifkin's *The Empathic Civilization*, this book has a perspective on tragedy that makes it seem downright fortunate when you look at the big picture. The primary blockage to the accomplishments of these long lists of wonderful pioneers are corporate capitalists, who, if we don't take a bite out of, may prevent progress necessary for our survival.

We merely need to reshuffle significantly—and according to new rules—who owns and who owes. The mythology of money has to change as the main players change and we can't change it without changing the main players. We need to make money be secondary to, rather than determinant of, the well being of living creatures, including ourselves.

The Indian Ten Commandments[6]
Sent by Jack Bloomfield of One Planet United

1. Treat the earth and all that dwell thereon with respect
2. Remain close to the Great Spirit
3. Show great respect for your fellow beings
4. Work together for the benefit of all mankind
5. Give assistance and kindness wherever needed
6. Do what you know to be right
7. Look after the well being of mind and body
8. Dedicate a share of your efforts to the greater good
9. Be truthful and honest at all times
10. Take full responsibility for your actions

These ten items could well become the basis of a new financial order, because they don't mention money at all.

Now I want to turn to Tom Atlee again, who, in this next essay, provides an overview of these kinds of things being put into motion.

Democracy in Crisis: Breakdown and Breakthrough
By Tom Atlee (*Co-Intelligence Institute newsletter*, May 2010)[7]

I'll talk about democracy in a minute. But first a note about crises and evolution. Evolutionary science tells us that crises and catastrophes are cauldrons of co-creativity, generating new forms. Perhaps the most dramatic example is how the seventy heavier-than-iron elements get created in supernovae explosions of dying stars, some of which burst so violently they are as bright as a whole galaxy. You can't get much more catastrophically creative than that.

Here are two potent examples from the deep history of our own planet:

1. Over a billion years ago there was an "oxygen crisis," in which existing photosynthetic bacteria cranked out so much oxygen into the ocean it was toxifying the planet. It was rusting all the nutrient iron out of the water, eating away at the bacteria themselves—remember anti-oxidants? —and depleting methane from the atmosphere, dangerously cooling the planet. Bad news! Luckily, oxygen-breathing bacteria evolved right at that time to change oxygen to carbon dioxide, putting things back in balance.

2. Hundreds of millions of years later an unfortunate concentration of meteor strikes and volcanoes apparently triggered climate change so serious that it wiped out the dinosaurs and most other species on earth. That cleared the way for the emergence of big mammals like us. Our rodent ancestors' underground lifestyle apparently helped them survive that global calamity sixty-five million years ago, releasing a whole new

era of evolutionary creativity, out of which we showed up very much later.

It is certainly something to think about: If it weren't for these three horrendous catastrophes (among many others), we wouldn't be here. For better and worse, the crises keep coming.

Which brings us to today, sixty-five million years after the dinosaurs left the stage. And what do we find? The U.S. Supreme Court has just decided that giant special interest groups like unions and corporations deserve the same speech rights as ordinary citizens and that money is speech. Tossing aside major laws and legal precedents, a 5-4 majority stripped away all limits to corporate partisan activity in federal elections (opening the way for similar legalistic unleashings in state and local elections). Talk about a catastrophe!

If all of us could buy hours of TV advertising and legions of lawyers to beat opponents in court and lobbyists to beat opponents in politics and buy off government official with campaign contributions, that might be one thing. But we don't have the same economic and social power as insurance conglomerates, oil companies, and Wall Street. And the idea that corporations are persons—nailed down explicitly in this decision—is patently absurd. The Bill of Rights gets stretched to the breaking point when a multinational corporation is given the same rights as you and I. Somehow I can't imagine the USA's Founding Fathers had this in mind when they said "We the People."

Maybe it would be okay if all bloggers and media were created equal and everything was presented in rational arguments. But that's not the way it is. And it is getting worse: Add to that the rapidly growing ability of political advertising literally to get inside your brain, totally bypassing your rational mind so you think you know why you're making a decision to buy or vote, but you don't have a clue—a practice known as neuromarketing—and we have the makings of a political system light years more manipulated and out of control than it is now. The prospects for an appropriate balance of power vanish in an explosion of polarizing language, compelling imagery and potent networking.

Some folks are calling this sea change in our political landscape the end of American democracy, as we know it. At the very least, it is a rapidly growing obstacle to our already struggling collective intelligence and community wisdom.

Okay, so we have a catastrophe in the making. Where's the opportunity?

I see an unprecedented surge of democratic consciousness-raising and creativity in the last few months and going off the charts in the last week. The Supreme Court decision directly inspired a few of these efforts, but by its extreme irrationality it also releases powerful energies that could support any number of significant initiatives and radically shift democracy in participatory, answerable, collectively intelligent directions. Anything could happen. Right now is what evolutionary political theorists call "an evolutionary moment."

Here are some of the more promising wise-democratic initiatives I see emerging to give a voice to "the people" as a whole, awaiting your support and participation. I'm confident there are hundreds of others that I don't know about or have overlooked. This tip of the iceberg suggests there's a significant shift developing under the surface...

1. Inspired by a David Sirota article "Seeing Red and Feeling Blue in Purple America," a new "Purple Alliance" is coming together to "convene concerned individuals and organizations from anywhere on the political spectrum; consider every issue that anyone cares enough about to defend or advocate; and connect everything and include Congress." I'm not sure how exactly they plan to do this, but the intention is clear. As purple movement leading light Bruce Schuman says, "The way I see it—there's a new wind blowing. I think there are new ideas in the air. I think there are emerging new political forces—that aren't about "Republicans" and "Democrats". We need a political system that is about "the people" and about "democracy", not the two-party system—and about the right way to run this country, and how we can come together as a nation, to be stronger, to be better..."

2. The Transpartisan Alliance has already had remarkable success bringing together leading progressives and conservatives for creative conversation. It is now exploring the possibility of convening Citizen Leadership Councils and Citizens Assemblies of people from all parties—Democrats, Republicans, Greens, Libertarians, Independents, etc. —to discuss issues of public importance and advise government and the public with common ground solutions.

3. Steven Kull, a leading international pollster at World Public Opinion wrote to me, "I have found very strong support [among citizens] for the public having a much greater role in governance and strong support for informed representative samples [of randomly selected citizens] playing an advisory role to government. In the US, 68 percent support the idea and three quarters say they would have more confidence in the views of such a group than the views of Congress." So Steven is developing a major pilot program to create a Citizen Advisory Panel of thousands of citizens at a state level (randomly chosen, one-third turnover each year) to serve as a pool from which people would be picked for occasional phone surveys, online surveys and deliberations, and face-to-face citizen deliberative councils. (His proposal is not yet online.)

4. The Co-Intelligence Institute's research project called the Whole System Initiative envisions multiple simultaneous but independent citizen deliberative councils and stakeholder dialogues tackling a single subject. The outcomes of all of them could be compared for instructive similarities and differences. Then the participants would be mixed and matched into a final round of conversations using Dynamic Facilitation—all in an effort to see if any particular series of "convenings of the whole" would result in similar outcomes. If some form of citizen dialogue and deliberation could produce replicable results like public opinion surveys do, it would

be a major breakthrough for democracy. The specific process described in the project is offered more as a starting place for wise-democratic research than as a final proposal for wise-democratic process.

5. Promise USA proposes a networked series of national conversations, hosted by Michelle Obama, inviting citizens to explore questions of importance to all. The questions would be posed by Michelle and explored in World Cafe-style conversations in which people talk in small groups for half an hour and then switch into new small groups, going through several cycles of this before all together harvesting what they learned or created in their groups. Conversations could be as small as a few people in someone's home to thousands in large auditoriums or convention centers. With several national conversations each year, each conversation would begin with a report from the First Lady about what actions individuals, groups, and the government had done that arose out of the last conversation. Initiated by facilitators who have used World Cafe with the Girl Scouts of America, Promise USA's initial conversations would be facilitated by girl scouts themselves, to help the adult citizens stay focused on long-term common-welfare solutions that will serve the next generations well.

6. Ballot Initiative Process Reform. The main project I'm familiar with here is the Oregon effort, Healthy Democracy Oregon (HDO) to institute a Citizens Initiative Review (CIR) in which citizens juries review every ballot measure that qualifies for the ballot—interviewing advocates and opponents of the measure, deliberating together and then publishing their findings in the official voter information pamphlet. The Oregon State government last year authorized an official pilot of the proposal, which will review three ballot initiatives during this year's election. The folks working on this have also been invited to a International Forum on Direct Democracy whose main focus is on ballot measures, and their use to change constitutions. Two major subtopics are the use of technology in changing the initiative process, and efforts to reform technology.

7. Repair California, a movement to create a Citizens Assembly to rewrite California's dysfunctional constitution that is at the heart of the state's current mess (bordering on collapse). The Assembly would be "randomly chosen with five delegates from each of California's eighty assembly districts, a four hundred-person sample large enough to be representative. The initiative that calls the convention can define an open process that adds webcasting, blogs, social networking, and hearings to build a consensus. Citizen delegates will earn a stipend so they can take a leave of absence from work, have a budget to hire the experts, and travel around the state in hearings and meetings."

8. Wisdom Councils use dynamic facilitation to help a periodic group of randomly selected citizens to articulate citizen concerns, dreams, and creative solutions. Held regularly (ideally, quarterly for a community, annually for a state or nation), Wisdom Councils serve to develop the collective voice, self-awareness, and agency

of We the People, both through the councils themselves and through the impact they have on the community's ongoing conversations and activities. While this American idea has been around for over a decade, it is beginning to gain traction particularly in Canada and Europe.

Although each of these (and a number of other existing "voice of the people" programs from Public Agenda to AmericaSpeaks to National Issues Forums) arises from a different sense of what, exactly, is needed and how to achieve it, they all seem to be grounded in a shared desire to access the common voice and wisdom of the whole society—We the People. That such a collectively wise voice is even possible to achieve is an idea new in our adversarial political culture, stuck as it is in "May the best man win" or, at best, "The art of politics is compromise."

The fact that so many visions of real public judgment and community wisdom are showing up makes me wonder if it is time to connect them all together, to create a larger conversation among those who believe it is both possible and desirable to call forth a legitimate, wise, empowered voice of We the People. What would such dialogue and networking come up with that would be more practical, powerful, fundable and broadly attractive than any of the proposals so far put on the table?

I can imagine (just for example) a system for broad spectrum citizen input grounded in an expanded form of Steven Kull's already broad vision, including not only a variety of survey channels and types of citizen deliberative councils, but also crowd-sourcing software to collect and evaluate bright ideas and proposals from the public, integrated with direct democracy systems for online voting, as well as leading edge research into how we can best generate a legitimate, wise "voice of the whole" that appropriately includes experts, stakeholders, and policy-makers, as well as average citizens. This whole system could be woven into the political and governmental process in many ways, from advising the public or policy makers, to actually passing laws or budgets. It could address policy issues, proposals, candidates, evaluation of government or corporate operations, and constitutional amendments; you name it.

Steven Kull notes that public wisdom on many issues can be discovered inexpensively using online surveys, while other topics—like budgets, highly technical subjects, and very polarized issues—may best be addressed using face-to-face, in-depth, deliberative approaches, which would be less frequent due to their expense. In some places approaches would become institutionalized, while in other places such a process may be stewarded by the grassroots, and backed by a network of We the People lobbyists and organizers. In any case, a very committed and enlightened grassroots movement is needed to push such a People's Voice system into existence over the resistance of entrenched special interests. It would require activists who realize that creating new, wiser, more answerable democratic structures is far more important than any other issue because it will determine how all other issues are dealt with.

Other responses to the Supreme Court's decision that don't involve creating a "wise voice of We the People" include:

A. *Strengthen Conflict of Interest Laws*: Doris "Granny D" Haddock, who ten years ago—at ninety years old—walked across the U.S. for campaign finance reform, now suggests "a flanking move that will help [campaign finance] reforms move faster: We need to dramatically expand the definition of what constitutes an illegal conflict of interest in politics" to include anything that significantly benefits a corporation. "Should you ethically vote on health issues if health companies fund a large chunk of your campaign? The success of your campaign, after all, determines your future career and financial condition. You have a conflict." Interestingly, this conflict-of-interest approach serves to facilitate the evolutionary activist agenda of "aligning the self-interest of individuals and corporations to the well-being of the whole society."

B. *Ban Corporate Personhood:* Ralph Nader writes, "This corporatist, anti-voter decision is so extreme that it should galvanize a grassroots effort to enact a Constitutional Amendment to once and for all end corporate personhood and curtail the corrosive impact of big money on politics. It is indeed time for a Constitutional amendment to prevent corporate campaign contributions from commercializing our elections and drowning out the civic and political voices and values of citizens and voters."

I agree and think this is one of the most basic reforms needed. Wikipedia provides a detailed discussion of corporate personhood and a list of organizations already working on it

C. *A Constitutional Amendment*: Pass an amendment to allow Congress to limit corporate involvement in elections. FreeSpeechForPeople.org and People for the American Way are pushing this, which complements the Nader approach, above.

D. *National Politicians Respond.* Sen. Chuck Schumer and Rep. Chris Van Hollen have attacked the Supreme Court ruling and pledged to push through legislation to combat it. President Obama said he can't "think of anything more devastating to the public interest" than the Supreme Court's decision, and he will make it a priority to address it.

Other organizations responding rapidly to this include Alliance for Democracy, Public Citizen, The Community Environmental Legal Defense Fund, New Coalition and Liberty Tree.

Again, Reality Includes the Best and the Worst

The list of inspiring developments generated by Tom Atlee can give us heart, and maybe help us to see that the source of real power in the world could be just us. His list of things that are beginning to make a difference in perspective on ourselves and our friends and even our enemies is heartening.

While it is important to point out, as I have in the biggest part of this book, how even if we win we lose, my friend Jack Stork points out that even if we lose we win sometimes. Life is in charge of life...

From Jack Stork[8]

Even those among us who can see, who can observe the hardening condition induced by the enemies of human liberty and well being, feel powerless in the face of this darkening and omniscient order. Despite the quadrennial claims of our political parties during national election years, no savior has arrived and none is coming. No Obama, no miracle of "green science," no national genius will emerge to lead us. We have only the simple, direct, undeceived intelligence of ordinary men and women to rely upon. We must regain respect for the seemingly meager and often lonely powers an individual does have, and choose work and a way of living upon which we can all rely.

Acknowledgment of that, and living accordingly, engenders humility, success and the physical and spiritual thrivance of men and women and children everywhere. It is the animating spirit of socialism.

The Universe is eruptions, fire, collision, destruction, rebuilding, reordering, beauty, and chaos. From a distance, this chaos is beauty, magnificence. Up close, it is unnerving and gives rise to the impulse to instill order.

Life is chaotic, always has been and probably always will be. The impulse to instill order is strongest in the young who have been prepared to live in a neurotic, predictable, Walt Disney world. All over the world one can see college students carrying signs that say, End War, End poverty, and so on. Really saying, "Fix the world to be like the liars told me it was so I can live in the world that I was prepared for."

Instead of ordering the chaos, it is wiser to order one's self to live in chaos. In spite of the dangers, outside, inside, and all around, plus the ones that we ourselves create. The human race has increased to a dangerous size.

If half of the human race were eradicated, there would still be too many people, but the planet would be healthier.

Tom Atlee is on the right track. All living things share a desire to achieve a healthier state of being, including the planet. It is what makes the potted plant on the kitchen counter lean toward the window. It somehow knows that it needs light.

If our world is in grave danger from humanity, it will simply shrug off however many of us as is necessary.

CHAPTER 17

A Final Framework for a Feasible Failure: What I Have Said, What I Have Said about What Others Have Said, and What We Should Do About It

This is the last chapter. There is a theme to it. The theme is that there is not enough time left. I think we have less than a generation's worth of time left before the damage of all previous generations does us in.

What we have to place our hope in is the capacity of old dogs and new kids to learn and apply the solutions of deep democracy. And it must be done aptly enough for a new human community to arise, thrive, and work for us to care for each other instead of keep on killing each other. I don't think there is enough time for that.

Still, I know that what I have learned over the course of my lifetime works for personal and social change, and what I have learned more recently works to speed it up.

I became an advocate for Radical Honesty more and more over the course of my life. I did so as a social activist, a clinical psychologist, a seminar leader, and a writer. A lot of people like Radical Honesty. Some don't. Some don't like it at first and then come to like it more as it soaks in. Our motto, which summarizes the evidence, is: "Radical Honesty! It works pretty good... most of the time!"

When George Monbiot says that democracy is the "least-worst" system of government, I take him to be making an analogous statement to mine about radical honesty. We could say that radical honesty is the least-worst rule of thumb for relationships—or that democracy works pretty good… most of the time. So, I think, the least-worst new system we can come up with now to save the world of humankind from itself and much allied life from extinction due to our destructiveness, is what we could call a radically honest deep democracy, which would be the least worst form of governance for our time and work pretty good… most of time!

The Wider Definition of Cannibalism

This book is obviously not just about cannibalism in the narrowest sense of the word. It is, however, very much about cannibalism in the broadest sense of the word. I have cannibalized some of the best thoughts and practices of many of my peers during my time.

The perennial ongoing argument between the protection of property and the life of the community has produced the emergencies facing the world and also the ideas to solve those problems. The shit I make out of digesting all of this stolen produce is pretty rich, and it has a chance of being the fertilizer for one of the best new dysfunctional systems ever devised by humankind!

Here is how I suggest we go about creating a world of less destruction and to avoid terminal entropic payback:

Rob from the filthy rich and give to the dirty poor, both money and protein. By mutual agreement simple delete the power at the top, take their shit and start over.

Organize immediately so as to take care of each other best by including each other in the design of how we get cared for.

Develop a new system of justice based on sustainability, and protect against the excesses of capitalism growing back again.

Synthesize all research on honesty and lie detection and build a Truth Machine (combining people and technology) that is highly accurate and can catch almost all liars before during and after agreements and actions they have made in the world, so that lying becomes futile.

Set up a form of government that utilizes dialogue and deliberation techniques like the World Café and its offshoots. This jury duty kind of service has term limits and people are drawn at random for it and asked to volunteer for a few months at a time. Their expenses will be covered, including at least part of what it costs them for being away from their jobs, homes, or businesses for a while.

Establish some form of world government to guarantee protection of world citizens from nation-states and corporate conspiracies.

Outlaw financial contributions to campaigns by vested interests, with real teeth in the law for violators (heh heh). If necessary, kill, eat and have a ritual to acknowledge the violators.

Design an educational system, and childrearing practices, that maximize the opportunity for the growth of human empathy, compassion, and intimacy. Raise children and heal adults raised in old cultural ways to advance their capacity for empathy using a loving learning system to replace what used to be called education. Establish from this a meritocracy that includes at the top level of evaluation, evidence of compassion.

The Limited and Limiting Ongoing Argument

The system of justice we have now is reflected in the Supreme Court. Current members and all recent nominees are significantly biased toward profiteers on issues of conflict between the wealthy and the community in general. No court member really sees in the precedents of the court any justification for opposing property ownership in favor of general community well-being at the expense of those with property. Liberals and Conservatives, Democrats and Republicans all fuss at each other cozily within the limited context of that ongoing argument.

No transcendent perspective will occur unless and until there is a global threat that everyone agrees upon. So these upcoming tragedies I have reported on may turn out to be our best hope. At this point it seems inevitable to me that a lot of people are going to die. It also seems clear to me that many fewer would have to die, and that those surviving would be happier and safer, if we chose who to kill selectively, using common sense in the best sense of the word. The logic of this is irrefutable.

It doesn't really matter whether or not we barbeque these people. I was just being practical. It is time to rob the robber barons and redistribute the wealth and the responsibility. And this needs to start immediately, if not sooner.

Stages of Incline as We Fall Together to Replace the World That Is Falling Apart

There is a progression through stages of personal growth written about in all the books we've put out on Radical Honesty. These same stages can be used to infer the path of growth needed for our upcoming quick cultural evolution.

Personal growth starts with the neurotic and unhappy individual life of the person who has been conventionally raised in the standard socially acceptable forms of abuse: working parents, families of fragmentation, the standard dumbing-down form of schooling, drugs, rock and roll, and so forth (the whole nine yards).

This person is the Toyota recall of the early twenty-first century—trying to solve the problem of being trapped in the jail of his or her mind, using his or her mind to try to escape. The process is to lose your mind and come to your senses and then repossess the mind while grounded in experience, so you can *use it* instead of being trapped in it.

There are billions of such "trapped in the jail of the mind" people, and millions trapped in the jails created by the minds of others who are equally confused.

We have a way to make most of these people happy, eventually productive and co-intelligent, and then politically powerful and contributive to others.

We can break what we do down into segments. Each of these segments stands alone and is also an invitation to the next segment. Each rewards the person with a modicum of improvement on their standard issue unhappiness and *substitutes a new kind of trouble*. The new trouble, the person is responsible for creating and proud to have. The trick is to choose new trouble to take the place of the previous misery. New and better misery, we might call it. Happier misery.

The sum of new and happier misery eventually results in social reform. It may lead, eventually, to the greatest human happiness ever known, from participating in an ongoing compassionate, loving community based on contribution to others. It generally starts with a lot of trouble.

Personal Transformation from Fairly Miserable to Pretty Happy, Even in Times of Trouble

The sequence of development in this "growing to full humanity" progression, is a kind of repair and replacement program with parallel segments, or pods, or programmed learning units, which can be roughly outlined like this:

1. *Grounding*: Interruption of the mind and discovery of the noticing being. Learning and using techniques and practices in noticing sensation and gravity and attending to personal experience. This is where you lose your mind and come to your senses and identify yourself as a noticing being with a mind, rather than a mind dragging along a body. This sounds easy, but is a lot of work because we are up against a brainwashing that exists even in the minds of the teachers, based on a lifetime of poisonous contextualizing of sensate information with cognitive "understandings" that are themselves poisonous.

2. *Relating and Forgiving*: Developing the capacity for intimacy—in a community of at least two—means going deeper through Radical Honesty. The subparts of this training are based on learning how to take charge of the flashlight of our attention. Once we learn how to take charge of our attention and can focus on either the external world, internal sensation or internal thought, we then shift the flashlight of attention from thoughts in the mind, and interpretations of emotions that live in the mind, to sensations in the body. The shift of the light of noticing from categories of the mind to sensations allows for the experiential resolution of emotions usually known as anger, embarrassment, grief, shame, horniness, joyfulness, and so on.

When people learn how to go into and pass through intense emotions—when life is just sensational—they become powerfully human and open to new experience. This is also called forgiveness. Forgiveness is possible because life is just sensational. Forgiveness leads to the possibility of love in community.

3. *Conscious Cooperation* (Co-intelligent Co-creation in Community—CCC) (Si, Si, Si! Amigo!): The building of a community of noticers who support each other and play together using each other's *beings and minds* to design each individual future, and then to design their future together. This is a co-creative process, based on caring for each other, paying attention to each other, listening to each other and playing with each other using all these capacities. Life purpose statements, project

write-ups, and time and money investment commitments and contracts come out of this for individuals. New organizations not yet known will be born out of this for communities. Children are sometimes better at leading this process than adults. Childlike adults and children therefore will trade off leadership in this process and all hierarchies are temporary.

Herd of Us? How to Be an Open Loving Happy Human Being Most of the Time, and Having a Community of Support to Prove It

The design of renewal of the process of liberation from the mind, done by the community of caring and care giving—is what education really is. We can establish a cooperative system of ongoing planning and sensitivity training about how to help each other pass the opportunity for the good life forward. This is about political and social reform through planning and action, but not like we have ever done it before. It is about alignment with each other and others we have not met, though we intend together to build the empathic civilization—the takeover of the world from the careless and giving it to those who care by either converting the careless or killing and eating them and taking all their wealth to put back into the commonwealth.

An Idea Whose Time has Come

Radical Honesty for personal happiness and community organizing is an idea whose time has come. It may also be an idea whose time has come too late. To actually attempt to change the world by loving and helping many people and killing a few other people is obviously one way to go about assisting the mass of human beings to save themselves from each other. But to do this on a large enough scale and quickly enough to actually turn us back from the path to extinction is the greatest challenge so far in the history of humankind.

Each of these things (with the exception of the empathic civilization on a world scale), have been accomplished by people who have attended Radical Honesty workshops in the past, generally over the course of a couple years or so. (See my book *The Truthtellers: Stories of Success by Radically Honest People,* for details.)

When people get some idea of the sequence of things (honesty, forgiveness, intimacy, community, co-creation, co-intelligence, and common work for community change and justice), they often enroll other people they know in reading the books and taking a workshop to practice the skills of radical honesty.

Out of Conflict, Wisdom. Out of Trouble, Peace

The process of undoing poisonous cultural conditioning and reframing the world is difficult. It takes persistence and requires psychological change even more than intellectual learning—a process that, so far, still takes a lot of time.

People come to the Center for Radical Honesty because they are not happy. They are rich and middle class people, privileged people of the world, and they are not happy. But they are entertained. Rich people are pleasantly distracted. After a while entertainment doesn't do the trick of distracting us from our alienation, but that takes a while to happen.

Unhappiness and dissatisfaction are built into our dysfunctional attempts to control and/or dominate or use other people while faking that we care—the standard operating procedure taught by our culture.

This is the way to "happiness" in our culture that doesn't work, but it takes a while to learn that it doesn't work. By the time we get that what we do to try to be happy doesn't work, really, for anyone, even for those "on top," we resist acknowledging what we know to be true. We have to bang our heads on the wall of life for a while. All these things take time.

What implications does this have for saving humanity and its millions of victims among our fellow species? A lot depends on whether all these long progressions from dumbed down to enlightenment must be followed without any shortcuts—in order to get enough of us to wrest control from, or educate and train (or some combination thereof) the rich people who are in charge.

In order to impact and change the ignorant pell-mell trip into hell we are in a race with each other to achieve or prevent, we need to act more quickly than we have ever acted before to bring about a change of heart and perspective in our enemies and ourselves.

And we must learn how to be happy personally, and start a contagion of curative happiness that cures the low level depression that most privileged people of the world call "life," while they rob and kill others to maintain their lifestyle. What can we do?

The Taoists say the way to find out what to do is meditate and reflect on and attend to water. "To the Taoists, water's intuitive, harmonius flow was wiser than the rational attitudes of a linear, man-over-nature mind. Thus, according to the ancient Taoist master Kuan-Tzu, as quoted by Brenda Peterson in *A Change of Heart: The Global Wellness Inventory*, "The solution for the sage who would transform the world is water." Our present day willfulness has taught us much about our own separate selves and little about how to live wisely and at one with the world. Only now are we recalling that there is a Tao at play in the world; and understanding its way may well help us find reunion with our own, and the earth's body."

We have to learn from water, and we have to learn from animals. And from children. And from people who have forgiven and become grounded in their experience. For animals, it's different than it is for us. Animals live in a world of now, which can allow them to experience being happy but perhaps not happiness.

Psychologists say that the emotion of feeling happy is generally a feeling that lives briefly, based on present circumstances. Happiness, on the other hand, is drawn from an overall assessment of one's life. That assessment, in turn, is based on myriad factors, including age, marital status, societal expectations, and health. Happiness is a summation, a conclusion over time. Animals don't worry about it because animals generally don't worry. People do. We have to have people see clearly the possibility of flowing like water and being like an animal as a path to happiness. And they have to see how they can be happy along the way to happiness from both having the vision of where they are going and the experience of helping and being helped along the way.

Our empathic brain, our limbic intelligence, integrated with our cognitive brain and utilizing our ability to be present to life and love and other people, done quickly and repeatedly, moment by moment, is the path to our salvation.

Overall Happiness

Recent studies in England indicate that each person has an average overall level of happiness at any particular period of life. If you ask someone if he or she is happy, the answer tends to be given quickly, without hesitation, reflecting the person's review of many years of life. Researchers say that this accounts for the incongruous situation in which someone who has recently lost a beloved pet or learned bad news can still answer that, in general, their life is a happy one. This average state, or baseline, has been defined as a "set point" of happiness, like the set temperature for a refrigerator.

Another study published in The British Medical Journal in 2008 announced that happiness spreads through groups like a viral contagion. Researchers following individuals found that happiness from one person was transmitted through close relationships with friends, siblings, spouses, and neighbors.

Moreover, feeling happy tended to spread more consistently and easily through the network than unhappiness. The closer an individual is to the center of the network, in other words the more friends and connections he or she has, the more likely they are to be happy. Those at the outskirts of the network, with fewer friends and acquaintances, are significantly less happy.

The majority of rich people, as well as many, many poor people, are on the outskirts of happiness, if we mean by that, actually joyfully living life.

We all need to fight the primary control system that keeps misery in place. Happiness requires knowing and admitting unhappiness, yet getting joy out of working to make things better for others and us. Like they say in AA, we have to admit that we have a problem. Then we have to support each other in not letting our problem run our lives.

Conscious Misery as One Key to Happiness

We need to generate *awareness* of unhappiness in order to generate happiness. We need to acknowledge misery and work with others to do something about it. We need to make people unhappy enough to change.

This rationale is the same as that of Muslim terrorists. They are right. If you cause enough misery things do sometimes change. The problem is, what they do (killing innocent people) hurts too much and takes too long as well. (It is important to mention here that not all fundamentalists are alike. The terrorists that bombed the Pentagon and the World Trade Center were smart and picked the right targets. They had accurately diagnosed the source of what keeps most of the world's misery in place. They are not as stupid as Baptists.)

Terrorists as well as all other propagandists are fundamentally educators. What they do is much too slow as well. It just takes too long.

So, what is an educational effort that can work quickly enough to save us from ourselves? It certainly looks like there is simply not one that works quickly enough. It appears that everything we have delved into here takes too long to bring about the amount of change of heart and mind needed quickly enough to save us from extinction.

Political change, terrorism, personal growth, spiritual development, and education for understanding (this book, for example) all are leading in the direction of what needs to change, but all of them together, even if in the flow of things they are really in accord, still are going to take too long. We are probably not going to blog, vote, pray, buy, fight, kill, or work our way to salvation, even if we step up to everything.

Some say the Internet will be our salvation because it allows for more empathetic learning and communication than ever before. That is true. But the most likely story about the Internet is that it will amuse us on the way, but will not change the structures of world oppression quickly enough to prevent our extinction. There is one hope. It is that *all of these things with cannibalism added to them might work!*

The Formerly Missing Link

Korporate kannibal cannibalism is the answer because it is the most efficient and direct route for world and personal reorganization. Change can happen fast enough to save us only if we eat the rich, or let them bribe themselves out of it, and then we cannibalize all they have. That, along with all the other combined efforts of humankind empathetically to recreate how we live together, I say, could work.

Korporate kannibal cannibalism is the missing link. This is the answer to doing things quickly enough to have them count. All of the wealth stolen from the world that can be restored can only be restored by taking it away from the most successful selfish bastards among us, the bullies, and their psychophants, who took it from the other "children" and lied to Mother Earth about it (and about stealing from her purse). We must kill and eat the folks in the seat so the human in the street can stay on her feet.

So, please ask yourself, *is it not true that we must do this in order to change quickly enough to not kill all the innocents and preserve primarily the ugly selfish bastards amongst us?*

Tom Atlee says (In the newsletter of the Co-Intelligence Institute): "So a crisis is upon us. If not addressed soon and well, it will almost surely morph into a catastrophe. If it is addressed in the right way, we could end up with a stronger, wiser democracy than we've ever had before. It is an evolutionary moment.

"Democracy is in crisis.

"Crisis presents opportunity.

"Opportunity opens the door to co-creativity.

"It is time for breakthroughs.

"It is time to move."[1]

As you know by now, I couldn't agree more. I am volunteering to be the biggest self-contradictory asshole of my time, advocating murder of killers who most don't recognize yet as the killers they are. It is fine with me if cannibalism is eventually viewed by history as simply a necessary stage of growth for the maturation of humanity rather than a permanent arrangement. We might leave in the rule that anyone keeping over a hundred million dollars gets eaten, and keep that in place for a hundred years or so, and then we can be done with it.

I just think cannibalism would give us a law that has some teeth in it, and it has a chance of getting the attention of people who don't think they have to pay attention to a damned thing.

Consider it. Then, as I said before, if you can come up with an idea that works any better than this, I am listening. Thanks for listening to me.

—Brad Blanton

NOTES

FRONT EPIGRAPHS

Woodrow Wilson, "A great industrial nation is controlled by its system of credit…" and "We are at a parting of the ways…" are quotes from separate speeches made during Wilson's 1911 run for the presidency. Often they are mistakenly cited as one quotation. A discussion by Andrew Leonard can be found online: www.salon.com/tech/htww/2007/12/21/Woodrow_Wilson_federal_reserve.

Ralph Waldo Emerson, "Self-reliance."

Charles Eisenstein, "The Ubiquitous Network of Lies" *Reality Sandwich* (June 24, 2009). Website: www.realitysandwich.com.

Dresden James. After repeated searches to ascertain the source of this quote, I have not been able to find any information on a man by this name, nor evidence that such a person has ever lived. It has gone viral among the blog community and I found the words powerful enough to include them in my book.

George Bernard Shaw, Annajanska (1919).

PREFACE

1. "The money powers prey upon the nation…" This quote is often attributed to Lincoln, when in fact William Jennings Bryan uttered it, probably during his run for the presidency. Source: www.referencecenter.com/ref/reference/Bryan-Wi/ William_Jennings_Bryan?invocationType=ar1clk&flv=1.
2. Joe Bageant, *Rainbow Pie*. Portobello Books, 2010. Viewed in advance of publication.

INTRODUCTION

1. Clinton Callahan, *The Power of Conscious Feelings*. Prescott, AZ.: Hohm Press, 2010. Viewed in advance of publication.

PART ONE

CHAPTER 1 GETTING HANGRY

1. Raj Patel, *The Value of Nothing: How to Reshape Market Society and Redefine*

Democracy. New York: Picador USA, 2010: pp. 88-9.
2. Paul Krugman, "Betraying the Planet," *New York Times* (June 29, 2009): p. A21.
3. Time to Eat the Dog? *The Real Guide to Sustainable Living*. Brenda and Robert Vale. New York: Thames and Hudson, 2009.
4. Susan Campbell. Private correspondence.

CHAPTER 2 FEEDING RICH PEOPLE TO POOR PEOPLE

1. George Monbiot and Paul Kingsnorth, "Is There Any Point in Fighting to Stave off Industrial Apocalypse?" *The Guardian/UK* (August 18, 2009). Website: www.guardian.co.uk.
2. Adam Sacks, "The Fallacy of Climate Activism," *Grist Magazine* (August 23, 2009). Website: www.grist.org.
3. Adam Sacks writes: "Many thanks to Richard Grossman, who posed that question fifteen years ago with respect to corporate domination of governance and culture when he founded the Program on Corporations, Law and Democracy (poclad.org). He understood that we must take the time to stop and penetrate beyond the obvious if we are to think outside of the cultural prescriptions that constrain our ability to act differently. Many thanks as well to Ross Gelbspan, a courageous and ground-breaking journalist, who early on investigated the forces driving the fossil fuel machine and has been sounding the alarm for almost two decades. See his excellent article, "Beyond the Point of No Return," (Grist.org) December 2007, which inspired many of the ideas in this piece."
4. Adam Sacks writes: "I would like to express deep gratitude to John A. Livingston, pioneer environmentalist, preservationist, teacher and writer. In 1981 he wrote "The Fallacy of Wildlife Conservation," which inspired the title of this piece. The fallacy that Livingston was referring to is well-described in the foreword by Graeme Gibson: "The Fallacy of Wildlife Conservation, as a statement of belief, is one of the fiercest and most uncompromising of John Livingston's convictions. Had he entitled it 'The Failure of Wildlife Conservation,' we might have tried again—without having to think too much about it. But he didn't. ... As a result of the word fallacy, we are confronted with an insistence that we rethink everything." *From The John A. Livingston Reader*, McClelland & Stewart, 2007, pp. xiv-xv. So it is, with the fallacy of climate activism, that we must rethink everything."
5. Adam Sacks writes: "Endless (exponential) growth is an impossibility in a finite physical system (planet earth), and we have a wealth of examples of overshoot and collapse, non-human and human, all of which are fully predictable. Our cultural inability to grasp such an obvious reality is a primary obstacle to progress in addressing climate change and its root cause. Indigenous cultures tend to have much better understandings of these things. See Herman E. Daly

and Kenneth N. Townsend, "Sustainable Growth: An Impossibility Theorem," from *Valuing the Earth: Economics*, Ecology, Ethics, MIT Press, 1993, p. 267 ff. For a wide-ranging discussion of the demise of civilizations, see Jared Diamond, *Collapse*, Viking, 2005."

6. Adam Sacks writes: "James Hansen et al.(2007), "Climate change and trace gases," Phil. Trans. Roy. Soc. A 365: 1925–1954 (2007)."
7. Adam Sacks writes: "Alfred W. Crosby, *Ecological Imperialism: The Biological Expansion of Europe, 900–1900*, Cambridge University Press, 1986, p. 92. The actual quote, referring to population, is, 'Mother nature always comes to the rescue of a society stricken with the problems of overpopulation, and her ministrations are never gentle.'"
8. Adam Sacks writes: "A word here about the skeptics, with whom we are also obsessed: Forget about them. They may appear to have control of the public discussion, but they are babbling into the abyss. Our enemy is us. By our own unwillingness to face the profound implications of climate change—that we have to reject civilization as currently conceived and come up with something completely different—we are doing far more damage to the cause of preserving life on earth than the deniers could ever do."
9. Adam Sacks writes: "'One of the more peculiar traits of our society is its assumption—its insistence—on solutions. Just as there are reasons for all things, so there are solutions for all things. Always there are ultimate answers; there is no problem that is not amenable to logical reduction. This, as we have seen earlier, in spite of such bewildering enterprises as ecology. I have no 'solution' to the wildlife preservation problem [read 'global warming problem']. There may not be one. But given the somewhat shaky assumption that one exists, I sense that I can at least feel the direction.' John A. Livingston, *The Fallacy of Wildlife Conservation*, p. 151."
10. Adam Sacks writes: "Our culturally skewed and defensive view of pre-hierarchical societies, seeing only lives that were 'nasty, brutish and short' struggling to survive in 'nature, red in tooth and claw,' has distorted earlier human experience beyond recognition. See, for example, Riane Eisler, *The Chalice and the Blade*, Harper & Rowe, 1987; and Marshall Sahlins, *Stone Age Economics*, Tavistock Publications, Ltd. (London), 1974."
11. Adam Sacks writes: "Jensen is one of our most passionate and incisive cultural critics and environmental writers. His words are, 'For an action to be sustainable, you must be able to perform it indefinitely. This means that the action must either help or at the very least not materially harm the landbase. If an action materially harms the landbase, it cannot be performed indefinitely ...' From Derrick Jensen and Aric McBay, *What We Leave Behind*, p. 56."
12. Adam Sacks writes: "Although, as I indicate in footnote 12 [*which is my note 14 here. —Brad*] in a brief discussion of holistic management of grasslands, we can

and must repair enough of the damage so that the infinitely complex self-organizing systems of nature—the systems that gave life to all living creatures—can begin anew.

13. Adam Sacks writes: "For example, consider hare-brained schemes from very smart scientists, some of whom know that the schemes are hare-brained but in their desperation see no other way. A recent article in *Rolling Stone*, "Can Dr. Evil Save the World?," has an interesting overview of the geo-engineering debate. The bottom line seems to be that we currently are able to do and think anything except changing the way we live, and risking the existence of life on earth is simply a chance we have to take (although 100 percent odds of failure is hardly a bet one should want to take, assuming there are any rational moments left). See also Ross Gelbspan's article, 'Beyond the Point of No Return,' footnote 1 [*which is note 3 here. —Brad*]."
14. Adam Sacks writes: "Glimmers of hope lie in the remarkable restorative powers of the earth. One such phenomenon is ancient pre-history but new to us. That is the relationship between grazers and grasslands. Whereas conventional grasslands management destroys soils and diversity, nature's way sequesters vast amounts of carbon in soils, with photosynthesizing plants as intermediators along with fungi, micro-organisms, insects, animals and birds—and creates productive and healthy land that, unlike forests, can bind carbon for thousands of years. We have the potential to remove gigatons of carbon from the atmosphere, reducing greenhouse gas concentrations by many parts per million with proper land management. Beyond grasslands, the planet's power of regeneration, despite our assaults, remains extraordinary. See HolisticManagementInternational.org.

   "Another example is the dramatic restoration of denuded rainforest in Borneo after only six years: 'Planting finishes this year [2008], but already [Willie] Smits [the Indonesian forestry expert who led the replanting] and his team from the Borneo Orangutan Survival Foundation charity claim the forest is 'mature', with trees up to 35 metres high. Cloud cover has increased by 12 per cent, rainfall by a quarter, and temperatures have dropped 3-5°C, helping people and wildlife to thrive, says Smits. Nine species of primate have also returned, including the threatened orangutans. 'If you walk there now, 116 bird species have found a place to live, there are more than 30 types of mammal, insects are there. The whole system is coming to life. I knew what I was trying to do, but the force of nature has totally surprised me. ... The place became the scene of an ecological miracle, a fairytale come true,' says Smits, who has written a book about the project.'"

CHAPTER 3 DISCONTENT AND ITS CIVILIZATION

1. Adam Sacks, "The Fallacy of Climate Activism," *Grist Magazine* (August 23, 2009). Website: www.grist.org.

2. Charles Eisenstein, "The Ubiquitous Network of Lies" Reality Sandwich (June 24, 2009). Website: www.realitysandwich.com.
3. "My Dinner with André," a 1981 motion picture directed by Louis Malle. Script by André Gregory and Wallace Shawn.
4. Joe Bageant, Personal Communication
5. Joe Bageant, "Raising Up Dead Horses" (October 19, 2009). Website: wwwjoe-bageant.com.
6. Randall Amster, "Empire of the Sun" *Truthout* (February 10, 2010). Website: www.truthout.org.
7. Daniel Quinn, "If They Give You Lined Paper, Write Sideways." Steerforth Press, 2007.

CHAPTER 4 OKAY, OKAY, WE CAN'T EAT 'EM

Epigraph: Peter Tosh. Lyrics from "Equal Rights," *Talking Revolution*. Pressure Sounds, 2005.

1. Joe Bageant, *Rainbow Pie*. London, U.K.: Portobello Press, 2010. Viewed in advance of publication.

PART TWO

CHAPTER 5 A NEW STORY FOR A NEW BEGINNING ON THE OTHER SIDE OF CIVILIZATION

Epigraph: Marilyn Ferguson, "Our past is not our potential..." *The Aquarian Conspiracy*. New York: J.P. Tarcher, 1987.

1. E. E. Cummings. *Complete Poems 1904–1962*. New York: Liveright, 1994.

CHAPTER 6 THE WORK OF STANLEY MILGRAM

Epigraphs:

Samuel Adams, "If you love wealth more than liberty..." Label on a Beer Bottle Adolph Hitler, *Mein Kampf*, from volume 2, chapter 2, "The State."

1. Roland Lloyd Parry, "Contestants Turn Torturers in French TV Experiment," *Agence France-Presse* (March 16, 2009). Website: www.afp.com.

CHAPTER 7 THE CONSERVATIVE WAY: THE PATHWAY TO OBLIVION

1. Gary Shepherd, "Ptolemy, Copernicus, and World Government," *United World Newsletter*. gshepher@verizon.net.

2. Davej, "Reagan Revolution Home To Roost—In Charts," Davej.dailykos.com. Originally published in *Campaign for American's Future, Blog for Our Future.*
3. Andrew Bolt, "TITLE," *Herald Sun* (Australia) (June 18, 2010) Bob Metcalfe
4. The End of the American Dream Staff, "50 Statistics About The U.S. Economy That Are Almost Too Crazy To Believe." Endoftheamericandream.com/archives/50-statistics-about-the-u-s-economy-that-are-almost-too-crazy-to-believe.

CHAPTER 8 AS LONG AS YOU HAVE OBEDIENT SERVANTS YOU CAN FORGET ABOUT JUSTICE

1. Derrick Jensen, *Endgame, Volume 1: The End of Civilization.* New York: Seven Stories Press, 2006.
2. Buckminster Fuller. *Grunch of Giants.* Design Science Press, 1983.
3. "Top Ten..." *Project Censored* (December 31, 2009). Website: ProjectCensored.org.
4. Allison Kilkenny, "Police Use Painful New Weapon on G20 Protesters" AlterNet (September 28, 2009). Website: AlterNet.org.
5. Amanda Ripley, "The Lesson: Passengers Are Not Helpless" *Time* (December 30, 2009). Website: Time.com.
6. Jensen, Endgame.

CHAPTER 9 THE TRUTH MACHINE

1. Ronald Bailey, "A Truth Machine: Can Brain Scanning Technologies Stop Terrorists—or Just Threaten Privacy?" *Reason* (November 14, 2001) Website: Reason.com.
2. fMRI
3. Emily Saarman, "New Lie Detection Technology Worries Stanford Ethicist" *Stanford News Service* (May 3, 2006). Website: News.stanford.edu.
4. Alexis Madrigal, "Lie Detection Brain Scan Could Be Used in Court for First Time" *Wired Science* (May 4, 2010). Website: Wired.com.

CHAPTER 10 CALLED BY EACH OTHER TO OUR HIGHER SELVES

Epigraphs:

Joseph Chilton Pearce, "In knowing ourselves as an integral function of a multifaceted Human Family Self..." *The Biology of Transcendence.*
Starhawk, "We are all longing to go home to some place we have never been..." From an email to her supporters.

A. J. Jacobs, "I need self-delusion..." *The Guinea Pig Diaries*. New York, Simon & Schuster, 2009: p. 98.

John Margolis, "Would you rather have health and wellness..." Private communication.

1. Wikipedia.com. Search phrase: collective wisdom.
2. Dave Pollard, "a young man from Newfoundland," contributed the comment in quotations to Wikipedia and his bio was subsequently deleted. Whether he or someone else removed it, we do not know.
3. Wikipedia.com. Search phrase: collective intelligence.
4. Norman Lee Johnson is the founder of the Symbiotic Intelligence Project, which is an investigation into the combination of the unique abilities of the Internet and human problem-solving to create a capability greater than the sum of the parts. Since September 11, 2001, he has integrated his diverse interests to address the national need for a response to biological and other threats. Website: CollectiveScience.com.
5. Terry Flew, *New Media: An Introduction*. Melbourne: Oxford University Press, 2008.
6. George Pór, Blog of Collective Intelligence: www.community-intelligence.com/blogs/public.
7. The Center for Collective Intelligence at the Massachusetts Institute of Technology. For a list of faculty, visit cci.mit.edu/people/index.html.
8. D. Tapscott and A.D. Williams. *Wikinomics: How Mass Collaboration Changes Everything*. New York: Penguin, 2008.
9. Ibid.

10 A. Weiss. *The Power of Collective Intelligence*. Wikipedia.com. Search phrase: deliberative democracy.

12. Jim Rough, *The Future of Public Participation*. Structuring for Collective Wisdom Blog (May 8, 2009). Website: http://blog.tobe.net. Viewed in advance of publication.

    As the conclusion of his full blog post, Rough mentions two resources. First, the Center for Wise Democracy, which helps helps governments and citizen groups employ these new social innovations (www.wisedemocracy.org). Second, Dynamic Facilitation Associates website (www.dynamicfacilitation.com). In particular, see the article "Dynamic Facilitation and the Magic of Self-organizing Change."

CHAPTER 11 THE MACHINE STOPS

1. E.M. Forster, "The Machine Stops," *The Oxford and Cambridge Review* (1909)

PART THREE

INTRODUCTION

Michael Jackson (song lyrics), "Earth Song," History—Past, Present and Future—Book I. Epic, 1995.

Rudyard Kipling, "If—," (1899). First published in the "Brother Square Toes" chapter of *Rewards and Fairies* (1910), a collection of short stories and poems.

CHAPTER 12 A SIMPLE QUESTION

Epigraph: George Leonard

1. George Leonard on Fritz Perls article.

CHAPTER 13 RADICAL HONESTY AS A PRELUDE TO DEEP DEMOCRACY

1. Brad Blanton, "Subject: Dear Republicans," Bart.com (2009).

CHAPTER 14 EXAMPLES OF CORPORATE HARDHEARTEDNESS AND IRRESPONSIBILITY

Epigraphs:
Frederic Bastiat
Joe Bageant. Personal communication.

1. George Monbiot, *The Age of Consent*. New York: HarperPerennial, 2004.
2. Ibid.
3. Ibid.
4. Ibid.
5. Multinational Monitor List of the Ten Worst Corporations of 2008.
6. Jeremy Scahill, "The U.S. Is Shipping Tons of Deadly Weaponry to Pakistan," *The Nation* (May 12, 2010).
7. Website: PolluterWatch.com.
8. Derrick Jensen. "Resistance Resisters: It's Time to Lead, Follow, or Get Out of the Way," *Orion* (March/April 2010)

PART FOUR

INTRODUCTION

1. Naomi Shihab Nye. "Kindness," *Word Under the Words: Selected Poems*. Portland, OR.: The Eighth Mountain Press, 1994: p. 42.

Chapter 15 Conscious Participation in Evolution

1. Taber Shadburne. Private correspondence.
2. Ignatius O'Reilly. "Sudden Mass American Enlightenment Puzzles Congress and Causes National Security Alert," *Signs of the Times* (April 1, 2010). Website: SOTT.net.
3. Jack Stork. Private correspondence.
4. Taber Shadburne. Private correspondence.
5. James Howard Kunstler. "Babbling on in Babylon—What If We Go Sane?" Kunstler.com (March 29, 2010).
6. *Public Education and Empowerment Resource Service newsletter*. Website: PeerService.org.
7. Ibid.
8. "U.S. Flag Recalled After Causing 143 Million Deaths," Onion News Service (April 13, 2010).

Chapter 16 The Pathway to Salvation

1. Rabbi Michael Lerner. "Personal Environmental Commitment," *Tikkun* (2010).
2. Charlie Bloom. Bloomwork.com newsletter (May 2010).
3. Ed Greville. Personal correspondence referring to Willie Smits' presentation, "Willie Smits Restores a Rainforest," at the TED2009 conference (filmed February 2009). To view the video: ted.com/talks/lang/eng/willie_smits_restores_a_rainforest.html
4. "Willie Smits: Conservationist." TED speaker profile. http://www.ted.com/speakers/willie_smits.html.
5. The People's Agreement. From the World People's Conference on Climate Change and the Rights of Mother Earth in Cochabamba, Bolivia, 2010.
6. Jack Bloomfield of One Planet United. Website: OPUnited.org.
7. Tom Atlee. "Democracy in Crisis: Breakdown and Breakthrough." *Co-Intelligence Institute newsletter* (May 2010).
8. Jack Stork. Personal correspondence.

Chapter 17 Summary of What I Have Said, What Others Have Said, What I Have Said about What Others Have Said, and What We Should Do About It

1. Tom Atlee May Newsletter 2010

About the Author

I ran for United States Congress in 2006 with radical honesty as a platform and I lost. It was one of the best unsuccessful campaigns anyone has ever run. There are bios of me in my former books, on our website, and all over the place. I like this one, which is excerpted from my campaign brochure at the time I ran for Congress. I have updated it and tinkered with it a bit to add in the four years since then.

My name is Brad Blanton and I'm running for United States Congress.

Heaven: I was born in Staunton Virginia on September 8, 1940, into a family with two parents and a sister who was nine. My brother was born fifteen months later. My father was a lineman for the telephone company and my mother was a homemaker, a poet, and a songwriter. We lived in a small house in the middle of an apple orchard and, as far as I can remember, we were in heaven.

Heaven Interrupted: When I was not quite six years old, my father dropped dead from a heart attack at thirty-seven years of age. Everything changed. A year later, my mother, who felt desperately alone and was grieving, and had three children to raise, married a shell-shocked veteran who had just returned home from six years in the Pacific. He was a machinist, she became a secretary, and they both became alcoholics.

Hell: Our heavenly family became the family from hell. The social security checks for us kids went for liquor; my stepfather beat my mother, sometimes putting her in the hospital, and causing her bodily injuries, broken bones, and three miscarriages. My little brother, Mike, was born a couple of months premature after a beating and survived. When I was nine, I became his primary caretaker until he was four and a half years old. My sister, who was sixteen, left home right after my brother was born to escape my stepfather's sexual advances.

Raising Hell: When I was twelve and my little brother was three he got rheumatic fever and it damaged his heart. The doctor said he needed to have rest and quiet to have a chance of healing. I became then not only his caretaker, but his protector from the chaos of our family. When I was thirteen years old, I interrupted one of my stepfather's violent attacks by picking up a stick of firewood and breaking three of his ribs and fracturing his skull. A few weeks later, I stole the social security money, went to the hardware store in town, bought two shotguns and two cases of shells for me and my eleven-year old brother (along with a basketball, a basketball hoop, a backboard, and a rod and reel), and I took over the family at gunpoint for a while and got the house cleaned up.

I told my stepfather to his face when he was cold sober that I was going to kill him the next time he laid a hand on anybody, and it became clear the family had to come to an end one way or another. I called in my grandparents and we split the family up. My little brother Mike went to live at his grandmother's house in Virginia, my younger brother Jimmy went to an aunt and uncle in Tennessee, and I went to Texas to live with my sister. My mother and stepfather stayed together for a couple of more years before she left him.

Forgiveness: I forgave my stepfather for almost everything before he died. It wasn't easy. And beating the hell out of him was a part of the process of forgiving him. Also included in the process of forgiving him was my coming to understand all the sadness and heartbreak and damage done to him by the life of killing he had been thrown into as a teenager when he spent six years in the Pacific slaughtering human beings. I learned the truth of the bigger story that had crippled him. The hatred that could have consumed me didn't. Compassion won out over vengeance. It was almost accidental. But I am not stupid. I was certainly struck by how brilliant our human arrangements for war work as a way to do religion and property settlements! That really works well doesn't it? And I can testify it lasts for generations to come—a gift that keeps on giving.

I forgave my mother for everything before she died, as well. Forgiving my mother and stepfather benefited me more than them. I learned that if we are able to forgive we can make a new beginning. I also learned that forgiveness is a very tough process, sometimes including things I myself need forgiveness for along the way. I learned that love happens when forgiveness is a two-way street, and that there is probably nothing more important than forgiveness and letting love happen.

Gratitude for Direction: I am grateful for the grace and luck of my whole childhood and for the path of life it put me on. I started college in Texas when I was sixteen, and I was clear and unhesitating about the direction of my life. I knew I wanted to help people who were helpless and protect them from the mean people. I have done that and am still doing it but I found that often the mean people and the helpless people are the same people. So helping mean people not have to be so mean is also good work that helps everyone, when I can do it.

My Dilemma and Our Dilemma: Helplessness and meanness are almost always in the same person. The helpless people are the mean people. The mean people are the helpless people who haven't learned how to forgive their cripplers. (Newsflash: "Childhood is hell, reports former child!") Some mean people are in denial about being mad at their parents and teachers to such a degree that they profess to love and honor them. These people are generally called neo-conservatives and they are in severe need of psychological help. They are the sickest among us.

In the course of figuring out how to help the helpless mean people, I got a doctorate in psychology when I was twenty-five years old. I have worked as a psychotherapist in private practice inside the beltway in Washington, D.C., for over twenty-five years, a seminar leader, and a trainer of psychotherapists. I worked with the helpless and the mean and their mates and families—the victims and oppressors produced by our civilization. I saw a lot of lawyers in therapy. Most of what they say about lawyers is true: ninety-nine percent of them give the rest a bad name. They are our professional liars, and it costs them their lives, just as lying does for most people.

How Lying and Secrecy Prevent Forgiveness: Out of that practice of psychotherapy and from my own life I learned that (1) the key to forgiveness is honesty, and (2) the secret to meanness is lying, and that (3) most of us are trapped into lying most of the time by the way we are raised, and that (4) the major injustices of the world come from our systematic instruction in lying, and the unresolved anger and hurt continuously perpetrated on all of us by the culture in which we are raised. The culture's agents of instruction are the previous generation of cripples, parents, teachers, and peers, who suffer from a disease called moralism, an illness that lies at the heart of civilization, our mutual sickness.

Based on that insight, I wrote a nationwide bestselling book called Radical Honesty, which has now been published in about a dozen languages. I created a seminar which has been conducted around the world called "The Course in Honesty" (Sometimes called, "The Curse of Honesty.") I have written five other books since starting and conducting that workshop on an ongoing basis about twenty years ago. I have helped thousands of people live happier lives. I have helped people overcome depression, anxiety disorders, chronic conflict, damaged capacity for intimacy and other forms of self torture and torture of others.

I have also been a political activist all my life. I joined the civil rights movement is 1959 when I was nineteen years old and stuck with it until we passed the civil rights acts of 1964. Integration has still not yet occurred, but segregation is over. I put my ass on the line to make that happen.

I refused to serve in Vietnam and I was in the anti-Vietnam war movement for ten years, a couple of those years full time. I put my ass on the line over and over again, and it still took forever to end that stupid fucking war. And it only took a few years between when that one ended and the bullshit continuation of the murder-based economy of the United States to work us into perpetual conflict and anti-terrorist terrorism still being perpetrated now in Iraq and Afghanistan and Pakistan, and elsewhere (God only knows where).

I have been arrested, jailed, beat up, bombed, tear gassed, shot at, fired from several jobs, received threats on my life, and been indelicately treated. I took it. I survived. I fought back. I wish I had done more of it more violently.

I was a hippie and lived in a school bus and drove all over America and I have taken nearly every illegal drug known to man, usually more than once. I did not exhale. I learned a hell of a lot. I have flaunted, opposed and broken laws all my life and I am not ashamed of most of it.

I have been married five times. I have fathered and helped raise six children, who are wonderful, loving contributors to the world. I am proud of them and of my ex-wives and of the job we did, and are doing, of raising those children together, and of supporting them after they have grown up.

I want to protect the future for all our children and stepchildren, and for my two grandchildren. I realize that the future of the people I love is in danger, and I hope you do too and that we can do something about it together.

I Am Damaged Goods: I can understand how some of you may feel it is a bit of a stretch to forgive me for the kind of life I have lived and vote for me to become a Congressman. I have overcome some of the hurts of my childhood, but you may not like the way I did it. And along the way and while doing that I have also made mistakes and been unkind, and lied and cheated, and stolen and been a hypocrite about professing love and acting hatefully.

Regardless of whether you agree with all of how I have lived or what I have done, I would like for you to understand that we can probably agree on a very important point: we are living in a damaged society. And I want you to know that I know how to help. I have broken some rules, and I have hurt some people, but I cannot hold a candle to the immense depravity, injustice, and murderous criminal behavior of the United States Government during my lifetime. Forgiving me for my past may be a challenge, but it is trivial compared to what it will take for both of us to forgive, for example, Bush, Cheney, Congressman Cantor, and the whole cabal of sick people who surround them, and the goddamned Democrats who have aided them.

The meanest people in the world are the ones considered morally righteous in a sick society. That is nowhere better demonstrated than the record of the Bush presidency and all the righteous people who have helped him in his meanness and the furthering of his ignorance. Someone ought to take a stick of firewood to the whole damn bunch of them. (This wasn't in italics in the notes for the speech, but I put this in italics now to point out that I have not come very goddamned far!)

I know the value of forgiveness and I am in the process of trying to forgive the neoconservatives for their ignorance, malice, heartlessness, greed, and stupidity. Even harder, I am trying also to forgive the lying purveyors of hope who call themselves Democrats. Since I can't beat the hell out of them and get by with it, I have to use the process of getting to forgiveness by telling the truth. And you need to have the truth told to you as much as I need to tell it. So, for the benefit of both of us:

This Is the Truth: You are the one responsible for keeping this hell in place. It is time you did something about it. What you do and don't do makes a difference. Your vote or lack thereof set this crap in motion. Not voting is a vote for business-as-usual: corruption, corporate welfare, deficit spending, war and the occupation of foreign lands, the most expensive and yet least fair health care system of all nations in the industrialized world, and an educational system that is dumbing kids down instead of inspiring them and us to think.

Right here in Virginia, in District 7, our quality of life is at risk. The divide between the wealthy and the poor is ever-widening, and the middle class is an endangered species. Paychecks don't buy what they used to, and if you lose your job you're unlikely to find another. Our traditional family farms are being swallowed up by the

Pro-Development Super-sizing Machine built by hypocrites preaching smaller government. Do you know who is responsible for that? It's you. And it's me. It's up to us to set things right.

We Don't Have to Live This Way. We don't have to have these troubles. We can lift ourselves out of this tragic failure of democracy by bringing into being a new vision. I hope you share this vision. The vision is to turn hell into heaven, and the time has come for us to proceed. I, personally, am committed to service and leadership in a world that works for me and everyone I know, and everyone they know—until together we bring into being out of our co-intelligence and common vision heaven on earth. The purpose of my life is to use every bit of my perceptiveness, intelligence, love of children, love of people, love of life, and sense of humor by writing books, designing and conducting workshops, giving talks, making media appearances, sharing honestly with friends, being with my family, running for public office, and helping with the raising of children and grandchildren in such as way as to create the possibility of a lifetime of play and service for every human being on the planet. (That's what I call heaven: the possibility of a lifetime of play and service as an open option for every human being on earth.)

I invite you to share this vision with me and help me bring it into being in the real world. If we can picture this together we can make it come true together. Imagine: Every little baby born, every little child alive, every adolescent, and every adult in every family on every continent living together in a world where all they have to do is play—and serve each other in the process of playing—because it is fun, it's the best way to learn, and it makes for the greatest possible life with others.

The stretch from what is so now to what we can envision is not as far as it looks. A great reconciliation under the duress of global warming may at last deliver us from our worst enemy: ourselves.

I am a lucky person to have lived during the times I have lived and to have had the friends and lovers, and little children who loved me. They helped to sustain me and help me thrive within the context of the poisonous cultural conditions of my place of birth in the shameful thieving murderous heart of corporate capitalism, the United States of America in the twentieth and twenty-first centuries. I live in the country owned and operated by corporations who have no conscience. There was love there in the very heart of evil. So I dedicate this book to the great God of evolution, in prayer for having our mutual human conscious participation in alliance with the Great Chaos to bring things forward to a locus of love in this starry little teeny place in eternal time within whose greater context our little activities play themselves out. I dedicate these words and all the information they convey to the God beyone God, in hope that the love of God so bastardized in our culture could really miraculously work out to be the actual love of God after all, the love to us from reality, and our love back for reality. In the words of Job, "The Lord gave. And the Lord taketh away. Blessed be the name of the Lord." I dedicate my books and my life to the whole trip.

Bibliography and Recommended Reading

in Addition to Chapter Notes

Peter Block "The Abundant Community: Awakening the Power of Families and Neighborhoods"

The Truth Machine, James L. Halperin, 1996

Thank God For Evolution, Michael Dowd, 2007

Endgame, Derrick Jensen, 2006

A Language Older Than Words, Derrick Jensen, 2000

The Crisis of Global Capitalism, George Soros, 1998

The Age of Consent, George Monbiot, 2003

Failed States, Noam Chomsky, 2006

Fondling Your Muse, John Warner, 2005

Wreckage With a Beating Heart: Poems by Redhawk, Robert Moore, 2005

Heart Politics, Fran Peavy, Myra Levy and Charles Varon, 1986

Deer Hunting With Jesus, Joe Bageant, 2007

Walking with the Wind, John Lewis with Michael D'Orso, 1998

Drug War Addiction, Sheriff Bill Masters, 2001

The Road, Cormac McCarthy, 2006

Directing The Power of Conscious Feeling, Clinton Callahan, 2010

Daily Afflictions, Andrew Boyd, 2002

The Value of Nothing, Raj Patel, 2009

Out of my Mind, Pila Hall, 2010

Biosphere Politics, Jeremy Rifkin, 1991

Jacob's Dream, Gene W. Marshall, 2008

Running On Empty, Peter G. Peterson, 2004

Big Bush Lies, Gerald R. Barret, 2004

Beyond Good and Evil, Brad Blanton, 2005

Rush Limbaugh Is A Big Fat Idiot and Other Observations, Al Franken, 1996

A Thousand Names For Joy, Byron Katie with Stephen Mitchell, 2007

Lies and the Lying Liars Who Tell Them, Al Franken, 2003

The Truth, Al Franken, 2005

Blessed Unrest, Paul Hawken, 2007

The World Café, Juanita Brown, David Isaacs and the World Café Community, 2005

The Empathic Civilization, Jeremy Rifkin, 2010

Other Books by Brad Blanton

Radical Honesty: How to Transform Your Life by Telling the Truth, Brad Blanton, Ph.D., Sparrowhawk Press, 2005 (New Revised Edition).

Practicing Radical Honesty: How to Complete the Past, Live in the Present and Build a Future with a LIttle Help from Your Friends. Sparrowhawk Press.2001

Radical Parenting: Seven Steps to a Functional Family in a Dysfunctional World. Sparrowhawk 2003

Honest to God: A Change of Heart that Can Change the World. (with Neale Donald Walsch) Sparrowhawk 2002.

The Truthtellers: Stories of Success by Radically Honest People, Sparrowhawk, 2004.

Beyond Good and Evil: The Eternal Split-Second Sound-Light Being. Sparrowhawk 2008.

Presentations and Websites

http://www.boingboing.net/2010/07/04/econopocalypse-the-m.html

http://www.davidicke.com/articles/media-and-appearances/36265-even-the-troops-are-waking-up-a-fantastic-video